BRUNO

SUNY Series in Hegelian Studies

Quentin Lauer, S.J., Editor

F·W·J·SCHELLING

BRUNO

OR

On the Natural and the Divine Principle of Things
1802

edited and translated
with an introduction by
MICHAEL G. VATER

State University of New York Press · Albany

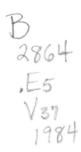

Published by
State University of New York Press, Albany

© 1984 State University of New York

For information, address State University of New York
Press, State University Plaza, Albany, N.Y., 12246

Cover and text design by Bruce McPherson

Library of Congress Cataloging in Publication Data

Schelling, Friedrich Wilhelm Joseph von, 1775–1854.
Bruno, or, On the natural and the divine principle of things.
(SUNY series in Hegelian studies)
Includes bibliographical references and index.
1. Metaphysics, I. Vater, Michael G., 1944–   .
II. Title. III. Series.
B2864.E5V37   1984   110   83–5101
ISBN 0–87395–793–8
ISBN 0–89395–792–X (pbk.)
10   9   8   7   6   5   4   3   2   1

To Jeremy

Contents

BRUNO, OR ON THE NATURAL

AND THE DIVINE PRINCIPLE OF THINGS.

A DIALOGUE.

Abbreviations

BRIEFE F.W.J. Schelling, *Briefe und Dokumente* II & III, edited by Horst Fuhrmans, (Bouvier, Bonn, 1973/1975).

CRITIQUE Immanuel Kant, *Critique of Pure Reason,* translated by Norman Kemp Smith, (MacMillan, London, 1963).

DIFFERENCE G.W.F. Hegel, *The Difference Between Fichte's and Schelling's System of Philosophy,* edited by H.S. Harris & Walter Cerf, (SUNY Press, Albany, 1977).

ETHICS Benedict de Spinoza, *Ethics,* edited by James Gutmann, (Hafner, New York, 1949).

ESSAYS F.W.J. Schelling, *The Unconditional in Human Knowledge: Four Early Essays,* translated by Fritz Marti, (Bucknell University Press, Lewisburg, 1980).

FAITH G.W.F. Hegel, *Faith and Knowledge,* translated by Walter Cerf & H.S. Harris, (SUNY Press, Albany, 1977).

F. WERKE J.G. Fichte, *Ausgewählte Werke,* edited by Fritz Medicus, Band IV, (Meiner, Hamburg, 1962).

PHENOMENOLOGY G.W.F. Hegel, *Phenomenology of Spirit,* translated by A.V. Miller (Oxford University Press, Oxford, 1979).

SCIENCE J.G. Fichte, *Science of Knowledge,* translated by Peter Heath & John Lachs, (Appleton-Century-Crofts, New York, 1970).

SPIEGEL Xavier Tilliette, *Schelling im Spiegel seiner Zeitgenossen,* (Bottega d'Erasmo, Turin, 1974).

SYSTEM F.W.J. Schelling, *System of Transcendental Idealism,* translated by Peter Heath, (University Press of Virginia, Charlottesville, 1978).

WERKE F.W.J. Schelling, *Sämtliche Werke,* ed. K.F.A. Schelling, (Stuttgart and Augsburg, 1856ff.).

Preface

THE PRESENT TRANSLATION is based on the text published in *Schellings Werke*, edited by Manfred Schröter, (Beck, Munich, 1965), = the Jubilee Edition of 1927, Vol. 3 of the major series. Citation of texts is according to the original edition of 1856ff., edited by K.F.A. Schelling. The ornate style of the original has been sacrificed in favor of a more conversational style. It is my hope that greater conceptual clarity will be achieved thereby. To that end, I have also been quite liberal in interpolating clarifications into the text, and supplying transitions where they seemed lacking. All such interpolations are enclosed within brackets. I have learned much from recent translations of Fichte, Schelling, and Hegel by Peter Heath, Fritz Marti, Henry Harris, Walter Cerf, and A. V. Miller. I have sometimes altered their translations of technical terms in citing their texts, but that is only for the sake of preserving a uniform terminology. I have adopted the convention of not capitalizing terms that refer to the absolute, since I feel that capitalization often interferes with the work of coming to a philosophical understanding of what the term signifies.

The help and encouragement of many different people comes to fruition in this volume, though I alone am responsible for its accuracy and intelligibility. The research on the Schelling-Hegel collaboration in Jena was done on a Marquette University Summer Faculty Fellowship in 1975. Reduced teaching loads granted by the Marquette Philosophy Department enabled me to revise the translation in the Autumn of 1981, and a grant from the Dean of the Graduate School assisted editorial preparation in the Summer of 1982. Miklos Vetö graciously supplied copies of rare historical sources, and Joseph Bracken, S.J. and William E. Dooley, S.J. assisted me greatly by reading preliminary versions of the translation and offering helpful suggestions. Professors Quentin Lauer and Robert Brown furnished helpful, and, I am afraid, needed, direction for the revision of the Introduction and the Translation respectively. David Latuch, Kerry Walters, Jerry Witkowski, and Anne Maloney provided enthusiastic and accurate assistance in research and editing, as did Keith Pheby, who is responsible for the index. Finally I must acknowledge the generous help given me by Sandra Brown, Tom McFadden, and Ann Mallinger of the Marquette Computer Services Division on the word-processing program on which the translation was executed.

Acknowledgments

I wish to thank the following publishers for permission to reprint copyrighted material:

Associated University Presses, Inc. for quotations from F. W. J. Schelling, *The Unconditional in Human Knowledge: Four Early Essays,* translated by Fritz Marti (Bucknell University Press, Lewisburg). © 1980 by Associated University Presses, Inc.

Oxford University Press, for quotations from G. W. F. Hegel, *Phenomenology of Spirit,* translated by A. V. Miller (Oxford University Press, Oxford, 1979). © 1977 by Oxford University Press.

MacMillan Publishing Co., Inc. for quotations from Benedict de Spinoza, *Ethics and On the Improvement of the Understanding,* edited by James Gutmann (Hafner, New York). Copyright 1949, Hafner Publishing Company. By permission of MacMillan Publishing Co., Inc., New York.

State University of New York Press for quotations from G. W. F. Hegel, *Faith and Knowledge,* translated by Walter Cerf and H. S. Harris (State University of New York Press, Albany). Translation © State University of New York 1977. Also for quotations from G. W. F. Hegel, *The Difference Between Fichte's and Schelling's System of Philosophy,* translated by H. S. Harris and Walter Cerf (State University of New York Press, Albany). Translation © State University of New York 1977.

University Press of Virginia for quotations from F. W. J. Schelling, *System of Transcendental Idealism,* translated by Peter Heath (University Press of Virginia, Charlottesville). Copyright © 1978 by the Rector and Visitors of the University of Virginia.

I also wish to express my gratitude to Bouvier Verlag Herbert Grundman for permission to translate materials from F. W. J. Schelling, *Briefe und Dokumente,* edited by Horst Fuhrmans, Volumes II and III (Bouvier Verlag Herbert Grundman, Bonn). Volume II © Bouvier Verlag Herbert Grundman Bonn 1973. Volume III © Bouvier Verlag Herbert Grundman Bonn 1975.

INTRODUCTION

You are right, the spirit of Schelling killeth the letter of Kant!

JOHANN MICHAEL SAILER[1]

The Revival of Metaphysics

IN THE SUMMER of 1801, Schelling formed the idea of casting his new system or 'identity-philosophy' in the form of a dialogue. The immediate occasion was the receipt of a letter from Fichte, written late in May but not posted until August, wherein Fichte voiced his fears that Schelling had never properly understood his system. In placing a philosophy of nature alongside transcendental idealism as a parallel system, he charged, Schelling had abandoned the standpoint of idealism and was instead pursuing a metaphysic of being. Fichte wrote, with characteristic bluntness, "I think that your system, by itself, has no evidence, and I think I could prove it. It can have absolutely none, unless you tacitly introduce clarifications borrowed from [my] Science of Knowledge."[2] The two philosophers who for eight years had labored in common to construct a comprehensive system of Kantian idealism had privately come to a parting of the ways.[3] Early in October Schelling penned an even-tempered and genial reply which discussed their differences at some length before avowing that it was impossible to settle all their misunderstandings in one letter. "I must place," he said, "my hopes [for resolving our differences] on future discussion between us on this central point [namely, whether an idealism can coexist with a realism]. Meanwhile, you will shortly receive a philosophical dialogue of mine. I wish you would read it."[4] The dialogue referred to is the *Bruno,* which appeared in April of 1802, in which Lucian represents Fichte's position in the dispute and Bruno (loosely patterned on Giordano Bruno) represents Schelling's. Though Schelling's announced intentions were conciliatory, and though large portions of the dialogue seriously explore grounds for reconciliation, there was to be no rapprochement between the two thinkers. Schelling closes his reply to Fichte of 3 October with the curt

3

announcement, "Just today a book appeared, written by a very bright fellow, that bears the title *Difference Between Fichte's and Schelling's System of Philosophy*. I had no part in it, but I could in no way prevent it."[5] The "bright fellow" in question was Hegel, and what the essay's publication signaled, other than the obvious public criticism of Fichte, was the collapse of Fichte's long-standing dream of establishing with Schelling a yearbook for critical philosophy, to be called *Review of the Progress of Philosophy*.[6] The alliance had shifted; 'Critical Philosophy' no longer meant Fichte and Schelling. It now meant Schelling and Hegel, and the first number of their *Critical Journal* appeared in January of 1802. And rather than facilitating the reconciliation of Kant's heirs and reestablishing the continuity of the Kantian tradition, the *Bruno* stands along with Hegel's *Difference* as a watershed, a break with the past, the sketch of a new direction, the manifesto of "Absolute Philosophy"—a philosophy now commonly called absolute idealism, but which was loathe to call itself idealism at the start or to acknowledge anything other than a dialectical debt to Kant and Fichte.

Indeed some of the most interesting features of the *Bruno* stem from the forceful, even vehement, way that Schelling expresses the discontinuity of his thinking with Fichte's. In attempting to systematize Kant's philosophy, Fichte had remained faithful to the transcendental stance which Kant first brought to philosophical inquiry, the investigation of consciousness with a view to uncovering, not metaphysically but heuristically, the underlying structures governing consciousness. Thus the *Science of Knowledge* took the form of a genetic deduction of the structure of empirical consciousness from the postulate of an original self and an equally original, though derivative, not-self. The spirit of Kant's philosophy was faithfully preserved; even though the postulated self and not-self seem to be rather otherwordly and metaphysical entities, philosophy was in effect confined to the domain of consciousness.

But in attempting to place a philosophy of nature alongside transcendental philosophy, and even more so in trying to speculate about a world order behind appearances which unites the realms of nature and consciousness, Schelling places himself squarely in opposition to Kant's restrictions upon the domain and the method of philosophy. In order to systematically explain the whole of appearances, he must surpass the limitation of inquiry to the experiencing subject and investigate the law-like ordering of nature, the domain of nonconscious reality. And in order to investigate reality outside the context of experience, he must abandon the Kantian path of transcendental questioning and the merely heuristic answers it obtains, and boldly operate as a metaphysician, that is, seek to generalize certain features of experience and fashion a comprehensive account of all the domains of reality in terms of these generalized features. As will become apparent, the features Schelling chooses to generalize are logical relations, the identity-and-difference of the subject and object in the situation of knowing, and that of the mental and physical aspects of the self-conscious organism. The fact that his metaphysical models are logical relations rather than properties may make Schelling's endeavor less suspect to Kantian eyes, but the *Bruno* abundantly and pointedly states Schelling's conviction that philosophy must once again acquire a metaphysical foundation if it is to be a systematic account of reality. The real target of many of Schelling's arguments is, therefore, Kant, not Fichte. Fichte's philosophy of consciousness is objectionable only in that it is a limited and regional stance, thus a willful refusal to think reality in all of its domains into a systematic whole. Schelling's adversaries are those "who make their fear of reason into the content of philosophy itself" (4:308).

Closely connected with the anti-Kantian and forthrightly metaphysical stance is the anachronistic cast of the dialogue's thought, a feature which is responsible for much of its charm but at the same time poses grave obstacles to understanding its philosophic content. Schelling boldly charges at Kant, leaps over his head, and runs—into the past! Echoes of the great metaphysicians of the past abound; Plato, Spinoza, Giordano Bruno, and Leibniz all contribute their doctrines and their distinctive vocabularies to the discussion. Their presence, which sometimes conveys the impression that the dialogue is set in the philosophers' Babel, is quite deliberate. Schelling wishes to vindicate the claims of metaphysics as such, to glorify the speculative courage of a Plato or a Spinoza, and to set their accomplishments above the petty attacks of a reason that cannot rise above the task of analyzing experience.

The metaphysicians of the past are present for another reason as well. A philosophical system that would claim to be absolute can establish itself in only two ways. Inside the system, it must provide a comprehensive and coherent account of everything that is. Outside the system itself, it must show that more limited philosophical stances are surpassed by being included in the system. To accomplish the latter task, systematic philosophy must argue that it is *the* philosophy or perennial philosophy, and that it alone can make sense of the bewildering variety of philosophic doctrines by providing the organizing principle for the history of philosophy. Insofar as it begins to work on this second task, the *Bruno* is one of the first modern documents that attempts to lay down the foundations of the history of philosophy, and Schelling's concern soon took firm hold on his philosophical colleagues as well.[7] Looking back on his identity-philosophy in 1827, when it was indeed only a surpassed moment in his thinking, Schelling credits it with two major accomplishments, a revitalization of the notion of nature as an organic whole, and the recovery of a vision of history that once again embraced the concepts of purpose and finality. He described the divided post-Enlightenment culture, the culture that evoked absolute idealism, in these terms:

> Just as previously one turned nature into a show of externality, into an illusory play without any inner life or any real life-interest, so one remained content, and to the same degree, with a history that seemed to be an accidental play of lawless arbitrary choice, a play of senseless and purposeless drives. Though its scholars were accounted the most learned, for the most part they accentuated the senseless in history, indeed the absurd! The greater the event, the more exalted the historical phenomenon, the pettier, more incidental, and worthless were the causes they introduced to explain events. And this attitude was pretty much the dominant spirit of the universities.[8]

One can perceive the whole spirit of Schelling's philosophy of identity in the above quote and in the *Bruno*'s subtitle as well, "The Natural and Divine Principle of Things." There is but one principle governing reality, not two; nature and the world of spirit, in its personal as well as in its institutional forms, are not ultimately different. There is no ultimate contradiction between the rule of necessity in nature and the freedom manifested in human life. Any apparent contradiction must be thought away so that the wholeness of the world can again emerge, so that eyes deluded by the double vision of an alienated, divided culture can begin again to perceive spontaneity and organic adaptation operative in nature as well as blind mechanism, and can perceive again the lawfulness and rational ordering operative in the world of human actions and institutions, not just the unpredictable spontaneity of self-interested individuals.

The lesson that Schelling's and Hegel's age needed, and ours no less than theirs, was the advice offered long ago by Plato: Look closely at the universe you inhabit. You will see two sorts of causes at work, one which necessitates its outcome, and one which is divine, which freely works for 'the best.' If our limited nature is to be capable of fulfilment, we must seek after the divine in all things.[9] This was indeed a hard saying for a culture that simultaneously believed in hard material particles and immortal souls, and it is still a hard saying for us today, for whom matter has become less tangible and more metaphysical, but whose concept of psyche has become more 'material,' more conformed to the mechanism of the rest of nature. The real scandal that we confront in reading absolute idealism today, which we encounter no less in Schelling's *Bruno* than in Hegel's *Logic*, is its commitment to the seemingly unthinkable proposition: Freedom and necessity are in some sense identical. If we lack the courage or the stomach to think through this gravely problematic proposition, then our world falls apart into irreconcilable halves and the morally absurd (though logically possible) consequence follows that our understanding and our action belong to flatly different territories, that our science and our self-knowledge simply contradict each other, that exact knowledge can have nothing to say to or about what is most important. Nietzsche and Wittgenstein, each with great clarity, drew the conclusion—nihilism, the intellect's silence about the ethical.

To the Future Through the Past

O N FIRST INSPECTION, the most striking feature of the *Bruno* is
that it appears to be a return to the substance of Plato's thought
as well as to its literary form. The great Kant was still alive,
neither Fichte nor Schelling had yet gone public on their dispute, and the
work was received with some surprise. A student at Jena writes to his
father, "Schelling is called 'Professor Murky-Mind' by many here. I do
not think he will maintain his academic reputation much longer."[11] Friedrich
Schlegel writes to his brother August, "Schelling's *Bruno* deserves much
praise. Of course I wish he would have presented the brave Italian himself
instead of a pale shadow of Bruno."[12] And Goethe, treated to a prepub-
lication reading of the dialogue on a visit to Jena, writes to Schiller,
"Schelling has written a dialogue, *Bruno or On the Divine and Natural
Principle of Things.* What I understand of it, or believe I understand, is
excellent and coincides with my deepest convictions. But whether it will
be possible for the rest of us to follow this composition through all its
parts and actually think it as a whole, on that score I am as yet in
doubt."[13] But the reaction to Schelling's philosophy that comes closest to
that of a contemporary Anglo-American reader is that voiced by Henry
Crab Robinson, a British student at Jena in the Autumn of 1802, in a
letter to his brother:

I shall at the close of this lecture instantly proceed to *Schelling* And
purify my fancy polluted by the inspection of rotten carcasses &

9

smoked Skeletons, by hearing the modern Plato read for a whole hour his new metaphysi[c]al Theory of Aesthetik Or the Philosophy of the Arts. I shall in spight of the obscurity of a philosophy compounded of the most profound abstraction, & enthusiastick mysticism; be interested by par[ticu]lar ingenious remarks & amused by extravagant Novelties. The repeated Assertion of *Polytheism* will indeed no longer surprise me; nor the development of the platonic Theory of Ideas. And the absolute *Reality* of the Grecian Mythology of Jupiter Minerva & Apollo & I shall be a little touched perhaps by the contemptuous treatment of our english Critics And hear something like his abuse of Darwin last Wednesday Whose *Conceit* concerning the influence of the breast in forming our sensations of beauty; he quoted "only to shew what *bestialities* (the very words) the empirical philosophy of Locke leads And how the Mind of Man is brutalised unenlightened by Science." For that there is no science in empir[ic]ism is a point settled even to *my* Satisfaction. I shall hear again Burke and Horne & the "thick-skinned" Johnson & the "Shallow" Priestley briefly dispatched And hear it intimated that it is absurd to expect the *science* of beauty in a country that values the Mathematics only as it helps to make Spinning Jennies & Stocking-weaving machines And beauty only as it recommends their Manufactories abroad. I shall sigh & say too true! . . . At 4 [?5] I shall return again to *Schelling* And hear his grand Lecture on Speculative Philosophy I shall be animated if I happen to be in an enthusiastick frame, at the Sight of more than 130 enquiring Young Men listening with attentive ears to the Exposition of a Philosophy, in its pretensions more glorious than any publicly maintained since the days of Plato & his Commentators: a Philosophy equally inimical to Lockes Empiri[ci]sm, Hume's Scepticism & Kant's Criticism, which has been but the ladder of the new & rising Sect. But if I happen to be more prosaically tuned, I shall smile at the good nature of so great an assembly; who because it is the fashion listen so patiently to a detail which not one in 20 comprehends And which fills their heads with dry formularies and mystical rhapsodical phraseology. At P[M] 6 I shall come home And exhausted with my fourfold dose of the day, try to gain some nourishment from my apple pye which I with some difficulty have taught the Maid to make.[14]

The critic's writing skills leave something to be desired, but he eloquently voices the scandal of the (apparent) mystical Platonism which the reader encounters throughout the *Bruno*. Were all the earnest labors of Kant in vain? Did his efforts to guard speculation from contamination by sheer imagination serve merely as a ladder for a revival of Platonism? Does the genial *Wunderkind* of German philosophy and letters in fact leap into an abyss of nonsense when he proclaims, "We shall not have scaled the summit of truth itself until our thought has reached up to the nontemporal being of things and to their eternal concepts. Only then shall we recognize things and explain them truly." (4:221)?

The *Bruno*'s Platonism is both real and apparent, a matter of polemical language, on the one hand, and the outcome of a considered decision, on the other, to contest Kant's claim that the boundaries of intelligibility coincide with the bounds of sense. Curiously enough, it is through Kant that Schelling returns to Plato, or rather, it is by standing Kant on his head that he does so. For Kant had consistently returned to Plato as a reference point in order to clarify his terminology and to elaborate the full-blown metaphysical counterclaims that stood opposite his critical positions. And it is this Platonic terminology, pedantically reintroduced into the philosophical vocabulary by Kant, that Schelling employs to combat Kant's Criticism, specifically the terms 'intellectual intuition,' 'idea,' and 'archetype.' Let us look at each of these in detail.

In 1770 Kant defined sensory intuition against the foil of a hypothetical 'intellectual intuition,' the sort of creative intuition a deity would possess and whose sole analogue in human experience is the artist's symbolic understanding, a knowing in and with the concrete singular, not mediated by abstract universal concepts.[15] Fichte and Schelling both employ the term to indicate a philosophical mode of cognition that (1) achieves full insight into philosophy's ground-principle (for Fichte, the self; for Schelling, the absolute) and that (2) establishes and realizes what it intuits. Schelling uses 'intellectual intuition' interchangeably with 'reason,' and he gives its most succinct and suggestive definition in saying, "One cannot simply describe reason; it must describe itself in everything and through everything."[16]

Kant had explicitly turned back to Plato when, in the *Critique of Pure Reason,* he uses the Platonic definition of 'idea' as a foil for elaborating his notion of a merely regulative employment of ideas. He begins his discussion with Plato:

> Plato made use of the expression 'idea' in such a way as quite evidently to have meant by it something which not only can never be borrowed from the senses but far surpasses even the concepts of the understanding. . . . For Plato, ideas are archetypes of the things themselves, and not, in the manner of categories, merely keys to possible experiences. In his view they have issued from highest reason, and from that source have come to be shared in by human reason.[17]

Kant later modifies the Platonic sense of the term to reach his definition of the ideas of reason:

I understand by idea a necessary concept of reason to which no corresponding object can be given in sense-experience. Thus the pure concepts of reason, now under consideration, are *transcendental ideas.* They are concepts of pure reason, in that they view all knowledge gained in experience as being determined through an absolute totality of conditions. They are not arbitrarily invented; they are imposed by the very nature of reason itself, and therefore stand in necessary relation to the whole employment of understanding. Finally, they are transcendent and overstep the limits of all experience. . . . The absolute whole of all appearance—we might say—*is only an idea.* Since we can never represent it in images, it remains a *problem* to which there is no solution.[18]

When he asserts that ideas alone are real and that appearances are but debased images of ideas, Schelling is simply standing Kant on his head, brushing aside the criterion of experience the latter employed, and emphasizing their origin in reason itself. Now there is very much of a polemical stance voiced in passages such as, "Things that exist and the concepts of these things do not subsist within the absolute any differently than do nonexistent things and their concepts, namely within their ideas. Any other sort of existence is illusion, mere appearance" (4:251). What is obscured by such a flagrantly paradoxical assertion that things really do exist in the full sense only in their ideas is the ground of agreement Schelling shares with Kant, namely that ideas "view all knowledge gained in experience as being determined through *an absolute totality of conditions.*" Schelling insists that ideas are not mere ideas because he thinks an absolute totality of conditions is no mere idea, but the fundamental underlying reality instead. Ideas cannot be sensed or demonstrated, but if reason's attempt to achieve wholeness in its vision of itself and its world is to be successful, they must be postulated. Schelling will not be content to regard unity and totality as mere regulative ideas, as did Kant.

But it would be misleading to suggest that Schelling returns to a purely Platonic sense of the term 'idea.' When he says, "Considered absolutely, true being is located only within the idea, and conversely, idea is substance and being itself" (4:303), the term carries Spinozistic connotations as well. For Spinoza, an idea was not primarily a representation, not a dumb picture, but an active mentation, a thinking which is a realization of what it thinks, a particular expression of substance's power. So too for Schelling, the true nature of a thing, its idea or its being "within the eternal," is an elaboration and unfolding of the absolute's essence, a particular display of its power. As opposed to the mere abstract representation that 'the concept' accomplishes, an idea is a being that is at the same time a knowing. It is endowed with subjectivity and life, as Hegel will later make evident when he takes over the term to describe the logical fulfillment and completion of the absolute. Hegel in fact introduces the term into his *Logic* in the very sense in which Schelling employed it:

> The idea is the *adequate concept,* the objectively *true,* what is true *as such.* When something has truth, it possess it through its idea, or *something only has truth insofar as it is idea.* . . . Inasmuch as the result follows that the idea is the unity of the concept and objectivity or what is true, it is not to be considered merely a *goal* to be approximated, but which itself remains forever something *beyond reach.* Rather, everything actual exists only insofar as it has the idea in itself and expresses it. The object, the objective and subjective realms generally, *should* not merely *harmonize* with the idea; they are themselves the congruence of the concept and of reality.[19]

A third point where Schelling employs Platonic terminology taken over from Kant is his assertion that the locus of ideas or archetypes is an 'archetypal intellect.' "Is it not rather the case," asks Anselm, "that all our effort is directed toward knowing things as they are exemplified in the archetypal understanding, of which we see only images in our understanding?" (4:220). Now in discussing the idea of a teleological organization of nature in the *Critique of Judgment,* Kant analyzed the idea of such an organization into that of the organism, a whole which is the ground of possibility of its parts. If nature were such an organism, it would have as its ground an "archetypal intellect." But Kant quickly qualifies this very speculative assertion, adding,

> It is here not at all requisite to prove that such an *intellectus archetypus* is possible, but only that we are led to the idea of it— which too contains no contradiction—in contrast to our discursive understanding, which has need of images (*intellectus ectypus*), and to the contingency of its constitution.[20]

Here again, Schelling takes what was for Kant a limiting concept, that which could be thought but never factually asserted, and asserts not only its reality but its preeminence over the empirically thinkable. Kant had used intellectual intuition, idea, and archetypal intellect as symbols of a thinkable, but never verifiable reality characterized by completeness, independence, and closure. Now for Schelling to assert the reality of what these Kantian terms suggested—a *constitutive* cognition, phenomenal experience as determined by a *totality of conditions,* the parts of nature determined in and through a *whole*—is to deny the fragmentary nature of experience with its inevitable subject-object dichotomy and to lay claim to an absolute stance. The philosophical motivation for such a claim is, as we have seen, the untenable cultural situation which imports double vision into man's self-vision and bids him consider himself a creature of necessity and of freedom at the same time, and in the same respect. Nonetheless, such a claim is grandiose, for absolute philosophy claims nonempirical access to a foundational reality that is an existing totality of conditions, a whole not made of parts, but organically specifying them. And to secure this access, this philosophy claims the competence that pious ages reserved to the Creative Word—intellectual intuition, a knowledge identical with the absolute's self-specifying knowledge. The boldness of these claims can best be seen by considering another seemingly Platonic aspect of the *Bruno,* the pervasive contrast between time and eternity.

Eternity is understood by Schelling in a Spinozistic, not in a Platonic manner. Eternity is simple existence as such or necessary existence, not qualified by duration or any other form of limitation.[21] It is not endless duration, an attribute that pertains to the second power or the domain of the concept. Subsisting in the third or eternal power, that is, as ideas, things are organic unities of the various possibilities and actualities which are displayed serially within appearance, in the causal-temporal order. And as simply and necessarily subsisting within the absolute, things are uncaused, or speaking more strictly, self-caused. For in eternity or the domain of the idea, the individual is its own ground of possibility. Furthermore, it is the ground of all the relations that within appearance seem to be external, for example, position in space, priority in time to another, or causal efficacy upon another. Schelling believes with Leibniz, then, that all relations are internal, at least within the absolute, and that internal relations are the foundation of apparently external ones. Schelling's metaphysics in fact commits him to the thesis that relations are more fundamental than entities, though he does not always seem to clearly grasp the point.[22]

If eternity is simple being without duration, and the individual subsisting as idea is a unitary nexus of relations, nothing more, then what of time? Time is the one metaphysical theme that Schelling treats most fully in the *Bruno,* and here again he pursues the strategy of using Kant to overturn Kant. He makes time into the primitive form of phenomenality as such: The thing is individuated by the act of its establishing its own time; it is time that externalizes relations which are unitary and internal in the absolute, thus producing the causal ordering of phenomena; it is time that establishes the phenomenal entity's individuality; and it is the independent and internal possession of time which makes certain high-level individuals centers of self-consciousness. In this complex doctrine of time, Schelling effects a simplification of Kant's epistemology which is comparable to Schopenhauer's elegant reduction of all forms of knowing to the one principle of sufficient reason.[23] Like the latter philosopher, Schelling's intention in reducing critical knowledge-theory to a simple formal scheme is to exhibit precisely the formality, the emptiness of the scheme, and thus to point to a more profound dimension of reality that escapes phenomenal knowing. Time and causal determination are the hallmarks of finite existence and experience; phenomenal knowing is but a constant juggling of temporal and causal relations, a continuous apprehension of an endless splay of different states ordered only by temporal-causal connection, a series in which the identity and substantiality of individual entities is only a vanishing moment. In a passage written later in 1802, Schelling succinctly states the relationship between time and eternity:

> There exists no real finitude, no finitude in itself.—What in every sense of the word is really real is neither purely ideal nor purely real, but an eternal and necessary union of the two. . . . This absolute and essentially eternal identity, once reflected in the finite or even in the infinite, becomes a relation of time, or one of cause and effect, insofar as time is the ideal aspect of the causal relation and causality the real aspect of time.[24]

In eternity there obtains a simple identity or indifference of factors that stand forth within appearance, namely the material and the mental, and an organic interrelatedness of what stands forth in appearance as discrete individuals. In eternity, everything is unitary and internally related. Within the phenomenal orders, however, or what Schelling terms the domain of 'reflection,' identity and internality appear only as the discrete serial connection of external differences according to the order of time and causality, a linkage of individuals and states of individuals according to the empty formulae supplied by discursive understanding.

Before we can philosophically assess this line of thought, we must turn to the dialogue's complicated line of argument and examine it in some detail. For, despite the apparent simplicity of the dialogue as a form of philosophical exposition, the *Bruno* is a tangled web of philosophical argument, reflections on the history of philosophy, explorations of possible grounds for reconciling Schelling and Fichte, and sheer polemics directed against Fichte's subjective idealism.

*Have you found out yet why Fichte
and Schelling are quarreling? The
one says: I = everything; the other:
Everything = I. Mathematically, it
is the same.*

ACHIM VON ARNIM[25]

The Argument of the Bruno

THE DIALOGUE has a nonspecific, though anachronistic setting. Anselm is a Platonist; his character betrays a fustiness and a longing to return to the past. His speech is grandiose and long-winded, and it is he who tries to steer the conversation back to arcane subjects such as the mystery cults. Alexander does not seem to have any specific philosophical allegiances; in contrast to Anselm, he displays an empiricistic and this-worldly bent, also indicated by the directness of his speech. Later in the dialogue, he becomes the mouthpiece for the mystical hylomorphism which Giordano Bruno presented in his dialogues, *On the Cause, the Principle, and the One*. Bruno and Lucian, whose disputes provide the major focus of the dialogue, represent Schelling and Fichte respectively, or the competing claims of identity-philosophy and criticism. The conversation takes place outdoors, throughout the courses of a night, a fitting setting for a discourse in praise of the celestial motions and of the "the divine intelligence" of Kepler, who first framed their laws.[26]

I. The Claims of Metaphysics Versus the Logic of Experience
[4:217–234]

The preliminary discussion of truth and beauty, led by Anselm, has a threefold function: (1) to mitigate claims Schelling made in the 1800 *System of Transcendental Idealism* about the superiority of the artist to the philosopher when it comes to intuiting and expressing the nature of the absolute, (2) to argue that metaphysical, or as they used to be called, 'transcendental' predicates such as truth and beauty must have an absolute or transempirical sense, and (3) to illustrate, in a preliminary fashion, the logic of indifference by establishing the nondifference or intersubstitutability of truth and beauty, each taken in the strongest sense. Only transcendental or purely metaphysical attributes—truth and beauty, identity and difference, reality and ideality, essence and form—can be indifferently related, i.e. 'identical' in the limited and technical sense of each member of a pair of opposites being equal and independent, while expressing the same content in irreducibly different ways.[27] As a contemporary review of the dialogue plainly stated, "The assertion that *indifference is the principle of philosophy* is the theme of this Platonic dialogue."[28]

But before Schelling can advance such claims, he must first argue against Kant's decree that terms such as 'identity,' 'difference,' and 'truth' are meaningful only within the context of experience. He must refute or in some way circumvent Kant's formulation of the logic of experience, with its insistence that the contents of cognition are ultimately heterogeneous, that experience rather than logical possibility is the touchstone of truth, and that the principle of noncontradiction is the ultimate law in the domain of concepts. The thrust of the dialogue's initial section, therefore, is to rehabilitate a metaphysical, or in Kant's terms 'transcendent,' meaning of 'truth.'

Schelling's discussion of truth (4:218–221) attempts to drive a metaphysical wedge between the sort of truth that is functional, exhibited in and confirmed by the coherence of experience, and a truth that is supposedly substantial and independent. Both correspondence and coherence are rejected as the marks of truth, and in their stead Anselm proposes the Cartesian-Spinozistic criteria of clarity, distinctness, and adequacy of knowing. More provocatively, he adds the requirement that truth in the fullest and the strict sense be atemporal or eternal. All connection between the truth of statements and ideas and the objects they represent is severed when Anselm then adopts the purely subjective criterion of certitude, and asks whether truth is to be viewed as a merely changeable certitude or as an inalterable one. When changeable certitude is rejected, so implicitly is the claim of all empirical or synthetic *a posteriori* judgments to be truths.

Alexander then proposes universality and omnitemporal validity as the marks of truth, thus narrowing the truth-claim to synthetic *a priori* or categorial statements that hold for all individuals and for all time, statements such as, "Every event must have a cause." But Anselm rejects these proposed criteria too, demanding that truth in the highest sense have no connection with time and finitude whatsoever. Eternity, absolute invariance, and the utter transcendence of finitude thus specify truth's nature.

Thus we can see that Schelling adopts a tenseless model of being in place of Kant's model of being as experience within time, the Spinozistic eternity of simple existence, unqualified by duration. In doing so, Schelling exploits the connection of being and time that Kant discovered at the basis of experience. For Kant, time is not only the fundamental form of intuition, it is the very nature of experiential synthesis itself, or schematization; time is thus the essence of phenomenality, or mere appearance. Schelling agrees, but argues that everything connected with time, even categorial concepts applicable to everything that appears in time, pertains to an inferior province of being. Absolute truth must "be independent of all time, without reference to time, wholly self-contained, and hence simply eternal" (4:221).

To this point, the argument has accomplished three goals: (1) In refusing to ascribe truth to the conceptual as such, the territory Kant called pure *a priori* cognition, Schelling implicitly criticizes Fichte's attempt to absolutize the domain of thought by attributing to it the fundamental role in the constitution of consciousness. (2) In illustrating how the pure concepts have an inbuilt reference to time and to sensory intuitions within time, Schelling demonstrates the necessary togetherness of conceptual infinitude and sensory finitude, and thus intimates that 'the eternal' is the indifference of the finite and the infinite, i.e. that the idea indivisibly comprehends both concept and intuition. (3) He effects the strict distinction of time and eternity, though it awaits the following investigation of imperfection to show that eternity is here conceived after Spinoza, and not as some all-perfect Platonic heaven. Eternity is simply the atemporal existence of the whole of what is; time is but the successive appearance of the severed parts, a dispersion of organic totality into externality.

At this point, Alexander inquires how one can attain this supposed region of eternal truth, but Anselm brushes aside the question, preferring to stick to the path of conceptual analysis. The question is important, however, and elsewhere Schelling provides a clear answer. The fundamental presupposition of all knowing, he argues, is reason, the abiding and eternal element in all cognition. And reason is nothing other than the identity of the knower and what is known. "The first presupposition of all knowing is that it is one and the same thing that here knows and that there is known."[29] This state is precisely the opposite of the stance of empirical subjectivity:

> In reason all subjectivity disappears, and this is exactly what our proposition [above] asserted. In reason, that eternal identity itself is at once what cognizes and what is cognized. It is not I who knows this identity, but this identity itself knows itself, while I am merely its instrument. Reason is precisely *reason* because in it the subjective

is not the knower. Instead, within reason the identical knows the identical and the opposition of subjectivity and objectivity balances itself out in its highest instance. . . . If there were not in our very spirit some sort of cognition that is completely independent of all subjectivity, one that is no longer a cognition of the subject as subject, but a cognition of that alone which is and that alone which can be known, a cognition of the absolutely unitary, we would in fact be forced to renounce the sphere of absolute philosophy. In that case, our thought and knowledge would forever lie enclosed within the sphere of subjectivity. As a result, we would have to acknowledge the Kantian and Fichtean philosophies as the only possible position, and immediately make that position our own.[30]

The proper answer to Alexander's query, then, is: Abandon the stance of subjectivity, the empirical self-consciousness! The advice seems preposterous, at first blush. It is only when the structure of consciousness has been studied, and self-consciousness exhibited as but a special case of the general structure of identity-in-difference, that this abandonment of self can be properly evaluated. In general, Schelling thinks that the 'I' that thinks is just as phenomenal, just as transitory, as the empirical objects it entertains. Fichte's 'self' offers philosophy no enduring and secure foothold.

Anselm proceeds to illustrate the difference between temporal cognition and eternal or holistic cognition by raising the issue of the reality of imperfection and evil (4:221–223). Though imperfection and error seem real to our eyes, in the perspective of nature as a whole, nothing is false or flawed, for in fact nothing could be otherwise than it is. An individual's psychological states, his statements, and his actions are all causally necessary within the order of nature, argues Anselm, and each failure or flaw can be explained by the agent's character or outside environmental influences. What is false and illusory is not this or that aspect of some concrete state of affairs, but the limited perspective of finite individuals as such, for only the whole exists as such.

Alexander objects that this theory makes imperfection and error necessary, and demands an account of their origin. Anselm employs a Kantian argument to sidestep this task: Imperfection, and more generally finitude, pertains only to phenomena ordered according to the law of cause and effect. To ask after the origin of finitude or imperfection is thus to pose an illicit question, for it is a causal question and, as Kant showed, causal explanation applies only to discrete elements within experience, not to the whole of experience. Anselm concludes that only *positive* logical, aesthetic, and metaphysical predicates can be ascribed to what is intrinsically real. All negation, including a privation such as imperfection, is a function of the limited temporal perspective of experiential cognition. In the perspective of time, everything is limited, flawed and debased. In arguing this way, Schelling seems to conflate Spinoza's dictum, "All determination is negation," with Kant's position that all determination proceeds by way of temporal synthesis.

Anselm underscores this association of time and imperfection by contrasting 'archetypal nature' to 'productive nature' (4:223–224), Platonic sounding terms for what Spinoza called *natura naturans* and *natura naturata* respectively. A nature composed of ideas or archetypes must be conceived as perfect, invariant, and without all reference to time, while the nature that embodies these types in individuals must be conceived as subject to the conditions of time and operating through causal conditioning. Thus an individual thing's existence in time, under the sway of causal necessitation, is in fact at variance with the thing's own nature, its eternal concept. A finite individual is never all that it can be, as Giordano Bruno put it.[31] Anselm concludes that imperfection is essentially tied to existence within time, and perfection to eternal being. This conclusion in turn will serve as a premise for the further argument that beauty is never created.

Anselm next tries to establish the claim that only the eternal concepts of things are beautiful (4:224–226). Beauty alone, among all other values, is an ontological excellence, for beauty is an intrinsic property and is never valued merely as a means to some other end. But since beauty requires independence from external conditions, it can never come to be within the temporal order. Strictly speaking, phenomenal objects existing in space and time cannot be called beautiful; beauty enters appearance only insofar as things are created which imitate beauty, and this imitation of beauty depends on the indifference that unites archetypal and productive nature. Aside from this phenomenal imitation, however, atemporal and ungenerated beauty is the very essence of things, freed from all limitation and negation, and this can only be the eternal concepts of things—Bruno will call them 'ideas.' They alone are properly said to be beautiful. And since a previous argument concluded that these same ideas are the sole criterion of truth, Anselm claims that the identity of truth and beauty is demonstrated (4:226–227).

It is important to note that the 'identity' of truth and beauty asserted is not strict identity, but indifference. 'Truth' means the invariant adequacy of eternal concepts, 'beauty' their ontological excellence and independence. Since both terms refer to a single set of entities, each expresses the essential nature of eternal concepts or ideas, but in irreducibly different ways. Truth and beauty are different angles from which to view the reality of ideas, so to speak, since they are different in meaning, but identical in reference. The 'identity' of truth and beauty thus furnishes the dialogue's first major instance of indifference, the relational structure of the absolute, and the bond between the absolute order and the phenomenal as well. This section closes with some comments on imperfect artistic approximations of beauty, which fall apart into the equal and opposite aberrations of naturalism and formalism. And so the focus of the conversation shifts to the practice of the creative artist.

Since truth and beauty have been shown to be equally profound and eternal aspects of the reality we could term 'absolute' or transphenomenal, the question arises whether it is the philosopher or the creative artist who more adequately intuits and expresses the nature of the absolute (4:227–234). Anselm begins with the nature of the work of art and its production. The work of art exhibits the identity of truth and beauty, but it does so as a thing, a spatio-temporal object which issues from the thought and work of a finite individual, and which represents various other finite objects or persons as well. The artwork is thus a paradoxical object, at once a limited thing and an exhibition of transfinite perfection. Anselm argues that the eternal must be considered the work's true creator, since only the eternal can unite the finite and the infinite. However paradoxical it may sound, the work of art is an infinite thing.

But the creative individual or artistic genius must be brought into the account as well. The only way, says Anselm, that the eternal can produce beauty while one individual produces this concrete work is if the eternal idea of the individual is really the creative agent. This move brings together the absolute order and the work of the creative artist, but unless another limitation is introduced, the artist's creation would be his self, not a work of art. The additional limitation is that beauty attaches to one or more *things* related to the individual's eternal idea. Thus three levels of being come together in the artwork: (1) the eternal or beauty itself, (2) as mediated through the personality of the creative artist, and (3) expressed within finite objects that represent other things, persons, or sensuous qualities.

Schelling notes that the more the idea of the creative individual is bound into the ideas of all other things, the more universal the artist's person will be, and the less the artwork will be a reflection of a limited and idiosyncratic personality. The work of art is thus the *Bruno*'s first example of the organic individual, the ideal form of individual existence wherein the individual is a recapitulation of the whole universe, a perspectival interpretation of an organically interrelated community of individuals. But Schelling's point is aesthetically valid as well. We may well be interested in some work wherein the artist has perfectly expressed the mood of his time in the language of his time, or in which he has literally poured out his small soul, but we are more profoundly moved by the creations of 'universal persons' such as Shakespeare or Goethe, artists who fabricate a whole world of distinct individuals and who voice the human sentiments in every dialect of their language.

A further problem arises in accounting for the universality of the creative genius's scope and for the rarity of such genuinely universal artists. Is it the case that in the process of artistic creation beauty itself is directly related to the artist's personality, to just this precise individual consciousness, or is it instead the case that the idea impinges on the creative individual in some absolute and global manner, but without full consciousness? Anselm opts for the latter alternative, emphasizing the ultimately unconscious nature of artistic inspiration. In the last analysis, then, the artist is possessed by the idea, but not fully in conscious possession of it. The artist is ultimately the tool of the absolute, and therein lies the key to distinguishing the artist and the philosopher. Since the former comprehends the absolute accidentally and unconsciously, his knowledge is said to be 'exoteric,' while the philosopher's, which is characterized by an inward and essential grasp of the idea, is said to be 'esoteric.'

The mention of esoteric knowledge brings the pedantic Anselm back to the theme of the mystery rites, and in describing their purported philosophical content, he presents a sketch of Platonism that is really the identity-philosophy in Platonic guise. In doing so, he touches on several noteworthy themes that will be developed later: (1) The self-identity of individual entities is an image of absolute identity (see 4:264–265); (2) it is the finite aspect or antitypal element of a thing that is responsible for its individual existence (see 4:316–318); and (3) the thing's separated existence is temporal because of the identity-in-difference of its psychical and material dimensions, the relative identity of its body and its soul (see 4:281–285).

II. *Indifference: The General Principle of Identity-Philosophy* [4:234–242]

Bruno now assumes direction of the discussion, and immediately dissociates himself from the peculiarities of Anselm's way of thinking. He is uninterested in historical surmise on the content of the mysteries, and promises instead the true philosophy, or at least a sketch of its foundations. In a poetic peroration he calls attention to the composite nature of the universe, which is neither finite nor infinite, neither material or spiritual, but is instead both at once. He thus distances himself from Anselm's Platonism, and from the simple dichotomy of the eternal and the finite that the latter's argument presumed. He admits, however, that the starting-point of his thought had been implicit in Anselm's treatment of the indifference of truth and beauty. Stated in its full generality, this is the idea of absolute identity, an intrinsic identity of opposites prior to any distinction of opposites one from another.

Schelling is emphatic on the point that this absolute identity is original and primary, not a result, not a synthesis of sublated opposites. Fichte had tried to describe consciousness in terms of just such a synthetic unity, yet the *Science of Knowledge* had ultimately been unsuccessful in its search for a ground for the synthesis of self and not-self.

There follows a highly abstract dispute between Bruno and Lucian on the logical status of a first principle. What is at issue within the dispute is whether the principle must be thought to be single, and philosophical procedure accordingly analytic, or whether a pair of ultimate opposites such as Fichte's self and not-self must be presumed, and philosophy's procedure seen as a progressive synthesis of these opposites. This is indeed a crucial decision point for any metaphysics. As Joachim said,

> For any monistic philosophy the fundamental difficulty is to find intelligible meaning within its system for the relative independence of the differences in the One. For any pluralistic philosophy the fundamental difficulty is to make any union of its ultimate simple entities intelligible without destroying their simplicity.[32]

Schelling argues that a metaphysics ultimately dualistic in its principles cannot provide a coherent or ultimately unitary account of reality. At the same time, he is aware of the difficulties monism must face in accounting for otherness or difference. Now while he wishes to reject Fichte's particular dualism, he must somehow build a principle of difference into his monistic principle and must argue that identity itself includes a dependent principle of limitation or differentiation. At first glance, the effort seems fraught with paradox. All depends, ultimately, on Schelling's establishing the plausibility of an absolute *identity of opposites,* that is, the ultimate nondifference of the absolute's identity *realiter* and its self-specification into a coordinated system of differences *idealiter,* in its 'form' or quasi-mental aspect. For the moment, let us take a closer look at Schelling's argumentation.

As he works to elaborate the conceptual definition of absolute identity as "the identity of identity and opposition" (4:235–239), Bruno argues that a first principle can have no opposite and that no pair of opposites can be fundamental, since opposition always obtains only within some embracing unity or synthesis. Lucian advances Fichtean-style arguments to the effect that, if identity is posited as the principle, its opposite must be posited too, since positing involves thinking, and the meaning of 'identity' is secured for thought only in virtue of its conceptual contrast to difference. The ideal or conceptual contrast of identity and difference, he suggests, implies that they must be equally fundamental and absolutely opposed in reality. Bruno responds with a complicated argument (4:236–238) that the logical and semantical opposition whereby a pair of opposed categories is meaningful need not be mirrored in reality. The contrast between identity and difference whereby the one term has meaning by excluding the other does not imply any real mingling of the two or any participation of the one in the other. Difference somehow depends on identity without modifying it, just the way that multiplicity depends on unity without destroying the fundamental character of the latter. In the course of this argument, Bruno specifies two different senses of 'identity' and 'opposition.' Relative opposites such as chemicals with widely differing properties can be brought to a relative identity (or synthesis) by reacting and forming a third substance, but absolute opposites such as an object and its mirror image can never be synthetically or relatively identified. Identity and difference are opposites in the latter sense; they are absolutely and infinitely opposed, and so can be united only in an absolute and infinite way. Lucian commits the fallacy of misplaced concreteness, conceiving identity and difference as if they were opposite things, capable of interacting and altering one another. This misapplication of experience-bound categories of substance, causality, and interaction to metaphysical fundamentals is typical of what Schelling will later attack as the standpoint of 'reflection.'

Lucian attempts to avoid the force of Bruno's argument by noting that, as the terms are defined, 'absolute identity' becomes synonymous with 'absolute opposition.' Surprisingly, Bruno agrees. Only absolute opposites can be absolutely identified, he says, and only the absolutely self-identical can be opposed to itself. He suggests a world order modeled upon the relation between object and mirror image: "If an object exists, so does an image, and if an image exists, so does an object. Necessarily, for that very reason, image and object would be together everywhere since they nowhere coincide" (4:239). The object-image model is significant, since the imaging relation prefigures Schelling's solution to the problem of the mind-body relation, and that of the natural and conscious orders of phenomena as well.

But we must ask by what logic Schelling can advance an assertion as paradoxical as, "What is absolutely self-identical and absolutely indivisible must, for this very reason, be absolutely opposed to itself." Kant had termed one species of judgment, negative in content, but affirmative in form, the 'infinite judgment,' reasoning that an assertion such as, "Soul is non-mortal" in fact asserts an infinite class in its predicate term.[33] And in the "Difference" essay of 1801, Hegel made the antinomy, the direct joining of opposites, the very paradigm of rationality.[34] The most probable origin, however, for the paradoxical assertion that self-identity is self-opposition, is Schelling's own prior reflections on the nature of the judgment. In a passage explaining how consciousness comes to represent its objects as external to itself or "in the world," Schelling reasoned as follows:

But now if concept and object originally coincide so far that neither of them contains more or less than the other, a separation of the two is utterly inconceivable without a special act whereby they become opposed in consciousness. Such an act is that which is most expressively denoted by the word *judgment* (Urteil), in that by this we first have a separation of what was hitherto inseparably united, the concept and the intuition. . . . . In the judgment, therefore, concept and object first come to be opposed, and then again related to each other, and set equal to one another.[35]

Judgment is therefore a function of differentiating the identical and reidentifying the differentiated. Now if the absolute is self-identical in a rational and expressive way, and not in the trivial way an inorganic object is, it will have this judgmental character, i.e. it will specify itself in an infinity of differences which are systematized or gathered back into identity. In the highest and most abstract case, the absolutely self-identical will be absolutely opposed to itself, or it will be indifference itself, or to say the same, the identity of identity and opposition. The formula aptly states the relation that obtains between the absolute's essence and its elaboration in 'form,' and between the absolute as a whole and the phenomenal universe; within the latter, the natural or finite order and the conscious or infinite order are related in the same way.

To this point, Bruno has argued that philosophy must be founded on one sole principle, the identity of the finite and the infinite or, borrowing Hegel's terminology, the identity of identity and opposition. Identity is the real essence of the absolute, difference a dependent modification. As ordinarily understood, namely as mere relative identity and difference which finite things exhibit, the concepts are meaningful only within this broader framework of absolute identity and absolute opposition. Schelling now turns his attention to the conceptual framework of Fichte's philosophy and attempts to demonstrate that the logic of indifference is fundamental to both their approaches (4:239–242).

Lucian asks whether Bruno's formula, the identity of identity and opposition, is sufficiently general to comprehend all conceptual oppositions. Bruno replies that 'identity,' 'opposition,' and 'identity and opposition' are perfectly general metaphysical predicates and offers to demonstrate that they will cover any pair of opposed categories put forward. Lucian suggests that the supreme identity should be conceived as the identity of the real and the ideal, or of thought and intuition. Schelling is here drawing upon sketches communicated to him by letter of Fichte's 1801 revision of the *Science of Knowledge,* where the formula, 'the identity of thought and intuition,' is advanced as the definition of absolute *knowing.*

Bruno first hints that Lucian's categories are one-sided and not sufficiently general, but he passes on immediately to the clarification of the terms 'intuition' and 'thought.' The discussants agree that intuition comes on the scene completely determined, specified in full detail. Bruno interprets this determination Spinozistically, as endless serial determination within the self-contained order of intuition, wherein one intuition i_n is determined by its predecessor i_{n-1}, which in turn is determined by i_{n-2}, and so on. Schelling has good reason to interpret intuition this way. Since for Fichte intuition is the first determination of what appears, the first production of a something 'there' for presentation, it is equally subjective and objective, and so may be viewed as *sui generis*.[36] Now since individual intuitions are completely determined and thus different from one another, Bruno reasons that the concept 'difference' is coextensive with 'intuition,' and that the latter may be substituted for the former.

Whereas intuition is seen to be equivalent to difference, the discussants agree that 'thought', the universal concept that is applicable to all appropriate determinate intuitions, is equivalent to indifference, for the concept applies to what is appropriate in a whole class of intuitions and is indifferent to what is individuating or ultimately specific in any given intuition. Thus the Fichtean notion of the identity of thought and intuition turns out to be the idea of the universal determining the particular, or the mutual establishment of concepts and objects in inseparable unity. Bruno finds this to be but another instance of the relation of indifference: The orders of general concepts and determinate intuitions are equal and opposed, each expressing the same content (from a different point of view, we might say). Because each is but an aspect or a facet of knowing, they are indivisibly united. Since the concept implies an infinity of as yet unspecified applications, while the intuition is the presence to consciousness of an individual finite entity, Lucian concludes that his formula—the identity of concept and intuition—coincides with Bruno's—the identity of the infinite and the finite. At this stage of the argument, Schelling eschews mention of the thoroughly subjective nature of Fichte's categories (but see 4:252–257, 303–307, and 326–327).

A noteworthy feature of the foregoing argument is Schelling's suggestion that the infinitude of the conceptual order is negative, not positive. Thought's infinity consists in the potentially endless repeated application of an abstract conceptual outline to a succession of determinate somethings. The concept's infinity is thus empty generality, abstractness, a standing apart from all content except in one general respect. It is Schelling's contention that Fichte's idealism attempts to absolutize this order of empty generality, an order that Kant saw was merely an aggregate of logical functions necessary to transform disparate intuitions into the continuous coherent totality we call experience.

III. The Idea as the Identity of the Finite and the Infinite
[4:242–247]

Lucian asks Bruno to clarify the notion of the union of opposites in the supreme principle. Bruno remarks that this question is central to all philosophy, since the whole enterprise is guided by a dialectical impulse, "the tendency to posit the infinite within the finite, or the reverse, to set the finite within the infinite" (4:242). And not only is this inbuilding of opposites central to our mental life, it corresponds to the absolute's eternal process of systematically specifying differences within identity, to its 'form' or quasi-mental aspect. Bruno suggests, rather elliptically, that since our cognition involves a process of continuously discriminating and identifying differentiated features, there must be an ultimate unity in which all differences are established, preserved, harmonized, and integrated. "It is necessary that there be one idea of all things, and hence that all things subsist in one idea, too" (4:243).

Now whereas the concept is an abstract unity set over against the multiplicity of intuitions, the idea comprehends and identifies both the unity of the bare concept and the multiplicity of objects furnished in intuition. The idea is therefore what the abstract formulae—the identity of the finite and the infinite, or of thought and intuition—indicated, and what Anselm suggested as well, in talking of "eternal concepts." The idea is the sole criterion of truth and beauty, for beauty is nothing else than the perfect identification of opposite features of reality, for example, of universality and particularity, or of the infinite possibilities of the species with the determinate nature of this one individual. The mature Hegel will call such an identity 'the concrete universal.'

Bruno proceeds to delineate the nature of the idea (4:243–245) and that of the concept (4:245–247) in some detail. First of all, the idea is situated within the nature of the absolute. The absolute has two aspects or poles, called 'essence' and 'form.' Essence is sheer identity; it is neither finite nor infinite, nor can it be characterized by any other disjunction of predicates. Form is indifference or identity-in-difference; it is both finite and infinite, and it can be characterized by *every* other conjunction of contrasting predicates. Form is the locus of ideas, for 'idea' signifies an individual entity within the system of differences elaborated in the absolute's form, while 'the idea of all ideas' indicates the absolute's form as such.

In the idea, all relations are relations of indifference. "Everything that is ideal is immediately also real, and everything that is real is directly also ideal" (4:243). The idea cannot be characterized as either real or ideal, and the same holds for less basic conceptual contrasts. It is an indifferent identity or, to say the same thing, a 'both . . . and . . . ,' of possibility and actuality, of unity and multiplicity, of limitation and unbounded reality. It is obviously inaccessible to finite cognition, which depends on the difference between conceptual counterparts to make sense of things. Everything fundamental to the comprehension of finite reality, the distinction of possibility and actuality, of being and nonbeing, even the modal contrast of possibility and impossibility, is without application to the idea.

From the foregoing argument the conclusion follows that no concepts that depend on the principle of semantic contrast can apply to the idea. But how else are metaphysical categories meaningful except through such contrast? For plain and unequivocal instances of 'abstractness' and 'concreteness' cannot be furnished, while indeed those of 'house' and 'automobile' can. The upshot is that Schelling is forced by his logic of indifference to forego any positive metaphysical characterization of the absolute. In essence, the absolute is the 'neither . . . nor . . .' of all contrasting predicates, in form their 'both . . . and . . . .' It hardly needs mention that the coexistence of both aspects is formally a paradox. If the absolute can be indicated at all, it is solely in terms of logical relations, not in terms of metaphysical predicates such as substance, cause, or unity. Although this procedure does not violate Kant's prohibition against extending mere concepts beyond the territory of empirical use, the emptiness of such a formalism is evident.

Bruno then turns to discussion of the concept, the domain of infinity. The concept has a genuine and completed infinity, not the pseudo-infinity of an endless serial progression in time, which is indefinite in that it is incapable of completion. In virtue of its infinitude, a concept is applicable to all relevant finite individuals over the course of time. It is thus said to comprehend and indeed comprise the possibility of individuals, but only their bare possibility.

A comparison of the natures of the idea and of the concept yields this surprising result: The finite exists in or is expressed in the absolute in two distinct ways. Though the absolute's essence is a strict identity that excludes all difference, even the opposition between thought and being, its form or quasi-mental elaboration of differences will be both thought and being at one and the same time. Form or the idea of all ideas is thus both 'infinite thought' and 'infinite reality.'[37] The former is the foundation of the phenomenal order of consciousness, the latter the basis for the correlated order of things.

Now infinite thought and all the concepts it includes have essential infinitude and constitute the timeless possibility of things. But the absolute's form is unitary and undivided, thus an identity of infinite thought and infinite reality wherein concept and intuition, the finite and the infinite dimensions of a thing are indivisibly one. The individual finite thing, therefore, exists not only as finite in the phenomenal world, but is included in the absolute's form in a double manner—as infinite concept and as eternal idea. As idea, the thing subsists as a simple identity of its real and ideal factors, an identity of its possibility and actuality, lacking any relation to time. But this involves a striking paradox, for though we can readily comprehend how the finite individual subsists qua possibility in its concept, it seems to have a double actuality, once in its separated existence within time, and again in its eternal idea. This implies that its specifically finite elements, the moment Fichte would call 'intuition,' must exist as discrete, differentiated, and serially determined within time and yet subsist in an infinite and atemporal manner within its idea.

There is a good deal of obscurity in the foregoing argument, some of it caused by terminological slippage, and some caused by lack of clarity on the ontological status of the individual finite thing. The following table may clear up the terminological matter:

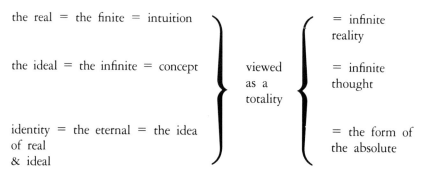

the real = the finite = intuition

the ideal = the infinite = concept

identity = the eternal = the idea
of real
& ideal

viewed
as a
totality

= infinite
reality

= infinite
thought

= the form of
the absolute

Some remarks on the table are necessary. Schelling faces no small difficulty in attempting to forge the convergence of his more naturalistic stance with Fichte's subjective idealism. Often he solves the difficulty *ad hoc,* sliding between Fichtean terms appropriate for the description of acts of consciousness to Spinozistic terms such as 'infinite thought' and 'infinite reality,' and to the quasi-Platonic terminology coined specifically for this dialogue, e.g. 'the finite,' 'the infinite', and 'the eternal.' This difficulty leads to the other mentioned above, a lack of clarity on matters of ontological commitment. To clear up this difficulty, we must anticipate Schelling's development of the concept of the powers (see 4:266–267 and 290–293) and state that all the triads in the above table name *aspects* of things, that is, features distinguished in philosophical analysis, but not distinguished in being. 'The finite' denotes the finite aspect of a thing, the sensuous content or actuality that appears in space and time. The term also refers more generally to the structure of appearance that involves individuality, materiality, and spatio-temporal existence, the first or finite 'power.' In neither case does the term refer to an individual or a thing. Schelling indeed faces the difficult task of maintaining a double ontological commitment, namely to the absolute and to individuals in the phenomenal order. But in talking, for instance, of intuition, concept, and idea, he is talking of aspects of entities distinguishable in thought; he is not talking of discrete entities. As we shall see, it is the third aspect or power, in other words the idea, that alone has any claim to being an entity in itself.

IV. *The Finite-and-Infinite Nature of the Finite* [4:247–252]

Lucian draws attention to the paradox implicit in the preceding discussion: How can the endless serial determination of things within appearances be reconciled with their eternal being in ideas? Bruno replies that neither the finite nor the infinite is intrinsically real; that is, neither things nor concepts are the fundamental entities. The eternal ideas alone are real, and they are the indifferent subsistence of the finite and the infinite. The finite and the infinite are not different in reality, for each is but a different expression of the same fundamental contents; their difference, the contrast whereby the one is what the other is not, is but the work of our limited understanding, or a function of reflection. If in any sense, therefore, one of the two can be said to be real, it possesses being only in and with the other. Things and concepts are not independent entities, nor are they individuals in their own right; they are but correlated aspects of phenomenal individuals, and, as we shall later see, the latter are but images of ideas, ideas perceived from the limited standpoint of reflection. Thus Bruno dissolves the initial paradox: The endlessly determined series of finite states or intuitions has real being only in and with its conceptual possibility in the identity of the ideas. Its existence as spread out in time is but a matter of appearance. But a new and deeper problem emerges here: Precisely how are intuitions and concepts identified in ideas? What common measure could there be between the finite and the infinite? What is it in each of the opposed orders that makes the identity of absolute opposites possible?

In answer to these problems, Bruno advances the paradoxical notion of 'the infinitely finite.' Within the absolute, he says, the finite possesses essential infinitude and lacks all reference to time, limitation, or difference, although it indeed remains finite. How this is so is best explained from the point of infinite thought, the aggregate of concepts, each of which is the ground of possibility for the succession of finite states of its object.

Within infinite thought, all finite entities are identical insofar as they are possible, argues Bruno. As merely possible, though not at all actual, there is no distinction between kinds of objects or between relations of priority and succession, as in the temporal sequence. The finite subsists atemporally in the absolute, then, so there is no intrinsic connection between finitude and existence within a temporal framework. Bruno concludes that nothing need interfere with the conceivability of the finite's possessing an infinite mode of being in the absolute. In fact the literally endless character of the time span exhibited in the phenomenal orders is only reflection's deficient manner of translating the infinite finitude of things in the absolute order.

The heart of the foregoing argument is the claim that there is nothing self-contradictory in the concept of an infinite finitude, once time is dissociated from the concept of finiteness. Schelling has not adequately argued for the latter condition, however. He intuitively perceives that it is the mutual externality of sequential states or events that makes phenomenal existence a deficient sort of being, but he nowhere makes plain in the *Bruno* how reason can overcome reflection and abolish the externality of relations—spatial, temporal, and causal—that are the framework of phenomena. The mature Hegelian system meets the same difficulty by advancing the methodological claim that thinking as such is the transformation of external relations into internal ones.

Another difficulty with the above argument is that Schelling has not yet clearly distinguished the powers or potencies from things, especially when talking of 'the finite.' The indifference of the infinite (or second power) and the infinitely finite (or first power) in the absolute means that the two poles of mentality and materiality which comprise the absolute's form are perfectly congruent; each expresses the same reality in decidedly different, though complementary ways. Schelling sometimes calls individuals 'finite things,' though, given that ideas are the only true individuals, they would be better termed 'phenomenal entities.' As we shall see, both the infinite and the finite power must be ingredient in any phenomenal individual, which is to say that each one will have a mental dimension of some sort and a correlated material one as well. Separated existence, or the individual's profoundly inexplicable apostasy from the integral life of the absolute, will involve a relative differentiation of its infinite and finite aspects, but no actual division. The finite simply never exists in and of itself.

Bruno proceeds to argue that since the finite (power) is both finite and infinite, finite entities or individuals will have a double nature (4:249–251). Examined in its concept, that is, within the limitations it establishes for itself, the finite entity is utterly individual; its ground of existence is external to its actual existence, its possibility divorced from its present actuality in time, and its concept an impoverished image of its essence. Its individuality, however, does not imply that the thing is independent or existing in its own right. Instead there is an endless diaspora of possibility and actuality that both interconnects finite beings and limits each of them individually. The possibility of some individual Y lies outside of it and behind it, in some other individual X, while it in turn bears the unactualized possibility of some future individual Z. Thus arises the sequential ordering of time and causality. "Since the finite individual is itself an actuality whose possibility is located in another individual, it will contain the endless possibility of other individuals, which, for the same reason, will contain the boundless possibility of still other individuals, and so on without end" (4:249–250). The dynamic nature of phenomenal existence stems from its deficiency, namely that the individual's full essence can never fully *exist* in any one moment or state. Existence in time means causally passing the buck.

Yet the individual's limited concept is at variance with its real standing in the absolute, where all divorce of actuality from possibility disappears, and only their indifference obtains. For within the absolute, the individual has its being as a member or a function of the whole, as part of the total organism in fact. Bruno argues that the organism is the most suitable sensible model for the absolute as form, for (1) organic interrelation is such that the possibility of the organism as a whole is vested in every part and function, while (2) it is the total pattern of interrelation among the various members and functions that establishes the function of any given member or part, and (3) the functioning part of an organism is indeed independent in its specific function, although only the organic totality exists as such. Anselm will later express this notion of organic individuality in Leibnizean terms, as the interdependence yet independence of all monads, each one a perspectival interpretation of the universe as a whole (see 4:318–320). For the moment, Bruno concludes that it is the organic character of the finite's infinite life in the absolute that requires an endless and indefinite span of development within time in order to phenomenally approximate its original and self-contained infinitude. Clearly, Schelling has grasped the difference between infinitude and endlessness, between what Hegel will call the real and the 'bad' infinite.[38]

Since the finite entity has a double nature, the question naturally arises of how individual existence is possible (4:251–252). This is clearly a difficult question for Schelling to answer; Kantian constraints on the applicability of causal or substantialistic explanation explicitly prohibit any explanation of the relation between the absolute and the phenomenal world in terms of concepts appropriate to explain phenomena. The best Schelling can do is to offer a two-sided explanation, a discussion of the conditions of individual existence from the point of view of the existing individual, and an account of the logical possibility of self-identity from the point of view of the absolute (for the latter, see 4:257–260). The connection between the two, the crucial 'why,' must remain essentially hidden and invisible.

Pursuing the first track of explaining the conditions of individual existence, Bruno argues that a finite entity is individual only within its own perspective, or, to say the same, that it is individual only insofar as it takes a limited perspective upon its real being within the absolute. Individuality is autolimitation. And this limitation of perspective is a temporal limitation, for the finite entity is in fact individuated in the act of generating its own time. The individual, explains Bruno, sunders the indifference of actuality and possibility in the absolute, interprets the logical priority of possibility over actuality as a priority of cause over effect, and places cause and effect within a schema of succession from prior to posterior. Thus it establishes its own time, for it posits the actuality of other finite beings, disconnected from their possibility, as its past. Likewise it posits the possibility of other things, disconnected from their actuality, as its future. Its view of the influence of other contemporary finite entities constitutes its present. Thus individuality is in fact explained as the collapse of the organic community of individuals within the absolute, the dispersion of their perfect coexistence without time into a temporal spread, whose measure is the distinction of past and future, and prior and posterior. From the point of view of the existing phenomenal individual, existence is time.

Bruno finds himself in the position to clearly outline the contrast between the temporal existence and the absolute being of things. In the absolute, the concepts of all things are inclusively or organically interrelated so that existent and nonexistent things subsist in an identical manner within their ideas, whereas the temporal existence of things involves the self-temporalization of each of them, the exclusion of all others as belonging either to its past or its future, and thus the generation of the whole continuous time series. Note that the general order of time as formulated by the abstract relation of prior to posterior is derivative, while the order of tensed relations among individuals is fundamental. The unique features of Schelling's treatment of time are thus (1) that each individual establishes its own time, since its separated existence is a temporal ecstasis, and (2) that the separation of one individual from the absolute precipitates the separation, or as Schelling later expressed it, the 'fall,' of all others. That one individual's attempt at self-realization involves the sequential realization of them all shows that separated, individual existence is an ontological irony; there is really no breaking of the internal and organic interrelatedness of everything, only a faulty translation of it into the medium of sequential differentiation. Separate existence is thus not real separation. Time may be the original form or framework of phenomena, thus the primary condition of reflection or discursive understanding, but it is an image of eternity as well.

Bruno concludes this section with a rhapsodic description of the absolute in the vocabulary of trinitarian theology. The strictly identical essence of the absolute is equated with the eternal Father, who in one single act of intellection (= the form of the absolute) generates the infinite and the finite powers. The infinite power is the Spirit, the unity of all, while "the finite, though in itself equal to the infinite, is yet by its own accord subjected to time and made into a suffering God" (4:252). Lucian suggests that Bruno's speculative fancy has soared into the incomprehensible and demands that the discussion return to the theme of consciousness. The stage is set for a confrontation of the claims of Fichte's phenomenalism with those of Schelling's identity-philosophy.

V. *Absolute Identity and the Domain of Knowing*
[4:252–257]

Lucian squarely poses Fichte's chief objection to the philosophy of identity, that it takes abstract formulae that legitimately describe the structure of empirical consciousness and extends them beyond the realm of evidence. Schelling's thought is apparently no longer transcendental idealism, but transcendent metaphysics. Lucian charges, "You have interpreted this identity [of thought and intuition I proposed] in such a way that it is no longer the principle of knowledge" (4:252). Bruno retorts that Lucian has done this as well, for he claimed not only that the identity of the real and the ideal is the structure of actual consciousness, but that it is the philosophical or metaphysical principle of consciousness as well. If Lucian in fact ascribes to absolute knowing the same structure of indifference that Bruno attributes to the absolute as such, then he has himself surpassed the territory of empirical consciousness and is operating as a metaphysician. Lucian explains that he employs the indifference principle transcendentally, as a heuristic device for examining empirical consciousness. Absolute identity is assumed as a principle in and of consciousness, nothing more. Philosophy, he concludes, has no warrant to entertain any notions of an absolute consciousness except in the context of explaining empirical consciousness. Having clearly stated Fichte's objection to his procedure, Schelling proceeds to ignore the considerable force of his argument. Fichte has *evidence* on his side, inasmuch as philosophy begins and ends with the given of consciousness; an absolute consciousness structured by relations of indifference is but a theoretical assumption in his philosophy. Schelling recklessly goes beyond the domain of consciousness and speculates about an absolute as such, outside of all relation to the territory of experiential consciousness.

Bruno argues his opponent into the position that consciousness is just a relative identity of thought and intuition, not an absolute one (4:254–256). Lucian concedes, perhaps too readily, that the identity of the principle of knowing is different from the identity exhibited in actual consciousness.

Bruno argues that empirical consciousness or actual knowing is but a relative, thus divisible, identity of its factors; only the metaphysical principle of knowing is characterized by complete indifference and indivisibility of its factors. But if there is one relative identity that exists outside the absolute, the ideal one or consciousness, there must be another one that does so too, a real relative identity, or *being*.

There are, claims Bruno, no real entities as such, nor any ideal ones either. There exists only relative identities of the real and the ideal. When one of the factors embarks upon separate existence, so does its correlated opposite; in fact they can exist only in and with one another. The general result follows that if the absolute enters appearance at all, it must appear as two distinct correlated points, one of which realizes the ideal by means of the real, the other of which realizes the real by means of the ideal. On the universal scale, these correlated relative identities are nature and spirit; on the individual scale, they are body and soul. Thus both orders of phenomena fundamentally belong together and reflect one another, for both nature and spirit display one identical process at work, the inbuilding of opposites, a process whereby totality is achieved whether the starting point be unity or multiplicity. It is this convergent process of the inbuilding of opposites from both directions that maps the absolute onto phenomenal existence and in fact connects apparently diverse regions of being. As we shall see in the sequel, Schelling finds much explanatory power in the complementarity of different orders of phenomena. It is this complementarity that enables him to avoid the phenomenological one-sidedness of Fichte's philosophy of consciousness and the crude materialism of its Enlightenment opponents as well. For intelligence will be seen to be equally founded in the body's capacity to represent its interaction with its environment and in the capacity of thought to detach itself from its immediate objects, representations of bodily states.

Bruno now proceeds to criticize the limitations of Fichte's subjective idealism (4:256–257). Fichte's programme, as Lucian represents it, is to reduce both being and knowing back to the structure of absolute consciousness. And yet he claims that absolute consciousness can be acknowledged as absolute only in and for the limited stance of knowing. This amounts to a reduction of being to knowing. Such a procedure, objects Bruno, abolishes the indifferent equality of being and knowing, and it is precisely this indifference that makes the absolute absolute. Whether Lucian is considering identity in its essence, as indifference, or whether he is talking of that identity's appearance within phenomena, there is no reason to restrict philosophy to an investigation of just one of the complementary orders. Neither the phenomenal order of being nor that of knowing stands on its own; each provides only distorted images of the supreme indifference.

Lucian concedes the argument at this point and moves to a conciliatory stance, though it is indeed doubtful that the philosopher he represents would have done so. There is no being as such, he asserts, only phenomenal being, nor is there any knowing as such, only the appearance of the cognizing self together with its objects inside consciousness. The contrast between being and knowing pertains to consciousness alone; the difference between the real and the ideal obtains solely within consciousness, and thus it has only ideal standing. And that, says Lucian, is precisely the meaning of the term 'idealism.' It signifies not the primacy of the ideal over the real, but the nonultimacy of the ideal-real distinction. Neither one of the two irreducible orders of phenomena is fundamental. Note that Schelling has Lucian state this point of agreement in rather idealistic terms. The rather broad definition of idealism advanced leaves a great deal of room for disagreement on what is fundamental, on what grounds the phenomenal togetherness of knowing and being.

VI. *The Logical Possibility of Separate Existence* [4:257–260]

Lucian asks Bruno to account for the possibility of the finite's departure from the absolute, that is, for the logical possibility of individuals' separate existence and for the ground of the two orders of phenomena as well. Bruno remarks that this question was implicit in Lucian's attempt to postulate absolute identity solely in reference to consciousness. He then clarifies what is to be explained, namely the exclusion of relative or nonabsolute reality from the absolute, or, what is the same, the division of nonabsolute reality into two opposite phenomenal orders. The task can be accomplished, claims Bruno, by a direct deduction of phenomenal reality from the idea itself. No transition from the absolute to the finite realm need be introduced, for the idea itself includes the distinction of the differing phenomenal orders as well as the individuals established by this distinction.

Although the eventual result of Bruno's extended argument is put forth as a 'deduction of consciousness,' the argument is rather loose and consists in an interconnected description of the mechanisms of inorganic nature, of organisms, and finally of consciousness (4:260–288). It is a deduction in the sense that its result, the triadic series of individual phenomena, is indeed implicit in its premise, the absolute idea, which is not only the organic union of all the levels or stages of appearance in general, but the union of all individuals appearing within those phases as well.

Now, for reasons we have stated above, the factual nature of individual existence is beyond explanation, but its logical possibility is subject to investigation and can be seen to reside in the nature of the absolute itself.

Schelling is not consistently clear within the *Bruno* about the difference between explaining factual existence and logical possibility, but at least some of his contemporary critical readers were.[39] J. J. Wagner points to the ambiguous nature of the relation between the absolute and phenomena as the work's central problem:

> As I embarked upon the reading of this work, I was filled with anticipation, not so much as to how the author would cancel the doubleness of reflection, but more so as to how he would reestablish it once again, after it had been abrogated.[40]

On Wagner's understanding, Schelling meets the problem not so much by a deduction of appearances as by a conceptual analysis of identity as indifference, the notion at the foundation of the whole discussion, but which receives precise and emphatic formulation only in the dialogue's closing pages.

> Schelling answers our question, "How does reflection issue from identity? How does the endlessly finite come forth from the eternal?" by establishing identity not as the sheer negation of what is different, but merely as the negation of [active] difference. So indeed, what is different is certainly not negated in the idea; it is merely sublated in its capacity to be opposed [to something else]. Its difference vis-à-vis other differences is preserved, and so too it is preserved for itself. Accordingly, differences are already contained in the thing's indifferent state or in its idea, but they are included as comprising [one] identical substance. They only become different insofar as they separate themselves [from the absolute]. The difficult point of the whole problem is thus the very act whereby something individual breaks away from the state of pure indifference for itself.[41]

Despite the fact that Schelling speaks of a "rule according to which the soul separates itself from the identity of all things" (4:284), Wagner claims no such rule is needed:

> So too our author often says that difference exists only in the perspective of the finite, but that it disappears in the sight of the divinity. Now if the divinity itself is posited in the perspective of differences as their totality (as is the case here), then difference is immediately established with the positing of indifference, and one can furnish no rule or measure that could mediate between the two. So too, one can provide no law for the separation of the finite from God. In the Schellingian idea of indifference one has already incorporated everything that should separate itself according to this so-called law. It is therefore superfluous to ask after such a law—just

as it is superfluous, once the concept of a triangle is fixed, to ask for a formula that would permit the deduction of its three angles. The concept of the triangle is itself this deduction.[42]

Alerted by Wagner's judgment that the logical problem of individuation is solved in the idea's indifference or in the absolute's formal aspect, and that the 'deduction' of phenomena is really a conceptual analysis of the idea, let us look to Bruno's argumentation.

He first offers an explanation of the difference between individual things and absolute identity in terms of limitation (4:258). In the absolute idea, the formal aspect of the absolute, the finite and infinite powers subsist in an indistinguishable unity, each one self-sufficient and unlimited. Neither factor can be distinguished from its conceptual opposite because both are unlimited. But finite things are distinguished because they reciprocally limit each other, and this limitation stems from the difference between their essence and their mode of being (or form). The succession of states necessitated by a thing's becoming in time means that the finite thing 'now' is but one aspect of its essence, of all that it can be. In the absolute, however, there is simply no difference between essence and form. Since its form comprehends the infinite and the infinitely finite in harmonious indifference, the absolute's form and essence are themselves indifferent. The absolute eternally is all that it can be.

Bruno then turns to a closer examination of the absolute's form (4:258–259). The absolute idea or its formal aspect is different from its identical essence only because it includes finitude in the first place. Of course it includes the finite as infinite finitude, thus as equal to the intrinsically infinite, and because of this equal inclusion of opposites it is itself indifferent with the absolute's essence. And yet it is because it includes the finite at all that the absolute's form becomes a community of perfect individuals, the locus of ideas. The absolute as form is thus an ideal evolution of individuals; it inchoately contains difference or the organic system of all the differentiated forms of appearance.

Things 'ideally' live a separated existence in ideas, therefore, although they are not yet actually separated and distinguished from one another. The absolute's form is the "womb of the universe," wherein things really exist as determinate relative identities of the infinite and finite powers, while ideally or 'for themselves' they are the difference of these powers. Now actual separated existence, as we have seen, involves each individual establishing its existence as the exclusion of other individuals, past and future. Evidently, in separating itself from the community of all things in the absolute's form, each thing chooses to affirm its ideal individuality instead of the essential interconnection of all things.

Let us pause to analyze this complicated web of concepts. For Schelling, each thing is at bottom but a relative identity of the finite or real power and the infinite or ideal power. As such it has both a real and an ideal dimension, and individuality logically depends on the coexistence but possible divergence of these two dimensions, which Schelling calls being *an sich* and being *für sich*. How every being can possess an ideal or for-itself dimension is not explained in depth, but Schelling clearly implies there is an incipient mental dimension to everything, and that in some sense this dimension is volitional as well as perceptive. Both in this distinction of real and ideal dimensions of all things and in the essence-form dichotomy as well, he presumes that the subject-object split fundamental to all forms of cognition characterizes reality as its most basic level. He also presumes that volitional characteristics such as having a point of view and perspectival self-assessment pertain to the mental or ideal aspect of every individual. At bottom, individual separated existence is something like self-will, a 'decision' to actualize the conceptual contrast of the real and the ideal, consequently a 'decision' to sunder the organic community of things in the absolute idea into the serial quasi independence of things under the conditions of time and of causal determination.[43] If the reader finds this course of thought puzzling and unclear, he is not alone. The problem of providing an adequate account of individuation furnished Schelling the chief impetus for altering and developing identity-philosophy in the years 1802–1806.

Bruno proceeds to explain that all things are ensouled through their subsistence in their ideas; that is, they are in living unity with the concept of all things. And it is this organic interconnection with all things that (1) makes them capable of separate existence, and (2) makes them manifest to some degree the interconnection of all within their very separate existence. For to the extent that a thing is individual and has achieved its own self-identity, it betrays the organic community of all things within the absolute. Phenomena as different as the animal's symbiosis with its environment, the motions of inorganic bodies in the system of universal gravitation, and the openness of all orders of phenomena to human cognition all testify to the mutual interinvolvement of all things.

Bruno concludes that there is a completely general structure common to all finite existence. To be finite means to be a relative identity of the finite and infinite powers and to be their difference as well. As a relative identity, the thing is individual or is its own identity; its self-identity is said to be the "image of the idea." But as a relative difference of the powers, the thing is finite, occupies space and time, and is subject to causal determination. There are both lifeless and living instances of this relative identity and difference, the former being material things, the latter acts of consciousness. What is expressed in the one is the same as what is expressed in the other. Even the general framework of phenomena exhibits the absolute's indifference, and so nature and consciousness constitute strictly parallel orders of appearances.

VII. *General Structures of the Universe: Individuation and Time* [4:260–263]

In a fairly disconnected set of remarks, Bruno addresses himself to those features of phenomenal individuals that are responsible for identifying their mental and material aspects, that is, the mechanisms for inbuilding difference or establishing indifference out of difference. Now the stars are perfect individual entities, for in their finite state they minimize the divergence between the finite and the infinite by infinitizing the finite. The way they equalize the finite and the infinite aspects of their existence is what makes them imperishable, and it establishes their living and animate character as well, whereby they are said to be immortal gods. But to some degree, every being approximates this perfection inasmuch as it is imbued with time and ensouled by its concept.

Switching to Fichte's idealistic vocabulary of intuition, concept, and idea, Bruno explains that the finite power or intuition is unitary, undifferentiated, passive and receptive of all, when it is confined within the absolute. Intuition becomes determinate—a presentation of a something—only in the particular thing, where it sets itself opposite to thought. Now neither intuition nor thought is intrinsically temporal; each becomes subject to time, and temporalizes the substance of the thing (the image of the idea) too, through their relative division from one another and their subsequent reunification (4:260–261).

Schelling is not very specific in this passage, but given the fact that Fichte interpreted the presentation, the basic unity of thought and intuition, as a wavering that is brought to a stand,[44] perhaps Schelling means that the division and reunification of intuition and thought generate the succession of discrete moments that constitute a thing's time. Time would then be an ongoing identification of the different, the process of inbuilding the finite and the infinite. It would be time that would translate the thing's essence or idea into its limited form of development and make it a relative identity and opposition of the powers. As we shall see, time, self-identity, and consciousness are all manifestations of the infinite power within finite appearances (see 4:265).

Bruno then turns the discussion toward the topic of the phenomenal individual's substance or self-identity (4:262–263). Since the individual is the relative identity and opposition of the finite and infinite powers, and since these powers appear as its physical and psychical aspects respectively, neither the physical nor the psychical can be real as such. Just as the idea welds the universal and the particular into an identity in the absolute, so there must be something in the individual that "imitates the idea and eternally establishes the universal within the particular and the particular within the universal" (4:262). This is the 'image of the idea,' in itself indifferent, but in relation to difference, an inbuilding force tending to produce indifference. It is the image of the idea that unites the infinite dimension of a thing, its 'soul,' with its finite or bodily dimension. It is the individual's substance, though it appears neither in the psychic nor in the bodily order.

Hence every individual thing exhibits a threefold structure. Its body or finite dimension is responsible for the thing's separated existence, while its soul or conceptual dimension makes continuance in separate existence possible by securing self-identity and individuality. In virtue of the latter, the individual, though self-excluded from absolute identity, is nonetheless its own identity. These two dimensions are united by the image of identity, whose function is to unify and integrate these two and to secure their togetherness. Individuation is primarily a function of the finite positing itself as perfectly finite, which in turn limits the associated infinite dimension to being the concept of but one individual, and subjects the third or idea-like element to a finite and temporal mode of existence as well. The individual thing's existence thus involves all three powers—the finite, the infinite, and the eternal—but all as subject to conditions characteristic of the finite.

VIII. General Structures of the Universe: Space, Time, and Gravity [4:263–266]

The same threefold structure of the powers, which will eventually be recognized as the basic pattern of the phenomenal universe, repeated on all levels of being and within all types of entities as well, is now seen to establish the continua which are the framework of all material appearances. Absolute (or empty) space is the perfect indifference of the finite, infinite, and eternal powers as it appears in the form of finitude. It is thus "the eternally resting and unmoved image of eternity" (4:263) or the dispersion of the perfectly internal relations that constitute the absolute's form into the form of externality.

The basic dimension of space is length, and it is the expression of the infinite or conceptual power, for not only is the endlessness of the line a finite analogue of the concept's infinitude, but the postulation of the line at the start of geometry is a pure abstraction, a purely constructive mental activity. Now indifference as such is incapable of being expressed in just one dimension, and so is imaged only in all three spatial dimensions together. Nonetheless the line is said to establish the relative identity of subject and object, the same identity that appears in individual things as cohesion and self-identity, and within nature as a whole as the affinity of things, of which the phenomenon of magnetism is but a special case.

Breadth, the second dimension of space, is the expression of difference or of the finite power. It is in virtue of the finite power that things are subject to time, for, when related to a determinate finite entity, the concept's essential infinitude is abolished. As the soul of this one individual, the concept becomes merely the idea of this body. In this case both the psychical and the somatic aspects of the individual are finite and stand opposed to the infinitude of the pure concept, and the individual, instead of containing its own time, is ruled by external or 'physical' time. This argument is hardly clear as it stands, but evidently Schelling thinks that the concept or infinite power appears within phenomena as time, "for time is the harmoniously flowing image of infinite thought" (4:265). Where the relative identity of subjectivity and objectivity, externally expressed in the dimension of length, is internally possessed by an individual, it becomes living time itself or self-consciousness.

Though Schelling here establishes the connection between the *concept, time-production,* and an entity's *self-identity* in a very loose and unsatisfactory fashion, nonetheless it is an important and suggestive idea in at least two ways: (1) Although Schelling directly borrows the doctrine of the parallel nature of the psychic and somatic orders from Spinoza, he gives it an idealistic rather than a naturalistic interpretation. Though the mental indeed mirrors the material inasmuch as the soul-concept is the idea of this one body, it is the mental, not the material, that is primary in this relation. The material (that is, discrete, completely determinate intuitions or presentations) exists in succession and is endlessly differentiated. It is the mental dimension that secures the individual's self-identity, connecting the various intuitions or states in a historical, not a substantial manner. Schelling thus provides an idealistic interpretation of Spinoza's mind-body parallelism, one more acceptable to Fichte than Spinoza's own naturalistic interpretation. (2) Though the association of concept, time-production, and self-consciousness seems a synoptic compression of all the epistemological apparatus of Kant's *Critique* into one idea, it is Spinoza's dynamic understanding of a concept (in his terms, 'idea') that permits the association. Only if a concept is an active thinking (of something), an expression of thinking rather than an impression of an object, can it be associated with time-production and the synthetic awareness of consciousness. Given this dynamic sense of Schelling's notion of the concept, one can perhaps see why Hegel, who in early works such as the *System of Ethical Life* employed the vocabulary of intuition, concept, and idea, chose in his mature works to call the self-developing absolute "the concept" and employed the term "idea" only for its static, unembodied logical side.

Bruno continues his exposition of the continua that link material phenomena by noting that it is the infinite power, whose clearest and definitive expression is self-consciousness, that is responsible for things being extended in space and enduring within time. Extension results from *extending*, time from *enduring;* both are synthetic and systematizing *activities,* despite the fact that their outcome is the framework of external relations between things. Light and gravity, their higher-order correlates, extend the scope of this systematizing activity, while abolishing the externality of things. Thus all the major components of the structure of the physical universe reveal that difference, individuality, and externality are but vanishing moments, not the ultimate character of things. "However much an individual being enlarges the sphere of its existence by departing from the absolute, eternity still holds it fast" (4:258).

Bruno then turns to the third dimension of space, depth, which unites the relative identity of length and the difference of breadth and thus extinguishes their difference. It is the expression of the third and highest power, the identity of the universal and the particular. In individual things, the third power or 'image of the idea' unites the opposed psychic and physical dimensions and secures the individual's self-identity; it is the idea within appearances, or rather *behind* appearances. For finite things exist as individual only in virtue of the opposition of the universal and the particular, i.e. of the concept and the material thing. Hence the individual as a whole is infected by difference and so stands opposed to its unity, which accordingly seems not to exist, but merely to be the hidden ground of existence. Within appearances, only the finite and the infinite power step forth; their unity, which is the sole real element, is a disappearing moment. The nonapparent character of the third and highest power is seen even more clearly in its universal function of binding the things of nature together into a system, namely gravity.

'Gravity' is the name Schelling gives to the activity of assimilating difference into indifference within the system of things as a whole. Gravity is the intrinsically indivisible tendency to identify all individuals and thus abolish their individuality, a uniform striving for identity over against every sort of difference. Among inanimate things, it is the force of mutual attraction we commonly call gravity; in individuals, it is the binding together of body and soul; within conscious individuals, it is the principle of intellection and volition.

In all of its forms, gravity remains hidden, a force observable only in what it does. Indeed, the striking feature of all manifestations of the third power—as the union of body and soul, the force that makes natural bodies a system, the synthetic connection of awareness and presentation in intuition, and the identification of concepts and intuitions in thought—is just this *invisibility*. Time, space, the individual's self-identity and cohesion, the forces that work the plurality of things into nature, the synthetic identity of self-consciousness, reason itself—these are the real structures that make phenomena possible, but they are themselves hidden, or, insofar as they do appear, empty and contentless 'things.' Within appearances, only differences stand forth, never the unifying structure of appearances. And on this fact rests the whole plausibility of Schelling's postulation of a nonphenomenal or absolute dimension where the indifference of things obtains as such.

The absolute is a logical domain, a fact apparent from its abstract definition as "the identity of identity and opposition." Though Schelling often seems tempted to hypostatize the logical and turn it into some metaphysical otherworld, his arguments capitalize on the mysterious non-appearance and nonpresentability of the connective elements which thought demands. For the logical, that which in bringing things to a systematic unity is tantalizingly everywhere and nowhere, is certainly never given, never an element of experience. The force of Schelling's argument is to convince us that Kant and Fichte were mistaken in attempting to locate the logical domain in the workings of the knowing subject and to force the logical to migrate from the territory of the synthetic *a priori* to that of 'the absolute.'

IX. *The Three Powers Generalized* [4:266–267]

Bruno now explicitly distinguishes the three levels of being that display the powers or 'potencies' with utmost generality—the inorganic, the organic, and the rational. The first power, or the inorganic, determines the spatio-temporal existence of phenomenal individuals; the second, or organic power, (equivalent to 'the infinite' or 'the concept') renders them intelligible; but the third, or rational power, is the real and substantial element of things. Thus all the general structures of appearance—space, time, gravity, individual identity, and the unity of consciousness—are images of reason, relatively differentiated forms of reason's pure indifference. Inorganic entities fill space and time because they establish a difference between the universal and the particular, and thus disrupt the purity of reason's fully internal identification of identity and opposition. Animate and sentient beings establish a difference between self-consciousness and sensation; in this case it is the subject-object difference which again disturbs the pure vacuity of reason and generates distinct acts of consciousness.

Schelling neglects to make sufficiently clear in the *Bruno* the notion of the powers or potencies he carefully elaborated in the 1801 *Exposition of*

My System. Each potency (*Potenz*) recapitulates and repeats the basic structure of indifference or the identity of opposites, but in a quantitatively different way. If the third power is indifference itself or a complete quantitative equality of universality and particularity, the other powers repeat the same structure, but with a quantitative imbalance toward one pole or the other. Thus in the second or infinite power, universality or subjectivity predominates over particularity, while in the first power, particularity or objectivity predominates over universality. Since each of the powers expresses the fundamental structure of indifference in merely quantitatively different ways, they are said to be 'powers' by analogy to mathematical powers. When the lowest or finite power, or rather the structure of indifference which underlies its predominant objectivity, is 'potentiated' or raised to the second power (or 'squared'), the opposite factor of universality or subjectivity predominates. And when the basic structure of indifference is raised to the third power (or 'cubed'), indifference itself stands out, without any quantitative imbalance of one pole over the other. While all this pseudomathematical language seems a bit fanciful, Schelling's basic idea is that the three levels—subjectivity, objectivity, and their identity—are (1) repetitions of the same logical pattern, and (2) involved, all of them, in each and every phenomenal thing. "Thus every single thing exhibits the universe, each in its own way" (4:267). The version of Leibniz's monadology that Anselm later presents (see 4:318–321) is meant to expand upon this point. For every phenomenal individual is but a limited point of view for intuiting the absolute, a perspectival interpretation of the totality of things. An individual exists within appearances only to the extent that it is a deficient translation of the organic interrelatedness of things within the absolute idea.

X. *Specific Structures of the Universe: The Heavenly Bodies*
[4:267–279]

Bruno now launches into a lengthy and highly poetic treatment of the most perfect sort of natural beings, the stars and planets. Although the idea of doing celestial mechanics *a priori* doubtless strikes us as humorous—a notable example is the deduction of sunspots (4:276)—it is safe to say that Schelling viewed this section as a literary-historical excursion, a poetic counterpart of his more sober endeavors to systematize the findings of empirical science in a "philosophy of nature."[45] Bruno's discourse combines the ancient view of the stars and their spheres as divinities, moving in perfect circles and driven by intelligence (the heritage of Aristotle, Ptolemy, and Dante), with modern celestial mechanics, as first formulated by Kepler. The section is intended to be a tribute to Kepler, and an anti-Newtonian polemic as well. Schelling views Kepler as a unique event in the history of ideas, the coincidence of the opposed tendencies of artistic creativity and the spirit of empirical science:

> From this, too, it is apparent why and to what extent there is no genius in science; not indeed that it would be impossible for a scientific problem to be solved by means of genius, but because this same problem whose solution can be found by genius, is also soluble mechanically. Such, for example, is the Newtonian system of gravitation, which could have been a discovery of genius, and in its first discoverer, Kepler, really was so, but could equally also have been a wholly scientific discovery, which it actually became in the hands of Newton.[46]

It is consistent with the *Bruno*'s rather vocal attack upon mechanistic materialism (see 4:305–315) that the general laws of nature be sketched out in the half-occult, half-mathematical manner of Kepler. The many direct citations and echoes of the *Timaeus* to be found within the account reinforce the impression that this treatment of nature is deliberately poetic. Space will not permit more than a mention of its chief points.

The heavenly bodies are the most perfect natural things, since they are directly ensouled by the infinite concept; thus they contain their own time and are self-conscious. They are the first individuals, and as befits the first images of the absolute, they are organic unities, populated with all sorts of individual entities, living genera, so to speak. "In short, they are blessed animals, and compared to man, undying gods" (4:262). Their perfection consists in their being natural beings but at the same time displaying the hallmarks of all levels of being, the inorganic, the organic, and the rational.

The planets are "sensible images of the whole real universe" (4:269). In their motion they imitate the idea and embody its activity, the inbuilding of differences. Any being that is not itself substance exists by fleeing its substantial origin and identity, for motion is the indifference of gravity expressed within difference. Such an imperfect thing flees the center in such a way that the time of its motion equals the square of the distance moved, for time expresses relative identity, while distance expresses difference or finitude. The nonsubstantial thing thus instantiates indifference within its very motion, or the identity of the second power with the square of the first, in that $t = d^2$. If the thing moves towards its center of being, the relation is reversed, and the distance moved equals the square of the time of motion. Thus the motion of imperfect things is governed by the inverse square law.

The planets or perfect beings, however, do not move in straight lines or in trajectories, but in circles. Movement through a circular orbit does not exemplify the inverse square law, but instead exhibits a perfectly proportional relation between the time and distance moved. Circular motion is thus the perfect movement, assuming that a body moves through a circular course at a constant rate.

But the planets do not in fact traverse circular orbits, nor do they move at a constant velocity. Here is where Kepler's laws come in, the laws which "seem to have been disclosed to us by a divine intelligence" (4:270). The first law states that the planets' orbits are ellipses, one of whose foci is the sun. The two foci that determine a planet's elliptical path represent identity and difference respectively; in virtue of the first, the planet inheres in the absolute, while in virtue of the second, it possesses self-identical individuality. Thus the planets symbolize the togetherness of the absolute order and phenomenal existence: "Things were so arranged that we might recognize identity within difference itself and appreciate the destiny of each of the heavenly bodies, that is, as particular beings to be absolute, and as absolute to be particular things" (4:271). Kepler's second law states that there is an unvarying proportion between the ratio of the time of motion and the distance covered in one arc and that of any other. In other words, though the times and distances covered in different arcs indeed vary, and the velocity of motion as well, there is yet a constant proportion among all arcs of the elliptical orbit, as if the body were moving at a constant rate in a perfectly circular path. "The stars, though they seem to traverse paths that are distorted circles, truly describe circular orbits in full conformity with the idea" (4:272). Indifference is again exemplified within difference itself.

To facilitate the transition from inorganic to organic nature, Bruno offers a general formula for assessing the perfection of individual entities: Things in the visible universe are perfect to the degree that they incorporate time, that is, to the degree that they approach or approximate self-consciousness. Now time is external to inorganic things; their difference can be assimilated into indifference only externally, through the force of gravity. But time is inherent in organic creatures; to be alive is to internally systematize and control different life-functions, to establish an indifferent continuity of life across continuously varying environmental conditions. Inorganic things indeed cohere into a system inasmuch as each one attracts every other, but this is merely passive inclusion into a totality. Organisms, on the other hand, are active systems, and not only within their own bodies but in their symbiosis with their environment. The inorganic system-principle is gravity, while that of the organic world is 'light.' Light is the "eternal idea of all corporeal things" (4:278), the ideal expression of the living unity of things. Now light is external to highly differentiated inorganic beings, just the way time is; dead things are passively incorporated into a system of visibility, just as they are incorporated into the system of gravity. Organic entities, however, contain their own 'light,' while conscious beings are capable of operating by the 'light of reason.'

XI. *Specific Structures of the Universe: Animal Life*
[4:279–281]

The fundamental difference between the things of inorganic nature and living things is their psychic dimension. Bare things are ensouled not by form or the idea, but by the mere concept; this concept, associated as it is with but one individual, is limited to expressing only so much of the universe as the body in question expresses. You might say the psychic dimension of bare things is pure feeling, without discrimination or awareness. The limited concept is merely a reflection of the isolated material body, and thus the thing remains disconnected from others.

The animal, however, contains time and light, both expressions of the second power, and thus to some degree embodies the idea, the living interconnection of all things. The animal in its very being is the interdependence of many different functions and it "contains within its concept the possibility of infinitely many things that lie outside its individual existence" (4:279), whether by way of propagation, motion and interaction, or by way of perception. Animals' actions appear purposive or rationally ordered; this is because in them the idea is the agent or intuitor, but not in a fully self-possessed manner. The idea is the animal's ground of being, thus distinct from it; the organism as such is not the existing idea, the way the rational and self-conscious knower and agent will be.

Both inorganic and organic nature, concludes Bruno, "reveal the mystery hidden away in God—the absolute identity of the infinite, which is the pattern, and the finite, which is the antitype" (4:281). As individually existing identities of correlated mental and material dimensions, all things exhibit the indifferent structure of the absolute idea. Precisely how all things are bodily and yet all are ensouled will unfold in the following section.

XII. *The 'Deduction' of Consciousness* [4:281–290]

Working toward the goal of elaborating the structure of self-consciousness, Bruno first spells out the double nature of the concept functioning as the soul of an individual and its strictly finite duration (4:281). It will be helpful at the start to recall that Schelling does not wish to accord priority to the ideal or the realm of consciousness, as did Fichte, and that, for him, the mental order is just as phenomenal as its material counterpart. Neither minds nor bodies are fundamental or have independent existence.

And since the mental dimension has been identified with the 'infinite concept' that ensouls the individual finite entity, Bruno's first step must be to establish the finitude of the soul.

As the 'soul' of an individual thing, the concept is potentially what the body actually expresses, or it is the possibility of the actual states (of itself and its surrounding environment) that the body expresses. This means (1) that the soul-concept is primarily the representation of bodily states and (2) that it is logically and ontologically prior to bodily states in that it grounds their possibility. The first point is a direct borrowing from Spinoza's psychology, the second an idealistic modification thereof.

The body is an infinite-and-finite sort of thing, a definite individual, yet capable nonetheless of exhibiting the whole universe (presumably by registering any change of state in its ongoing interaction with its environment). The concept that mirrors the body is limited or finitized in that very mirroring; even though it is the infinite concept of soul, it is at the same time the finite concept of this one individual. Thus soul exists in association with one individual in such a way that it is doubled, for it is at once the infinite possibility of cognition qua infinite concept, and the merely limited actuality thereof qua concept of this one body. "If you posit the existence of infinite cognition as the soul of one particular body, then you are positing a double soul, as it were, one soul embracing the [limited] actuality of infinite thought, the other soul its infinite possibility" (4:282).

The foregoing argument is difficult and highly abstract, yet one can see that in the split between the infinite possibility of cognition and its limited actuality, the structure of consciousness has already been articulated. For what is consciousness other than the ongoing synthesis of certain actual cognitions reflecting the state of the body (sensations) with the abstract cognition of universal concepts (categorial concepts, the infinite possibility of experience)? This will become clearer, in due time.

For now, it would be helpful to examine the puzzling notion of a 'double-soul.' It is introduced not only to account for the difference between sensory cognition and conceptual understanding, but to inject the symmetry of indifferential relations into Schelling's account of the psychic. Recall that though the finite appears phenomenally as simple finitude or isolated individuality, it exists in the absolute as the *infinitely finite* (see 4:247–252). In the same way, though the infinite or conceptual order is intrinsically infinite, it appears within the finite as *finitely infinite,* as associated with and ensouling one individual body. Though in general and in the abstract, concept and thing are simply opposed as infinity and finitude, when the one exists in and with the other under the conditions of appearance, each is *infinite-and-finite.* And this coexistence of the same and different furnishes another testimony that only the indifferent togetherness of the two is real and substantial. The finite and infinite powers are indivisibly united in the idea; within phenomena, however, they are merely relatively and divisibly associated. Hence neither acts of consciousness nor things are fundamentally real or exist independently of each other. "Indeed consciousness has no reality in the sight of the absolute, but, just like everything else that pertains to the image world, consciousness is real for itself and in its own perspective" (4:282).

In a phenomenal individual, therefore, the only real element is the identity of soul and body as it exists in the idea, an identity imperfectly imaged in appearances. Now soul and body exist solely within time, and this existence under the form of duration results from their mutual opposition—the way that physical states and acts of consciousness are distinct phenomenal occurrences, doubly yoked together in that the latter mirror the former, while the former realize the possibilities enunciated in the latter. Now soul is the infinite concept made finite by its association with an individual body. Insofar as it mirrors the states of the body, it is conditioned by duration and only in this manner can it exist as soul. It follows, then, that the soul is just as mortal as the body is. Neither is soul immortal as directly associated with the body, nor is the 'infinite concept of soul' either—soulishness in general, that which is common to all souls, that which is responsible for the abstract universality of thought. For just as the perceptual soul is directly related to and limited by the body, so the cognitive soul is directly related to and limited by the perceptual soul.

From this complicated description emerges Schelling's picture of the finite and merely phenomenal character of consciousness. The infinite concept in fact exists only as *sensation,* the empty infinitude of *abstract concepts,* and their thoroughly discursive synthesis in the *unity of consciousness.* Whereas Fichte would absolutize the domain of thought, Schelling insists that the infinite concept exists merely as the psychic dimension of this finite individual, inside a temporal process wherein one determinate concept is determined by a prior concept, and that one in turn determined by a prior one, and so on without end.

Bruno concludes his long exposition by noting that the opposition of the perceptual and the cognitive souls mirrors the opposition of soul and body as such. Since the infinite and finite powers are both variations on the fundamental theme of indifference, one can translate realistic talk of phenomenal individuals as soul-body composites into idealistic talk of the identity and opposition of sensations and concepts in the unity of consciousness. Though such a formula for conceptual mapping is hardly likely to dissolve all of Fichte's mistrust of a Spinozistic realism, it at least facilitates the transition from discussion of the phenomena of nature to those of consciousness. The deduction of consciousness which follows

(4:285–290) is really the discrimination of a fundamental opposition in the unitary act of consciousness. For the subject-object contrast is but a variation on the theme announced in the treatment of inorganic and organic nature, the relative identity and opposition of the finite and infinite powers (see 4:260).

Bruno and Lucian now join forces to clarify the double nature of soul. The opposition of the finite and the infinite aspects of soul, united only in the eternal idea, can express the soul-body opposition. Now the finite soul, which they term 'objective existing cognition,' stands to the infinite soul or 'the infinite concept of cognition' as actuality stands to possibility. Objective cognition, therefore, or the finite concept that mirrors the states of the body, is endlessly determined, sensation following upon sensation in the exact order that bodily state follows upon bodily state. The concept of cognition, on the other hand, the infinite concept which establishes the possibility of all of the determinate states of objective cognition, is complete, self-identical, and unchanging. The finite soul or objective cognition is thus the heterogeneous series of sensations, while infinite soul is the abstract identity of the concept as such. The double nature of the soul thus turns out to be the identity of thought and intuition, the formula Lucian previously advanced as his candidate for the first principle of philosophy. Bruno notes, now that this identity has turned out to be nothing more than a formula for the structure of consciousness, that the formula is strictly regional and lacks the generality requisite for the first principle of all philosophy.

Bruno then turns the discussion to the unity of consciousness (4:288ff.). Objective cognition (or sensory intuition) is finite insofar as it has the body as its object, but as related to the concept of cognition (or thought), it is infinite as well as finite. Now the concept of cognition is intrinsically infinite. Hence the unity of consciousness is an identity of two infinites— a knowing that unitarily comprehends two distinct knowings, one sensory, the other conceptual, one fully determinate, the other completely abstract and empty. The dynamic identification of these two different sorts of cognition is consciousness itself, or selfhood. Bruno employs the suggestive phrase "the infinite's coming to itself" to describe the process whereby objective cognition is transformed and infinitized, or transcends its finite condition of being merely the representation of a bodily state by being associated with the concept as such. Selfhood or self-consciousness is, therefore, the transformation of images of physical states into an active cognition, an emergence of a 'self' from the process of integrating sensations under concepts.

Schelling's account strongly suggests that the unity of consciousness, Fichte's I = I, is an emergent synthesis and not some logically prior pure act whereby cognition is first made possible. Sensations are first, then integration of sensations under concepts, then self-awareness. Implicit in this analysis of cognition is the view that the self is phenomenal and not fundamental, as Fichte would have it. No priority can be claimed for self-awareness over sensation. Both are strictly matters of appearance.

Bruno does not call attention to these implications, however, and allows Lucian to append the classical Fichtean description of the self to his account (4:289). The self, says Lucian, is the act of self-constitution, so that its being is its own deed. As the process of infinite thought's self-objectification, it is the identity of subject and object. This self-objectification is in fact the generation of appearances, for phenomenal things exist only in and through the discursive synthesis of sensations and concepts called the 'self.'

Bruno accepts these claims, yet subtly alters them by insisting that consciousness is not only the objectification of the infinite concept, but betrays the presence of the first and third powers as well. The concept is but the possibility of the manifold states of objective cognition, which serially actualize the abstract but universal possibility of the concept. And their necessary togetherness, the unity of consciousness, betrays the work of the third power, the phenomenal image of the eternal idea. Since the three powers together constitute the structure of consciousness and are found in all things as well, Bruno and Lucian can come to agreement on idealism as a methodological stance: "We can, therefore, comprehend the laws and conditions for finite things without having to extend our investigation beyond the question of the nature of knowing" (4:290).

The claim that knowing can by itself furnish the laws and conditions for the existence of things is a refinement of Kant's dictum, "The conditions of the *possibility of experience* in general are likewise conditions of the *possibility of the objects of experience*."[47] The agreement achieved is tenuous, though. Schelling can claim allegiance to idealism as a methodology because the structure of consciousness sufficiently exhibits the three powers, the conceptual tools for establishing a complete ontology. But Fichte would still want to emphasize subjectivity over objectivity and to ground objectivity in the self's original and founding activity. To prevent recourse to this sort of subjective idealism, Bruno reminds Lucian that it is neither self-awareness as such nor sensation that constitutes knowing, but only their dynamic identity. Further investigations of the elements of cognition will reveal the presence of the three powers inside the apparently simple elements of thought and intuition.

XIII. *The Domain of Knowledge* [4:290–297]

The basic claim of Schelling's philosophy of identity is that there exists nothing that is purely ideal and nothing purely real. Everything that we distinguish in phenomena is but an instance of indifference or subject-object identity, relatively differentiated from others by whether it exists under the finite power (as do bodies) or under the infinite power (as do minds). Thus no body lacks an infinite or mental dimension of some sort, nor are conscious minds ever found apart from organic bodies. The same hierarchy of potentiated instances of indifference manifests itself within the domain of knowing itself, where intuition and thought turn out to be not isolated, heterogeneous elements, but repetitions, on a more minute scale, of the subject-object identity that constitutes consciousness itself.

The investigation of the moment of *intuition* inside knowing (4:290–293) makes evident that intuition is not sheer finitude or difference, but is itself a structure that involves all three powers. Since in general there can be no strictly finite entity, there cannot be a purely finite moment in knowing. Bruno remarks that Lucian was correct in associating intuition with finitude, but not so in identifying the two, for intuition is really the coexistence of all three powers under the general preponderance of the finite. Intuition is the togetherness of sensation and awareness. Sensation is its finite factor; that is, it is a direct representation of a state of the body. The awareness of the sensory representation is the infinite factor, while their necessary togetherness, the intuiting agent or that which senses, is the eternal or rational factor. Only when all three aspects hang together as a whole do we have a case of intuition, an act of consciousness that is a presentation of a something.

Bruno notes that what is real in the unitary complex of intuition is the third element, the unity of consciousness. The remaining factors may indeed be analytically distinguished as sensation and awareness, sensing and what is sensed. However they do not exist independently or outside of the unity of consciousness; only within this unity can they step forth as opposite moments. A similar analysis applies to the intuited object. Since it can appear only within consciousness, and since it holds its status of objectivity only in and through the unity of consciousness, it is not a purely real entity, but one that is at once real and ideal. An intuition is, therefore, an intuition of a concept in an instance of being. And since the concept and the sensed something that falls under the concept have no standing other than as moments of the unitary act of intuition, Bruno is able to advance the paradoxical claim, "You never intuit anything other than concepts" (4:292). If that sounds shockingly Platonic, he stresses again that the only thing real in the act of intuition is the self that intuits, reason existing under the finite power. And reason, in all of its potentiated forms, is nothing other than the activity of inbuilding differences into one another; it is the dynamic identification of the universal and the particular which in each and every moment has indifference as its product.

Hence intuition as such is pure indifference; its object is space as such, the absolute space of geometry. Intuition as such is quite different from intuition of a particular thing or state of a thing, for the lucidity and transparency of pure geometrical relations becomes opaque and space becomes filled when the perfect indifference of the three spatial dimensions is shattered and reestablished in a purely contingent manner. Now what occasions the filling of space, and the subsequent subjection of reason to the merely finite function of intuition, is the basic condition of individual or separate existence, namely the immediate relation of the infinite concept to the finite individual thing.

Bruno notes that it is intuition operating in this subordinate capacity that Lucian previously opposed to thought. But intuition as such is not opposed to thought; in its structure and function, intuition is pure reason itself, whose differently potentiated form appears as thought. Intuition and thought turn out to have the same structure, then, and it is only as differently indexed forms of reason that the two can be identified within the unity of consciousness. Conversely, it is only within the unity of consciousness, the phenomenal correlate of pure reason, that the sensory presence of a something and the thinking of that something by means of a universal concept can be distinguished. In matters of epistemology at least, a contemporary critic's complaint rings true: "Schelling is reproached with almost always being in suspense between idealism, realism, and even materialism."[48]

Bruno now turns to the investigation of *thought,* which itself falls into three moments—the concept, judgment, and syllogism (4:293–297). His depiction of the interinvolvement of the three powers in the domain of the concept furnishes an interesting anticipation of the mature Hegel's *Logic,* despite his eventual judgment that logic pertains to the domain of phenomena and thus will not provide any ladder to the absolute.

Existing under the form of finitude, the knowing we call intuition is limited to the presentation of a succession of mutually exclusive states. "In each moment, only a portion of the entire universe falls within the scope of intuition" (4:293). Existing under the second power, however, the unitary complex of factors that constitutes the act of intuition becomes directly related to the infinite concept; thus it is transformed from being the intuition of a single something into an infinite capacity for intuition, or a thinking. And thinking itself again involves three distinct functions, corresponding to the three levels or powers. "The infinite that is posited as infinite we call 'the concept,' while the finite subsumed under the infinite generates the judgment, just as the eternal posited as infinite generates the syllogism" (4:293–294). All three of these forms of thought are infinite, completely general and valid for all objects and for all time. As will appear later, the infinity of the conceptual order corresponds to its emptiness (see

4:299–300). For the functions of thought stand in need of acts of intuition for phenomenal knowing to arise. Thought, though infinite, is limited by its abstract generality, and cannot attain to reason's real function, the integration of the universal and the particular.

Bruno then proceeds to a deduction of the pure concepts, or what Kant had called the 'categories of the understanding' (4:294–296). The modal concepts of possibility, actuality, and necessity stand in no need of deduction; Kant himself had hinted they were not exactly categories, but metacategories of a sort.[49] They are already adequately displayed in the component factors of intuition, namely sensation (actuality), awareness (possibility), and the union of the two (necessity). In addition, the modal concepts specify the various forms of thought: The concept is the possibility of intuitions (of such and such a type), a judgment is the determination of their actuality, while the syllogism establishes the necessity of intuitions in conformity with its conceptual connections.

Evidently, Schelling considers the modal concepts to be something more than concepts or categories. While the latter are mere logical functions necessary for the conceptual grasp of what intuition presents, actuality, possibility, and necessity seem to be part of the 'deep structure' of reality itself. They seem to express the three powers in their interrelations. For the infinite power is related to the finite as possibility is related to actuality, and just as necessity is the identity of possibility and actuality, so the eternal or rational power is the identity of the finite and the infinite. And within each triad of pure concepts, which are determined by the interpenetration of the powers, the members stand related as do possibility, actuality, and necessity within the triad of modal concepts.

The categories of quantity result from the expression of the three powers under the preponderance of the second or infinite potency. This potency is responsible for the generation of time, and so the possibility, actuality, and necessity of time furnish the pure concepts of *unity, plurality,* and *totality*. The categories of quality are the three powers indexed to the first or finite power. This power is responsible for the generation of space, and so the possibility, actuality, and necessity of space furnish the pure concepts of *reality, boundary* (or negation), and *determination*. Both of these triads equally exhibit the fundamental concepts of reason—identity, opposition, and the identity of identity and opposition—and in fact these triads seem to be different from the latter only because of the distortion introduced by 'reflection.' While a clearer definition of 'reflection' must await the following section, it is clear that the primitive phenomenal forms of space and time are what distort the pure rational concepts and transform them into quantitative and qualititative ones.

The categories of relation arise when the three potencies are indexed to the third or eternal power. Since the finite and the infinite potencies are already united in the eternal, relational pairs arise rather than single concepts, with the first related to the second as possibility is to actuality. Now the third or eternal power is reason. Reflected in the second power, it establishes the pure concepts of *substance and accident,* but in the first power, *cause and effect.* "Finally, the eternal expresses itself as necessity in the concept of a universal *reciprocal determination* of things. This concept is the highest sort of totality that can be recognized within the domain of reflection" (4:296).

Some brief comments on the nature of the judgment and the syllogism are appended, but here again the emphasis is on the function of the potencies, on how these structural variants of indifference permeate all the territories of phenomena and establish isomorphic relations between them all. When Lucian expostulates, "How admirable are the workings of the understanding" (4:297), the stage is set for Bruno to introduce the Kantian distinction between reason and the understanding, and to unfold his very un-Kantian argument that philosophy cannot be content to stay at the level of understanding and merely formulate the logic of experience, but must proceed beyond reflection to the proper totality of reason.

XIV. *Reason and Reflection* [4:297–310]

In the "Difference" essay of 1801, Hegel had coined the term 'reflection' for the attitude of the analytic understanding which seeks to simplify any complex, organic reality by reducing it to fixed moments completely external to one another. Its real-life result is an estranged culture, wherein human life perceives itself to be fragmented and doubled. Within the culture of reflection, the living identity of the 'rational animal' is sundered and compartmentalized, treated, for instance, as the territory of physics on the one hand and of morals on the other, or the domain of physiology on the one hand and of psychology on the other, each separate discipline or perspective upon human life laying claim to sole and exclusive competence.

Schelling adopts both his colleague's notion of reflection and of the culture of self-estrangement, and uses the conclusion of Bruno's discourse to underscore the main themes of the "Difference" essay. This is more than a show of solidarity with his colleague, for Schelling had sent Hegel's essay to Fichte with a disclaimer that he had no hand in it; at the same time, he had promised the *Bruno* as a vehicle for reconciling his views and Fichte's. Up to this point in the dialogue, Schelling has fairly represented both the style and substance of Fichte's philosophy, and he has exercised a great deal of ingenuity in translating his Spinozistic realism into terms more acceptable to Fichte. Now he turns sharply critical, attacking Fichte as no better than a materialist. What better polemical weapon could be found lying at hand than the arguments already enunciated in Hegel's *Difference,* that offensive document that announced to the world an irremediable breach in the ranks of critical philosophy. Then, too, Hegel's themes needed restatement; Fichte, among others, had not heard them, as a letter of J. J. Wagner written late in 1802 attests:

> Recently a traveler from Copenhagen, D. Oersted, sought me out. He had come from Berlin, where he had heard a private lecture-course by Fichte. Fichte stands stubbornly by his *Wissenschaftslehre,* as ever. He claimed Schelling never understood him, and that he had no need to read Hegel's *Differenz.*[50]

Bruno undertakes to distinguish reason and reflection (4:297–302), for unless a philosopher recognizes what pertains to reflection and what does not, he will never understand "those laws that are in God and that determine how things behave within appearances" (4:297). Reflection is what divides the phenomenal and the absolute; it is the source of the apparent mutual externality of individuals, and of their separated existence as well. The world of appearances originates in reflection, for it is not the realm of the finite as such, but only a fragmentary reflection of the finite as it subsists within the idea.

But the possibility of reflection is established in the idea itself, "for alongside the intelligible things, the true and substantial universe also includes the idea of the sort of being that was destined to perceive the universe through sensible images" (4:298). Reflection is thus an idiosyncratic way of seeing the universal light of nature, a seeing which involves not the intuition of ideas in their organic wholeness, but which depends on images and accordingly intuits things under the forms of externality, space and time, and so must think them discursively as well.

There is a certain vagueness in Schelling's concept of reflection, though it is not surprising, given the difficulties he encounters in explaining individuation or separate existence against the background of claims such as, "Absolutely, in the perspective of divine nature, nothing is external, either to itself or to that identity whence it derives its perfection" (4:298). At the core of the concept of reflection is the conviction Schelling shares with Kant that the human intellect is ektypal, not archetypal, and that it is thoroughly discursive. For, within the framework of idealistic epistemology which insists that objects exist and are determined only in and through consciousness, that they are utterly nothing outside of consciousness, not even sensory intuition immediately 'delivers' its object. Intuition, thought, consciousness itself all proceed by sundering and synthesizing, by differentiating and reidentifying in a progressive, that is to say, discursive and time-bound manner (see 4:288–293). The fact that all the elements of consciousness turn out, upon philosophical analysis, to be different complexes of the three potencies shows that there is nothing simple, nothing merely given, in the whole mode of cognition that Kant termed 'the understanding.' Reflection is thus the diametrical opposite of intellectual intuition of the idea, the disappearance of its simplicity and immediacy, and its replacement by various forms of temporal connection and cognitive synthesis.

One of the curious features of Schelling's thought throughout the period of identity-philosophy (1801–1806) is that he seemed to forget the simple truth, vividly grasped in the 1800 *System of Transcendental Idealism,* that one can approach 'the idea' only discursively, and that intellectual intuition itself can only be discussed discursively or adumbrated symbolically in the artist's creativity.[51] As early as 1801, Hegel makes reflection a certain limited function of reason, not its simple opposite; being both a deficient mode of cognition and a legitimate function of reason as well, reflection can function on a philosophical level as a bridge between the discursive and divisive work of the understanding and the negative work of reason itself. Schelling does not follow Hegel on this point, and his abstract opposition of reason and reflection, in effect a posited simple dichotomy of the absolute and the world of appearances, is philosophically unsatisfactory. A metaphysics that ultimately postulates an invisible and empty otherworld is inevitably suspect.

Bruno returns to the syllogism as an example of the poverty of reflection. The syllogism is indeed the rational identification of the three powers, but in a merely formal manner. Now reason permeates all modes of cognition: in intuition, it is the intuiting agent; in thought, it is what thinks. Yet in the syllogism reason appears as nothing but an artificial differentiation and reunification of the powers, accomplished in and for the sake of the analytic understanding. The logic of reflection resolves the organic totality of the absolute into eternally fixed moments, producing, on the formal side, the distinction of categorical, hypothetical, and disjunctive patterns of reasoning, and on the material side, the distinction of the concepts of soul, world, and God. "The understanding pictures these three moments as all separate and sundered from one another, which is the greatest possible disintegration of what is simply one within the absolute" (4:300). Anyone who hopes to fashion philosophy from the materials of logic is simply mistaken, says Bruno, for logic is merely a science of the understanding.

Reason and understanding can be definitively distinguished by the way they view the two orders of phenomenal reality. The understanding attempts to absolutize one of the two, that is, to locate the idea or identity of thought and being either within phenomenal being or phenomenal knowing. In its one-sided approach, it attempts to explain the union of concept and thing, which constitutes the individual, through the concepts of cause and effect. There results a simple idealism, or a simple realism, one just as false as the other. Both philosophies of reflection commit the same errors: (1) absolutizing one phenomenal order, (2) reducing one order to the other, and (3) employing the empirically valid schema of causality to establish the metaphysical connection between the supposedly primary and the supposedly derivative orders. "Such a procedure puts one the greatest distance from the truth. For, in the individual being, thing and concept are not united through the connection of cause and effect. They are united through the absolute, and, truly considered, they are but different aspects of one and the same individual thing" (4:302).

Reason's operation, however, is guided by the logic of indifference. Reason views the finite and the infinite orders as equally derivative, as co-primary expressions of the absolute within appearance. Instead of absolutizing either thought or being, it recognizes the idea, the identity of thought and being, within phenomenal things. Reason is able to intuit the ultimate metaphysical nondifference of thought and being, for it is itself the highest image of the absolute's indifference; that is, it is exactly the same sort of cognitive activity that establishes the absolute's form. It is indifferent with the self-knowing absolute idea, that which simultaneously establishes the difference between thought and being and secures their complete indifference. Reason is thus the absolute's self-knowledge, or to speak less anthropomorphically, its self-expression: "None of its images display the absolute in its perfect indifference, except the one wherein everything attains to the same identity of thought and being that exists in the absolute, namely reason. It is reason alone that knows everything divine, for in knowing itself, it establishes its native indifference as the matter and form of all things." (4:301).

Bruno then turns to direct criticism of Fichte's idealism and attacks the basic feature of the *Science of Knowledge,* its endeavor to eliminate the concept of being and replace it with that of activity (4:302–306). Language can but badly translate the insight of reason, he claims, for language is the tool of the understanding and dependent on images. It is therefore equally appropriate and inappropriate to try to characterize the absolute either as absolute being or as absolute knowing. "But the farthest removed from the true idea of the absolute are those philosophers who try to define the nature of the absolute as activity, in order to avoid speaking of it in terms of being" (4:303).

Activity, argues Bruno, is not a fundamental type of phenomenon, as are being and knowing. Just as there are finite and infinite forms of knowing, namely intuition and thought, so too there are finite and infinite forms of being, namely passive being and activity. Activity is thus the absolute identity reflected in the infinite dimension of things, and so it is the correlate of consciousness, while the passivity and receptivity of natural things is the absolute's expression in the finite dimension. Neither action nor passion can exist as such within the absolute, nor indeed can either member of the more inclusive contrast, knowing and being.

That the contrast between passivity and activity, the natural and the divine, the real and the ideal, has no ultimate truth is attested even by the nature of individual things, for they cannot be adequately understood through just one member of the contrast. This is plainly shown in those individuals that manifest the idea's indifference, for, within the order of nature, organisms exhibit an approximate coincidence of being and activity, just as the work of art does within the realm of spirit. For an animal is a thing that is what it is by reason of its functions and activity, and the artwork is a thing produced through conscious activity which preserves that activity in a state of rest. Bruno intimates that it is just this faulty urge to separate and abstractly contrast being and activity that tempts one into conceiving the natural world as pure passivity and the conscious realm as pure activity. To follow this urge is to break the one principle of things apart into two supposedly independent and opposed principles, one natural, the other spiritual. This represents an artificial and alienating division of the world into opposed domains, supposedly independent of each other. But the absolute is the one *natural and divine* principle of all things, as the dialogue's subtitle suggests.

Bruno proceeds to broaden his criticism of Fichtean idealism into an indictment of Enlightenment culture (4:305–310). The mentality of reflection is expressed on a grand scale in the conflict between French materialism and German idealism, and on the smaller scale in Kant's ambivalence about natural necessity and human freedom, the ambivalence that tempted Fichte into thinking away being for the sake of moral activity. Reflection thus interprets the world on the basis of a self-induced double vision. For it abstractly opposes the natural world, wherein states of passive being establish the possibility of activity, to the spiritual world, wherein actions establish secure and stable structures of social life. But phenomena such as the planetary motions and the self-regulating character of organic being show that nature is not dead or devoid of purpose. And phenomena such as artistic creativity, the moral order, and the historical life of social institutions equally show that the spiritual world is not spontaneity without structure, and that the rule-regulated character of conscious activity is not sheer freedom, but rational necessity as well.

The divisive mentality of reflection insists, nonetheless, on segregating the natural and the divine, and thereby it systematically misapprehends them both. God and nature are viewed as external to one another, nature being governed by the iron necessity of mechanism, while the divine is exalted beyond any contact with the world, banished from the earth, so to speak. The practical consequences show up in Enlightenment France, where the theoretical materialism of the intellectuals finds its counterpart in the lawlessness of the masses in rebellion, who quickly transform a revolution undertaken in the name of equality into the vengeful bloodbath of the Reign of Terror. But the absolute comprehends both necessity and freedom in such a way that the one-sided shapes they take on inside appearance disappear, namely, mechanism, on the one hand, and arbitrary choice, on the other. The only analogue within our experience for such a union of freedom and necessity is the feeling of destiny, an inchoate apprehension of some final nondifference between the results of causal determination and those of conscious purposiveness.

Bruno abruptly breaks off his long discourse, dismissing the question of what form systematic philosophy should take on as an irrelevant detail. Anselm intervenes, stating that the evolution of the form of philosophy is indeed an important matter. He then launches an attack on the contemporary state of philosophy, comments quite continuous with Bruno's attack on Fichtean idealism and the cultural situation which evoked it. Anselm's chief point in fact restates the conviction Hegel voiced in the "Difference" essay, namely, that a self-estranged culture is the precondition for the emergence of philosophy in its perfect shape. "As long as it [philosophy] lacks enduring form and shape, it will not escape corruption. Though perhaps the least perfect forms or systems of philosophy have perished and the noble matter once bound to them has been set free, it must still be alloyed with what is base, be sublimated, and finally be made wholly unrecognizable [before it can reach its true shape]. For philosophy is forever challenged to assume more enduring and less changeable shapes" (4:308).

Anselm proceeds to describe the need for establishing a meaningful history of philosophy, suggesting that only a perennial philosophy will satisfy that need. It is a common assumption, he says, that a philosophy is an idiosyncratic point of view, and that a philosophy should be original. But such an assumption makes a mockery of the one reality in which all philosophers stand. And the estate of philosophy is discredited as long as philosophies are perceived to be like comets, "transitory apparitions of fiery vapors" (4:308). Just as superstitious awe over the appearance of a comet is cured when one learns that comets are every bit as subject to the laws of celestial mechanics as the planets are, so too the ignorant adulation that greets each 'new' philosophy would be dispelled if one could see an ordered progression or pattern of elaboration that connects various philosophic doctrines. Schelling is here laying the foundation for the sort of historiography that Hegel will perfect with polemical zeal, and that, tempered by the objectivity of Hegel's pupils Michelet and Erdmann, will become the basis of our present history of philosophy.

Anselm vitriolically describes the contemporary state of philosophy as a sort of hysterical paralysis, induced by "fear of reason" (4:308). Both Kantianism and Fichte's subjective idealism are limited by their tendency to think in terms of polar oppositions and by their inability to conceive metaphysical relations on anything other than a causal model. He then proposes they close the discussion with an overview of the four chief shapes that systematic philosophy has taken on over the span of history—materialism, spiritualism, realism, and idealism. Not surprisingly, each turns out to be a version of identity-philosophy. This historical 'proof' that identity-philosophy is the common thread connecting all these diverse metaphysics suggests the possibility of an absolute philosophy, "the possibility of a philosophy without any oppositions, philosophy pure and simple" (4:323). However, the interpretation of the four positions that unfolds is anything but objective; few materialists or realists would recognize their philosophies in Schelling's formulation. Happily, the author uses the occasion for other purposes as well, a summary of the identity-philosophy and a clarification of difficult issues such as the status of the idea and the phenomenal individual, as well as a final demarcation of his position vis-à-vis Fichte.

XV. *Identity-Philosophy as the Perennial Philosophy*
[4:310–329]

Alexander begins this coda to the dialogue proper by recounting the decline and fall of the teachings of materialism (4:310–316). What he advances as 'materialism' is really the naturalism that Giordano Bruno put forward in his dialogues *On the Cause, the Principle, and the One*. Thus the genuine doctrine of the *Bruno*'s namesake is at least introduced into its contents, and a rich notion of matter as "itself the identity of the divine and natural principle, and thus absolutely simple, unchangeable, and eternal" (4:310) is advanced against the claims of modern mechanistic materialism.

As Alexander explains it, matter is itself the indifferent unity of all things. Now things are differentiated by their form (or mode of being), for though their essence or possibility is infinite, their actual mode of existence is finite. "Finite things as such are at each and every moment all that they can be at that moment, but not all that they could be according to their essence" (4:312). The difference between essence and existence in things generates time, the endless progressive approximation of the finite to the intrinsically infinite. The positing of time is thus the differentiation of indifferent matter, the transition from the absolute to the articulated totality of appearances we call the universe.

The first form or 'form of forms' is identical with matter, identical in the sense that, being all forms and being identical to no one specific form, it is as indifferent or nonspecific as is primitive matter itself. This form of forms comprehends both the psychic and the bodily dimensions of things, both of them equally being species of matter. But primitive matter, the unity of things, is not to be equated with vulgar matter, the bodily dimension of things. "Of course the point where matter and form are perfectly identical, where soul and body are themselves indistinguishable within form, is located above and beyond all appearances" (4:313). It is this hidden point of identity that makes the universe one eternal organism, not subject to change, motion, or any process of transformation.

Though the proliferation of terminology hardly contributes to clarity, it is clear enough that Schelling takes Bruno's 'matter' and 'form of forms' as equivalent to the 'essence' and the 'form' of the absolute (the latter is equivalent to 'the idea,' or more precisely 'the idea of all ideas'). The absolute's form indifferently contains the ideas of all things, not by being any one of them, but by being all of them nonspecifically. The absolute's form or mode of expression, then, is something like an ideal elaboration of specific differences, but one so inclusive that different specific ideas do not competitively exclude one another. The individual's form or mode of existence is, by contrast, an exclusive determination of specificity, one that forces the translation of the thing's unitary essence into the fragmentary reality of the present momentary state.

There is much that is obscure in the foregoing explanation, enough to occasion the question of whether the very project of thinking the absolute is self-contradictory. And the obscurity resides in Schelling's pivotal notion of the absolute's form. For little philosophical acumen is needed to apprehend the externality inherent in the very structures that connect phenomena, namely space, time, and causality. And logic can indeed tempt us to enter on the path to monism and to encounter at its end a quite Parmenidean absolute identity, the 'essence' of the absolute. But it is the connecting link that is problematic, the notion of the form of the absolute, wherein identity and difference interplay, wherein differences are indeed established but somehow remain mere conceptual differences. The origins of this notion are obscure as well. Schelling is too much of a Spinozist in his identity-philosophy phase to speak plainly of a divine mind or to refer back to Christological speculation in theology. Perhaps one can best elucidate this curious doctrine by viewing it as a metaphysical descendant of Aristotle's analysis of knowledge:

> Now, summing up what has been said about the soul, let us say again that the soul is in a way all existing things, for existing things are either objects of perception, or objects of thought, and knowledge

is in a way the object of knowledge and perception the objects of perception.[52]

There are certainly perplexities enough in Aristotle's account. Schelling's concept of the absolute's form seems to excel in perplexity, inasmuch as it omits the modest Aristotelian "in a way."

Alexander then employs Giordano Bruno's exotic version of hylomorphism to sketch the history of materialism. Originally 'matter' meant the living identity of all things, but the idea was eventually corrupted. Plato understood matter to be no more than the bare substrate of natural things, opening the door to the later identification of matter with 'body,' and its subsequent reduction to the concept of inorganic body. And once the idea of life was eliminated from that of matter, a debased hylomorphism arose which viewed matter as purely passive and external, and form as an eternally fixed difference impressed on the yielding material stuff from without. The notion of a living totality of nature was thus reduced to that of an empty space, a neutral background for various and sundry unrelated particulars. "The general conception finally prevailed that the living totality of the universe is like a receptacle or chamber, in which things are placed in such a way that they do not participate in one another, nor live in community with each other, nor interact with each other" (4:315). The epitome of the progress of modern materialism, whose outcome is none other than the "death of matter," is the reductionistic programme of modern biology, the attempt to explain the organic solely in terms of the inorganic. The procedure, says Alexander, makes the barbarian idolator or the primitive totem-worshiper seem in possession of superior philosophical and religious sensibilities.

Anselm employs his sketch of 'intellectualism' or Leibnizean monadology (4:316–321) to clarify the status of the idea as the identity of concept and thing, and to relativize the mind-matter dualism which was apparent in Bruno's discourse. He returns once more to the language of Platonic image metaphysics, but employs it in such a way that the distinction between exemplar and image falls apart. There is really only one exemplar, God or substance, and it pervades all derivative unities. There is much terminological slippage within this discussion; Schelling's attempt to map his identity-philosophy onto Leibniz's metaphysics is not without confusion.

There is a threefold hierarchy of being, claims Anselm: (1) the archetypal world or the absolute idea; (2) derivative unities or 'monads,' finite individuals existing at the levels of organism and of self-consciousness; and (3) the world of appearances, which arises because the monads are a finite and merely organic expression of the idea.

Ideas can be called archetypes, but they are the most perfect sort of archetypes, ones that do not abstractly stand over against their copies, but instead combine both exemplary and image aspects in themselves. Anselm calls the exemplary aspect of an idea the foretype or determining element, the image aspect the antitype or determinable element. Since these aspects are identified in the idea, any image of an idea, any derivative unity, will possess both psychic and somatic dimensions, and within the psychic, it will have both determinable and determining modes of consciousness, namely, thought and will. Now since the idea is a pure identity of exemplar and image, of determination and determinability, it is impossible to strictly separate the two aspects in any derivative unity or monad. A monad's body, therefore, will not be pure determinability, nor will its soul be pure activity or exclusively determinative. As tied to an individual body, the monad's soul will be a determinable determining, that is, a consciousness that is aware of itself and acts only insofar as it also passively represents the states of its body.

Anselm's definition of an archetypal idea as the identity of exemplar and copy is paradoxical, at least if the terms are understood Platonically. Schelling here wants to emphasize the difference between a concept, which abstractly stands over against the particulars it signifies, and an idea or living union of concept and thing. Now the concept possesses empty infinitude; it purchases generality at the cost of abstractness. Only the concrete generality of the idea can serve to connect the order of representation and the order of physical being, for the idea alone is a representation that is what it expresses or a reality that is and is what it is by thinking itself. It is clear that the concept 'horse' is but an auditory-visual image which has content in relation to thinking actual and possible horses; it suffices as a higher-order representation of many actual and possible horses because it concretely represents none. All this seems familiar and factual. But a horse-idea would be quite another critter, a self-thinking horse! The notion is ludicrous, except as a part of a more comprehensive reality, a scheme of ideas within a self-thinking and self-founding mind.

It does not make sense, therefore, to speak of ideas except in the context of the one idea, the idea of all ideas. For if there is such an exotic entity as a self-establishing thought, and if we need to posit such an entity to metaphysically connect the phenomenal orders of thought and being, surely there can be but one such thing. And this, says Schelling, is indeed the case: "Only insofar as the monads' representations are imperfect, limited, and confused do they picture the universe as outside of God, and related to God merely as its ground. But insofar as their representations are adequate, they represent the universe as existing in God. God is thus the idea of all ideas, the cognition of all acts of cognition, the light of all lights" (4:320).

Turning then to the third or lowest realm in the hierarchy of being, Anselm says that the world of appearances arises because the idea, the power active in all acts of cognition, is distorted by the contrast of determining activity and passive determinability in the monad. Operating in this distorted manner, the idea is limited to representing states of the body within time. It no longer represents itself to itself as substance, but instead perceives substance as the ground of being, equally present in itself and in other entities beyond itself. Thus the monad's thinking becomes an indistinct imaging, a representation of what is real in other things. In this way the world of appearances arises for each and every monad, each of which is a world unto itself. Since each monad is, at bottom, the absolute idea or the one substance, the causally unrelated monads form one world, their representations all private, but harmonized. God, the absolute substance, permeates them all, just as space embraces all the bodies that fill it.

At this point Lucian and Bruno take over the discussion and establish the nondifference of realism and idealism as general philosophical alternatives (4:321–326). Realism and idealism cannot be distinguished either in their aim or their object, argues Lucian, for both positions strive to attain knowledge of the absolute. They must therefore take different approaches to knowledge of the absolute, realism focusing on the absolute's essence, idealism on its form. It is the indifference of the absolute's form and essence, the fact that one and the same absolute is in one respect the 'neither . . . nor . . .' of all opposites and the other the 'both . . . and . . .' of all opposites, which makes realism and idealism equally valid endeavors and in fact opens the path to absolute philosophy, one that transcends all partial stances and that silences all sectarian disputes.

Bruno notes that though one can call the absolute's form 'absolute knowing,' this knowing is the infinite identity of the real and the ideal, and so both includes and cancels the opposition of thought and being. Neither thought as such nor being as such can be directly ascribed to form or absolute knowing. Absolute knowing is a knowing only in the sense that it is an ideal elaboration of the absolute's strict identity, an indifferent expression of its essential reality in the one idea of all ideas. In the absolute idea, there is no knower that stands over against what is known, as there is in phenomenal consciousness, and what is known is in no way distinct from absolute knowing.

One can also call the absolute's form 'absolute selfhood,' but one encounters the same limitations on the applicability of the term as obtained for 'knowing.' Since there is no duality nor opposition in the idea, neither thought, being, nor even their identity in self-consciousness can be literally predicated of it. For thought and being are first established as independent and opposite when knowing is related to appearances; in that context, too, only a relative identity (and difference) of thought and being stands forth, even in the case of self-consciousness. The self is indeed an identity of thought and being, but a thoroughly contingent and synthetic identity. In the idea or 'absolute selfhood,' however, the identity of thought and being is necessary and indivisible; 'selfhood' is general in this case, not located in one particular point of view by reason of connection with an individual body. In relative selfhood or self-consciousness, the self exists as the consciousness of phenomenal objects or appearances, and only within this context do selfhood and objectivity come to the fore and distinguish themselves as the opposite poles of experience. But within absolute selfhood, attained only in intellectual intuition of the idea, there is no self, no discursive knowing, no distinction of objects, and, above all, utterly no distinction of subject and object.

Bruno and Lucian agree that an idealism that is confined to the standpoint of philosophical reflection on the absolute idea will be congruent with a realism that reflects on the absolute's identical essence. The former will not be subjectivistic, nor the latter objectivistic or naturalistic. But both positions will be 'idealistic' in the sense that they equally deny the claims of naive realism, which takes the sensible world to be something in and of itself. Each position will have to admit that the phenomenal order of things and that of consciousness are equally primary, and that the two in their togetherness constitute appearances. Idealism thus becomes a philosophical tactic, an attempt to analogically expand the structure of empirical consciousness into a description of the metaphysical fundamentals. Like any other attempt to think analogically, idealism must conclude with a 'negative theology.' The absolute may indeed be viewed as an 'absolute knowing' for heuristic purposes, but idealism must finally confess that in the absolute there is no literal knowing and no literal knower.

But Schelling does not ultimately believe that Fichte is capable of the requisite methodological caution to use idealism as a partial approach to absolute philosophy. He is suspicious that Fichte's proposed, but unpublished, reworking of the *Science of Knowledge* will simply absolutize the stance of empirical self-consciousness. Bruno accordingly concludes the discussion with a final critique of subjective idealism, the philosophy of empirical self-consciousness (4:326–329). For a philosophy that limits itself to the standpoint of consciousness, absolute identity appears to be beyond the reach of knowledge. This position in fact becomes explicitly antitheoretical; it allows absolute identity to confront the subjectivity of empirical consciousness as something independent and objective only in the ethical command. Hence, "for ethical activity, absolute identity assumes the guises of the command and the infinite ethical task, while for thought, it takes the shape of faith, the end of all speculation" (4:326).

Lucian embraces this outline of Fichte's idealism with enthusiasm, but Bruno wryly points out that, since this position does nothing other than perfectly exhibit the structure of ordinary consciousness, it is not philosophy at all. An idealism of this sort, one that simply removes the absolute from the scope of theoretical philosophy and places it within the narrow confines of ethics, is far from a philosophical grasp of the idea. And in its willful ignorance of the activity and divinity of nature, it coincides with mechanistic materialism. "This philosophy considers nature dead, the bare object and material for an action which does not spring from nature itself and which is located beyond nature" (4:327). This idealism will inevitably conflict with realism, for it has lost sight of the absolute and contents itself with the limited study of empirical consciousness and ethics.

But idealism need not be such a limited stance, claims Bruno. An idealism that grasped what is essentially ideal, that is, the idea rather than self-consciousness, would set itself beyond all opposition to realism. For the idea, or absolute knowing (as Fichte would call it), is but one aspect of the absolute, and though it expresses the absolute's identical essence by translating its sheer identity into a systematic web of ideas, it is perfectly indifferent with that identity. Bruno now makes clear his central thought, that the absolute's double nature is the highest instance of the logic of indifference. For it is the indifference of sheer identity and the idea's systematic elaboration of identity within difference that makes the absolute the identity of thought and being.

> To come to know this indifference within the absolute—that character whereby idea is substance, the absolutely real, whereby form is also essential reality, and reality is form, each one inseparable from the other, whereby form and reality are not just perfectly similar likenesses of one another, but directly are one another—this is to discover the absolute center of gravity. To know this is to uncover the original metal of truth, as it were, the prime ingredient in the alloys of all individual truths, without which none of them would be true. (4:328)

Indifference is thus the principle of all philosophy, and the logic of indifference provides a clue to its methodology as well. For philosophy cannot be satisfied to observe and describe various phenomena without seeking to locate their ground of unity, nor can it be content with abstract conceptual unities unless it sees within them a self-specifying activity which establishes these differences. Philosophy's business is to simultaneously unpack indifference into difference and inbuild difference into indifference. Indifference in fact supplies a 'Jacob's ladder' to the absolute, as Bruno suggests in the allegorical concluding passage. "And as we move up and down this spiritual ladder, freely and without constraint, now descending and beholding the identity of the divine and natural principle dissolved, now ascending and resolving everything again into the one, we shall see nature within God and God within nature" (4:329).

This philosophy . . . should have acknowledged that it is a science wherein there is no mention of existence *or of what* actually exists, *or of knowledge in this sense either. It treated only the relations its object takes on in mere thought.*

F. W. J. SCHELLING[53]

The Significance of the Philosophy of Identity

SCHELLING HAD THE OPPORTUNITY, which many twentieth century philosophers would account good fortune, to outlive his philosophical positions. In fact he did so several times over, becoming, like Leibniz whom he greatly admired, a philosophers' philosopher, influencing great minds such as Marcel, Heidegger, Tillich, and Habermas, but lacking an audience within the general culture.[54] In 1827 Schelling said of the so-called system of identity, the projected system of which the *Bruno* is but a sketch, "On the one hand, it seems almost impossible that this system is false, but on the other hand, one will sense something in it that prevents one from declaring that it is the ultimate truth. He will recognize that it is true within certain limits, but not unconditionally and absolutely true."[55] Let us turn to the task of evaluating the success of this ambitious piece of metaphysics, while leaving the last word to its sternest critic, Schelling himself.

Recalling that the *Bruno* was penned as a vehicle for discussion between its author and Fichte, let us first address the question whether the dialogue advances any grounds for reconciling their conflicting positions. It is quite plain that it does not, and that the conviction that their differences were irreconcilable hardened in Schelling's mind even as he wrote. The argument makes clear that the only position Schelling and Fichte can share is phenomenalism, the belief that appearances are not what is fundamentally real. Schelling is unequivocal about his belief in the ultimate duality, equiprimordiality, and irreducibility of material and mental phenomena. His claim that the *Science of Knowledge* would reduce the material to the mental dimension is correct. There simply can be no agreement between a subjective idealism that would think away all being or materiality, including nature, and a methodological idealism that wants to preserve the difference of nature and spirit by interpreting them as equally well-founded orders of phenomena. Basic to the two philosophers' long-standing dispute is Schelling's insistence, not only that nature cannot be thought away, but that it is the very foundation for spirit or the realm of consciousness. Fichte had tried to fashion a self-contained philosophy of spirit with but two branches, epistemology and ethics. Schelling's more comprehensive and naturalistic vision of philosophy is well expressed in these remarks on the 'identity-philosophy' made in 1827:

> Thus it follows, from the foregoing determination, that the initial moments of the infinite's positing itself (or since the life of the subject consists in this self-positing, the initial moments of this life) are moments of nature. From this it follows, too, that this philosophy is in nature from its first moves, or that it starts from nature— naturally not in order to remain there, but to later surpass it in ever ascending steps, to emerge from it and become spirit, to elevate itself into an authentically spiritual world. In its beginning, therefore, this philosophy could be called nature-philosophy, but nature-philosophy was only the first part or foundation of the whole [system]. . . .
> At the start, it was difficult to find a name for this system, since it included the very opposition of all earlier systems within itself, as cancelled. It could in fact be called neither materialism nor spiritualism, neither realism nor idealism. One could have called it 'real-idealism,' inasmuch as within it, idealism itself was based on a realism and developed out of a realism. Only once, in the preface, thus the exoteric part, of my first presentation of this system, did I call it the 'System of Absolute Identity.' I meant that therein was asserted no one-sided real being nor one-sided ideal being, but that only one ultimate subject was to be conceived in that which Fichte called 'the real' and in that which we have become accustomed to call 'the ideal.'[56]

It is plain, then, that no rapprochement with Fichte is possible. The *Bruno* is to be read as the velvet-gloved counterpart of the obviously polemical attacks Hegel unleased in the "Difference" essay and in *Faith and Knowledge*.

Perhaps it was with some insight that contemporaries referred to Hegel as Schelling's henchman.[57]

Let us now consider the kind of metaphysics advanced in the *Bruno*. As we have seen, Schelling is quite vocal in his opposition to Kant, and quite daring in his attempt to steer Criticism away from epistemology and back to metaphysics. But the fact remains that Kant had set forth clear arguments that spelled the end of metaphysics, at least as a speculative, if not as a descriptive enterprise. Schelling's metaphysics is highly speculative, however, and the question naturally arises: How could anyone attempt to philosophize in this manner *after Kant?* The answer is very much obscured by Schelling's decision to turn back to the history of philosophy and present himself as Plato risen from the grave—a decision quite consonant with his flashy, arrogant personality. Nonetheless, the answer is simple: Schelling does *Kantian metaphysics*.

When Kant pronounced that "all metaphysicians are therefore solemnly and legally suspended from their occupations,"[58] he advanced two general lines of argument: (1) Metaphysics commonly takes categorial concepts meaningful in the context of experience and attempts to apply them beyond the bounds of sense. It errs in that it fails to realize that categorial concepts have no cognitive content; they are but logical functions which interrelate items of experience. Thus talk of substance, causality or a reciprocally determining community of things is meaningless if applied to what is behind or beyond experience. The metaphysician commits the fallacy of misplaced concreteness in his assumption that categories have some positive epistemic content. Hence, to ask after a 'cause of the world' is equivalent to asking whether the rules of chess move one space at a time on the board like pawns or along the diagonal like a bishop. (2) In fixing its sight upon supposed hyper-experiential objects such as the enduring soul, the cosmos as such, and the deity, metaphysics postulates totalities of experience which are not subject to any possible truth-test within experience. Such 'ideas of reason' involve an illegitimate advance from the experience of a finite chain of conditioned entities to a supposed totality of conditions. The ideas of immortal soul and of a personal deity involve the fallacy of reification as well, for 'soul' hypostatizes the empirical stream of consciousness, and 'God' hypostatizes the logical notion of the aggregate of all positive predicates or qualities.

Not only is Schelling keenly aware of Kant's arguments; he is convinced of their truth as well. Careful analysis of the *Bruno*'s argument shows that he indeed follows the limitations on speculation they propose, and that he avoids both sorts of fallacies through his logic of indifference. It is his genius (though some may think it a perverse sort of genuis) to have hit upon an *a priori* logical idea which is *nowhere* exhibited in experience, namely indifference or the identity of opposites. Within Schelling's theory, indifference functions both as a connective that links various phenomenal and nonphenomenal domains and as an explanatory device; Schelling need have no recourse to substance-accident or cause-effect relations except when he is talking of the serial interconnection of phenomena within time. As we have seen in detail, indifference explains and unites all the disparate regions of being—mind and matter, soul and body, intuition and concept within consciousness, nature and spirit as the universal orders of appearance, the absolute's form and phenomenal existence, and finally the absolute's form and its identical essence. It is clearly an elegant system, though perhaps a purely formal one, that can establish all these connections with one principle. Thus Schelling is able to avoid causal explanation except in its appropriate context, where one world-state is seen to be determined by another or one intuition determined by its predecessor. He is aware, as well, that questions such as, "Does the absolute cause appearances?" or "What is the cause of separated existence?" are metaphysical in Kant's sense and thus unanswerable, though he clearly shows some uneasiness about not being able to pose and answer the latter question.

Now Kant's first specific objection to metaphysics was that it lifted portions of the logic of experience and employed them out of context. The causal relationship, for instance, is exemplified in any experienced sequence of events where prior members condition or influence subsequent ones; it would therefore be illegitimate to ascribe causality to the unconditonal. But indifference or the essential identity of opposites is never clearly and unequivocally exemplified within experience at all. The prime candidate for an experienced instance of indifference would seem to be the correlation between the psychic and somatic aspects of some sensation, but it fails to exhibit indifference the way causally related events exhibit causality. Causality is the only categorial schema available for conceiving the connection of conditioning and conditioned events. The togetherness of psychic and somatic events, however, may be conceived in several ways, for example, (1) either by means of the categories of substance and accident, which leaves open several possible interpretations, namely (a) that both aspects are attributes of a common substance, (b) that the bodily aspect is substantial, while the psychic inheres in it as a quality, and (c) that the psychic aspect is substantial and the somatic accidental, or (2) by means of the logic of indifference. Then too, it is always arguable that psychic and somatic states are simply different. At any rate, if they are indifferently related, this is not *shown* by experience; it is a conclusion attained by pure thought alone, a metaphysical interpretation of the facts that experience furnishes. Schelling cannot, then, be accused of extrapolating a concept which is part of the logic of experience into a pure idea. Indifference may indeed be a pure idea, but since it contradicts the whole logic of experience, the claim can credibly be advanced that it is a genuine idea of reason, not a misplaced concept of reflection. Schelling thus manages to evade the first of Kant's general objections to speculative metaphysics.

Kant's second objection to metaphysics claimed that the ideas of reason are inherently dialectical in that they advance from the experience of conditioned entities such as personal self-consciousness, nature, and the logical ideal of totality to the unconditional posited as a totality of conditions, namely soul, world, and deity. Schelling's metaphysics escapes the fallacies of hypostatizing self-consciousness or the lawlike order of nature by steadfastly maintaining that both orders are strictly phenomenal. There is no nature-in-itself and no enduring or immortal soul. Neither knowing nor being can be attributed to the absolute, nor can either acting according to freedom or acting in conformity with causal mechanism.

But what of the deity, or the absolute, as Schelling calls it? Kant's criticism of conventional philosophical theism claimed that the idea of God illegitimately (1) represented the unconditioned as a totality of conditions, and (2) hypostatized all the positive items that an exhaustive table of contrasting predicates would exhibit. On the first score, the bipolar nature of Schelling's absolute seems to evade the objection, for the absolute is a strictly identical essence on the one hand, and the totality of all differences held together in the absolute idea on the other. The form-essence distinction, itself the highest instance of indifference and the ontological foundation for all other instances, seems to keep the unconditioned on one side, and the totality of conditions on the other. One cannot deny, however, that Schelling frankly portrays the absolute's form or the absolute idea as a totality of conditions. A Kantian would be justified in asking precisely how we can jump from the conditioned nature of experience to the idea of a totality thereof.

On the second score, Schelling escapes the charge that conventional theism is arbitrary and illogical in describing the deity in terms of positive predicates alone, for Schelling conceives the absolute's form as the totality of all differences, that is, of all contrasting qualities and attributes, positive and negative, held together in an indifferent unity. Theism conceives deity as infinite, perfect, and external to a finite, imperfect world, while Schelling's absolute idea is the indifference of the infinite and the finite, and the coexistence of what we term 'perfect' and 'imperfect' as well. But here again, the Kantian may object that it is precisely the ascent from the fragmentary and successive nature of experience to the idea of a totality that is objectionable.

It is evident, at least, that Schelling carefully considered Kant's objections, even if, in attempting to conform to their letter, he sought to evade their spirit, and that he was consciously working toward the invention of a Kantian-style metaphysics. Consideration of the predominance of speculation on time in the *Bruno*, and of the Kantian manner of that speculation, reinforces this impression. Time is the primitive form of appearance as such. It is what accounts for phenomena being phenomenal, for the durational rather than the eternal form of things' existence, and for the discursive nature of the understanding. Time is made virtually synonymous with individual existence, for the individual separates itself from the eternal community of all things in the absolute precisely by fashioning its own time. And yet time functions as a bridge connecting things' existence in their ideas with separate existence, for it is the expression of the infinite or conceptual dimension, it is responsible for the self-identity, coherence, and cohesion of things, and, in the highest instance, time is itself the stream of consciousness. Now it might be argued that this account of time is fundamentally incoherent, yet the attempt to make external or objective time the framework of finite phenomenal existence and yet make internal time the framework of the discursive synthesis of self-consciousness betokens a vigorous attempt on Schelling's part to bring unity and coherence to the Kantian account of mind.

In all the foregoing discussion of Schelling's attempt to formulate a style of metaphysics immune to Kant's critique, we returned again and again to the concept of indifference. We must now try to measure the validity of this central, enigmatic idea. We have already noted that it formulates a logical connection never exhibited in experience, namely the essential identity of properties that appear to be direct opposites. Only the connected opposites pertain to experience, never their hidden connection. Hence there is a curious invisibility that pertains to every instance of indifference. Within nature, gravity and light are systematizing forces, not things. They never come to appearance; instead, things appear within the systematic framework that they, and space and time as well, provide. Within consciousness, the unity that binds sensation and awareness into the one act of intuition never appears or presents itself as a distinct something, nor does selfhood or the unity of consciousness that connects the moments of thought and intuition. Within the self-conscious organism, body and the stream of consciousness indeed appear, but their indifferent union remains in the background and never presents itself as the substantial element it supposedly is. And the same occurs within the whole scheme of things; the finite and the infinite stand forth in appearance, but never the eternal. Experience exhibits both knowing and being in their distinctness, but never their indifferent or absolute union.

What are we to make of this invisibility of the indifferent? Clearly, it implies the invisibility, and ultimately the ineffability, of the absolute. A metaphysical foundation of appearances that is invisible and ineffable bears both positive and negative philosophical results. Positively, it is true that, if experience never provides a clear instance of an indifferent relation, one is 'safe' from Kantian attacks in characterizing the absolute solely in terms of this nonexperiential form of connection. But on the negative side, the possibility of *arguing* to the absolute is simply cut off, whether by analogical extrapolation from experience or by deductive proof. The absolute must remain a *postulated* otherside of the world of experience, quite beyond the truth-test of experience, and incapable of characterization by any quality or attribute which pertains to experience.

In the last analysis, the only thing that can be said of the absolute is that its nature is indifferent, or unitary and bipolar at the same time. Indifference is a purely logical entity; it involves no quality, mental or physical, for it is only a relation between some set of contrasting qualities.

The question then arises, 'What sort of logical function is indifference?' Is it a connective or a relation, a primitive connective or a derived logical function? It could be interpreted as a relation, but since it essentially involves the connection of opposites, it seems best to view it as complex logical function based on conjunction. As a logical function that simultaneously affirms and denies any and all opposed predicates, it is fundamentally a reversal of the logic of experience. If we denote two contrasting predicates by the functions Fx and Gx, we can represent their indifferent subsistence in the absolute by

$$\sim (Fx \vee Gx) \ \& \ (Fx \ \& \ Gx).$$

Using f(x) and g(x) to represent any and all opposed predicates, the nature of the absolute can be schematically depicted as

$$\sim (f(x) \vee g(x)) \ \& \ (f(x) \ \& \ g(x)),$$

where the left-hand string indicates the absolute's identical essence, the 'neither . . . nor . . .' of all opposed qualities, and the right-hand side the developed system of differences coexisting in the absolute idea.

Now the fact that we can represent the absolute in simple symbol strings indicates that Schelling's metaphysics of indifference is purely formalistic. And the fact that ordinary logic forces us to read these strings as simple contradictions suggests that the logic of indifference is parasitic upon the logic of experience, just one member of the vast domain of contradictions. Nothing is materially contradictory about $\sim (f(x) \vee g(x))$ as such; negative theology frequently has resort to such expressions. But $(f(x) \ \& \ g(x))$ certainly is a contradiction if g(x) is the denial of f(x), as is the conjunction of the two strings. Now the fact that any and every contradiction applies to the absolute certainly does supply Schelling with a defense against the charge of illicitly borrowing from experience. But that the absolute can only be described in logical terms, and even then only in terms of ordinary logic stood on its head, shows it to be a thin construct indeed.

Here we encounter the chief difficulty with Schelling's identity-philosophy, not that it is a formalism, but that it is an empty formalism, not that it approaches characterizing the *ens realisimum* logically rather than analogically, but that no suitable interpretation can be given to its formulae. Schelling attempts to mediate the opposition of abstract identity and sheer difference, and that of the interrelatedness of phenomena comprehended under scientific laws and their reciprocal exclusion in space and time. He is indeed ingenious in discovering the interrelatedness of things and in suggesting that an ultimate internality grounds all things. He is deficient as a metaphysician, however, in letting the contrast between the internal and the external remain a simple opposition. Schelling simply leaves the sheer identity of the absolute's essence something other than the inclusive difference of the idea; he leaves the absolute the mere unexplained otherside of the phenomenal world, which he correctly views as governed by exclusion and externality. Hegel will ultimately prove himself the more astute thinker by (1) seeing that the ultimate categorial contrast of internality and externality (or selfhood and otherness) must itself be philosophically explained, (2) that explanation of the internal-external relation must ultimately be in terms of one of the relata, and (3) that *thinking,* a rather garden-variety cultural activity, provides the paradigm case of the internal comprehending, or "outflanking," the external.

Though Schelling is ingenious enough to get around Kant's objections, or at least their "fine print," and to point out the path toward a logical metaphysics, he is not sufficiently abstract a thinker to see that his new path leads towards a metaphysics of relations, wherein individuals, either "in idea" or "within appearances," become purely derivative entities. Nor does he possess the foresight to realize that such a project which reduces all entities to complexes of relations and explains all relations through formal, not material, properties, might turn out to be an elegant, though strictly uninterpretable, formal construct.

We reserve the critical last word to Schelling himself, for he eventually became quite aware of the difference between a logical formalism and a philosophy that can claim to capture existence. In his *Lectures on Recent Philosophy,* given in Munich in 1827, Schelling offers a balanced evaluation of his identity-philosophy, though one slightly tinged by the tendency to conflate Hegel's system, characterized by dynamism, with his essentially static early system:

> (1) One cannot reject the system because of its compass or territory, for it encompassed everything knowable, everything that can in any way become an object of knowledge, without excluding any-

thing. . . . (2) As to its method, it was formulated to exclude any influence by the subjectivity of the philosopher. It was the object of philosophical inquiry itself that supplied the system's content, that successively determined itself according to an immanent principle, a thought progressively specified according to its own inner law. . . . Besides, when one considers how the authority of all natural modes of thought was undermined by Fichte's subjective idealism, how consciousness, dismembered by the earlier absolute opposition of nature and spirit no less than the crass materialism and sensualism, . . . felt itself injured and insulted, then one will understand why this system was initially greeted with a joy that no previous system ever provoked, nor any later one will again provoke. Nor nowadays one does not realize how much one had to *struggle* for what today has become the common good, and in Germany almost an article of faith shared by all high-minded and sensitive men—I mean the conviction that that which *knows* in us is the same as that which *is known.*[59]

Schelling proceeds to discuss the crucial limitation of this philosophy, that it failed to recognize that it was mere thought:

Now how did it come to pass that this philosophy, in the form in which it first exercised an almost universal attraction, was yet a short time later seen to be limited in its influence, and showed a repelling pole which was little noticed at first? It was not because of the attacks it received from many quarters. . . . It was rather a misunderstanding about itself, a situation wherein the system gave itself out for something (or, as one used to say, let itself be taken for something) that it was not, something that according to its original thought it ought not be. . . . An eternal event is no event. Accordingly, the whole representation of this process [of the absolute subject's development] and this movement was itself illusory. None of it really happened. Everything occurred in mere thought. This philosophy should have realized this; in doing so, it would have set itself beyond all contradiction, but, at the same time, it would have surrendered its claim to objectivity. . . . It should have *recognized* itself to be *pure negative* philosophy. In this way, it would have left a space free for a philosophy beyond itself, for a positive philosophy which considers *existence,* and not given itself out as absolute philosophy, a philosophy which leaves nothing beyond its compass.[60]

*I was amazed to see you mention in
your letter that you had not received
the latest fasicle of Schelling's
[Critical Journal]. You should have
had it by then. If only that damned
Hegel wrote better!—I often have
trouble understanding him. Because
of the wretched diction, I am certain
that Hegel, and not Schelling,
penned this piece [against you.]*
FRIEDRICH JACOBI[61]

Schelling and Hegel

WHILE SCHELLING'S AND HEGEL'S contemporaries were left to wonder which of the two had wielded the hatchet in the unsigned articles of the *Critical Journal*, scholars have been left the more difficult task of analysing the relationship between the two thinkers in the brief years of their collaboration, and that of assessing the difficult question of one's influence upon the other. Some scholars are of the opinion that the collaboration was a business-like and distant affair, lacking any deep cordiality or friendship.[62] Others see a very close working relationship between the two philosophers in Jena and speak of a marked mutual influence of one upon the other.[63] Most scholarship acknowledges the similarities between the themes of the *Bruno* and Hegel's *Difference* and *Faith and Knowledge*, but there is some speculation that Schelling's break with Fichte may have been occasioned more by Hegel than by Schelling himself.[64] But since the *Bruno* displays both conciliatory attempts at dialogue with Fichte and bitter polemics against his positions, and since their dispute had been long simmering—a marginal note in Fichte's copy of Schelling's 1801 *Exposition* reads, "Polyphemus without eyes"[65]—the safest and least speculative course of judgment would be to simply state that the three relevant works, as early statements of a new alliance and indications of a new path for philosophy, present a common front.

One can indeed point out Hegelian influences in the *Bruno* and essays Schelling wrote later in 1802,[66] but one must also acknowledge the continuing influence of Schelling's style of thought on Hegel throughout the years of his stay in Jena. Perhaps it is the critic closest to the scene that renders the best judgment on the Schelling-Hegel collaboration. Rosenkranz states that in his years at Jena, Schelling sought to lay out the critical and general foundations of absolute philosophy, while Hegel went to work on developing philosophy as a *cycle* of sciences.[67] He also notes that in his 1805–06 lectures on the history of philosophy, the crucial phase of Hegel's development in which he first elaborated his notion of dialectical methodology, Hegel warmly acknowledged his debts to Schelling, while criticizing the logic of indifference as an inappropriately quantitative approach to philosophy.[68]

The most important item to note in discussing Hegel's influence upon the *Bruno* is that in the early months of their collaboration, Schelling came to share Hegel's praxis-oriented vision of the task of philosophy. Pöggeler notes that Hegel's philosophic concern in the Jena years was the same as the youthful ideal of his seminary days—to secure the union of the divine and the human, of the finite and the infinite, and to overcome the ruling cultural division, the abstract opposition of nature and spirit.[69] Though his own concern with aesthetics from 1800 onwards and his friendship with Goethe may have nudged him toward the same position, the *Bruno* exhibits what is for Schelling an unusual awareness of the responsibilities of the philosopher toward his society. As eloquently as Hegel's "Difference" essay, it voices the hope that a philosophy which recognizes and respects both the material and the spiritual can serve as a propaedeutic to a cultural revolution that will cure the estrangement ruling human life.

There are important Hegelian terminological influences on the *Bruno,* as we have seen. The clumsy language of 'qualitative indifference' and 'quantitative difference' is put aside, and Hegel's description of the absolute as "the identity of identity and opposition" is adopted as the canonical expression for indifference. Schelling also adopts the Hegelian term 're-flection' as a synonym for Kant's 'understanding,' and speaks, as Hegel does, of the 'doubling' or 'self-estrangement' that rules the contemporary culture. Finally, in a note to the discussion of the movements of the heavenly bodies, he praises Hegel's dissertation on the orbits of the planets, though without specifically mentioning him by name. A further sign of Hegel's influences appears in Schelling's 1803 *Lectures on Academic Studies,* where he calls for the development of a "science of form," a "positive scepticism," dialectic—a task which Schelling himself never undertook.[70]

Hegel himself worked within the scheme of Schelling's philosophical concepts throughout his stay in Jena, albeit never quite comfortably, and certainly never gracefully. The 1802–03 manuscript, *The System of Ethical Life,* opens with the sentence, "Knowledge of the Idea of the absolute ethical order depends entirely on the establishment of perfect adequacy between intuition and concept, because the Idea itself is nothing other than the identity of the two."[71] The analysis of the social order in terms of the Schellingian triad, intuition, concept, and idea, is barely intelligible even if the reader is familiar with the *Bruno,* and Hegel proceeds throughout the piece to use the terminology of 'intuition,' 'concept,' and judgmental 'subsumption' in novel, if not bizarre, ways. The 1803–04 *First Philosophy of Spirit* depends on the following definition of spirit in terms of indifference or the identity of opposites: "The concept of Spirit as thus determined is *Consciousness,* the concept of the union of the simple with infinity; but in the spirit it exists for itself; or as the genuine infinity; the *opposed* [moment] in the [genuine] infinity in consciousness is this *absolute simplicity of both* [singularity and the infinite]."[72] The notion of 'infinity' displayed in this passage involves the perfect, immediate, and antithetical joining of opposites.[73] Thus the passage says that consciousness is the identity of identity and opposition, while spirit is that living identity doubled or united to its abstract counterparts.

The most interesting example of Hegel's dependence on Schellingian concepts and modes of thought, and of his increasing dissatisfaction with them as well, is found in the *Jena Logic, Metaphysics, and Philosophy of Nature* (1804–05). While the mediation of the judgment and the syllogism indeed provides part of the overall pattern of development in this difficult work, it is the 'infinite judgment' or direct joining of opposites that furnishes the predominant mode of logical transition, an obviously Schellingian method.[74] And in many sections of the manuscript where one expects to see mediation emphasized, it is either underplayed or entirely absent. Thus judgment fails to stabilize and fully realize the determinate concept; the middle term receives scant attention in the treatment of the syllogism, and the section on reciprocal determination includes a surprising critique of the poverty of the notions of mediation and transition:

> To the extent that this reciprocal determination is not a liveliness, to that extent it is not what it truly puts itself forth as being, namely an infinite mediation of transitions, a rational cognition. For cognition is precisely cognition only as infinite, in the situation of absolute opposition. As the other-being of spirit, nature possesses infinity only in this superficial manner of mediations within itself. Inasmuch as nature is this simple unity of opposites, it fails to represent this opposition as being inherently infinite, but represents it in a bare,

superficial manner, as being simple, a division, a determinacy in which the 'more' or 'less' of the production, and the predominance of one or the other of the opposites obtains. Cognition must absolutely tear apart this simplicity and exhibit the extremes pure and simple, and thus cancel them as qualitatively opposed. . . . What is essential to the idea does not come into consideration here, the relationship of determinate moments as a relation. It is considered only an appearance of determinacies, which exist here the way they do in all forms of mediated transition, and which are differentiated only by the 'more' or 'less' of one or the other [opposites].[75]

Hegel suggests in this passage that mediation or transition is an inferior or superficial form of connection when compared with the infinite judgment, the direct union of opposites. Only when the 'infinity' of absolute and immediate opposition comes to the fore will mediation be absolute cognition. Mediation is seen to be the inferior or natural form of rationally identifying opposites because it is fundamentally quantitative; the interaction of entities in nature proceeds by degree. But rational cognition is the identification of absolute, that is, qualitative, opposites. Indeed this seems a Schellingian pattern of thought.

But if this 1804–05 manuscript shows that Hegel has not yet arrived at his mature understanding of dialectical methodology, with its emphasis on mediation and its model of the 'rational syllogism' wherein every term mediates every other, it clearly shows Hegel's discontent with Schelling's early understanding of indifference as 'quantitative indifference,' especially as presented in the 1801 *Exposition of My System*. Quantitative relations, thinks Hegel, are not really relations, for they involve no real opposition. Real relations accomplish the identification of qualitative opposites. Passages such as the following discussion of quantitative difference show that Hegel was in search of some absolutely negative power that he could call the absolute, and that he could no longer be satisfied with Schelling's construct of the absolute, wherein the developed difference of the absolute's idea is in stark contrast to an utterly identical, undeveloped absolute essence:

But for that reason it might appear as if the correct way to express the nature of difference either in relation to the absolute or in itself would be in this form of a merely quantitative difference, as an external difference that never affected the absolute's essence itself. Inasmuch as the absolute essence is such that in it difference is simply cancelled, the illusion must be avoided that difference itself subsists outside it, that the cancellation of difference precedes it, that it is merely the cancelled state of difference—and not at the same time its existence and the cancellation of the opposition [as well]. In general, opposition is qualitative, and since nothing exists outside the absolute, it is itself absolute, and only because it is absolute does it cancel itself. In its rest as the cancelled state of opposition, the absolute is at the same time the activity of opposition's existence or the cancellation of the absolute opposition. The absolute existence of the opposites, if one wants to interpret the existence of opposites as itself the absolute essence, does not turn the absolute into an external, indifferent subsistence of its moments. Rather the absolute essence is precisely that wherein an external indifferent co-subsistence is cancelled, because the absolute is nothing quantitative or external.[76]

It is clear that at this stage Hegel rejects Schelling's way of expressing the absolute's identity as indifference, the nondifferent inclusion of quantitative opposites which actively exclude one another in phenomenal being. He poses the demand that an identity of opposites be an identity for itself, and that this identity actively sublate the opposition of its terms. Note, however, that there is no mention in this passage of mediating opposites or of some progressive, synthetic unification of them. In the *Jena Logic* Hegel battles to replace Schelling's vision of the absolute as static indifference with one of an immediate union of opposites. At the same time, he struggles to replace the notion that all differences in some sense ontologically reduce to a merely quantitative preponderance of subjectivity over objectivity or vice versa with the more lively notion that determinateness is real or qualitative on every level. These two endeavors give the long, twisted dialectic of the manuscript what cogency it has, at one and the same time to preserve the qualitative or for-itself status of the determinate on each and every level it appears and to lead opposed determinacies to an identity that is not merely a result, but which is truly substantial and independent. Schelling's system, reflected in Hegel's eyes in 1804, seems a blurred image of the truth, for Schelling variously seems to sacrifice the determinate and for-itself character of being encountered in experience to a determinate absolute, or to sacrifice the determinate qualitative richness of the absolute to the realities encountered in experience under the form of externality. Hegel will have both.

It is in the 1807 *Phenomenology of Spirit* that Hegel first achieves independence from Schelling's concepts and, to a certain extent, his vocabulary. Though the Jena writings of 1802–1805 display an ingenuity and an independence of mind, notably in their focus on metaphysical and social/ethical topics and in their developmental or dialectical style of exposition, Hegel remained an essentially Schellingian thinker. To the movement of philosophical exposition corresponds no movement of the content being expounded; transitions are all alike, an immediate slide from one antithetical opposite to its counterpart; whether Hegel talks of their unity as 'identity' or 'infinity' or 'relation,' the static Schellingian union of opposites suppresses all vitality. Hegel had not yet succeeded in formulating an alternative to the logic of indifference.

All that is changed with the *Phenomenology*, a vast, flowing and polymorphous work bursting with novel insights, bewildering terminology, dialectical somersaults, but, above all, with energy. The work was meant to be the history of consciousness's education into the absolute stance, but its writing was, I suspect, the philosopher's education into his own stance as well. Its overall philosophical achievement, realized with minimum consistency in its various parts, is a preliminary statement of a new method for systematic philosophy, a method that will achieve the realization of that goal of conceptual comprehension or 'idea' which Schelling's system had merely announced. It is convenient to apply the simple appellation 'dialectic' to this method, but difficult to pin down or formalize its elements and procedures. For this new method rejects the Cartesian idea of atomic simplicity in favor of holistic complexity, rejects the propositional form of truth for an elaborate, discursive style of description which Hegel termed 'syllogistic,' and everywhere prefers to sink itself in the detailed and the specific instead of ascending to the commanding terrain of the abstract and the general.

Hegel announces his grasp on the new dialectical method in the *Phenomenology*'s Preface, but it is important to realize that the Preface was written after the bulk of the voluminous work, not prior to it. In a sense, Hegel had to immerse himself in the whole tortured history of consciousness in order to ascend to clarity on his procedure in the Preface. For the work, I have said, is a vast flux of energy, forever transforming itself, taking on new shapes and discarding the old. Yet it is not pure flux; it is process and it has an end-state or result. Hegel could only come to clarity about his method and at the same time attain to a final judgment on Schelling, the pronouncement namely that "everything turns on grasping and expressing the True, not only as *Substance* but equally as *Subject*," because in the course of the *Phenomenology* itself, subject or self becomes substance. But more of this anon.

Traces of the influence of the *Bruno*, both positive and negative, abound in the *Phenomenology*. It might seem surprising that Hegel is still reacting to a document published four years earlier, but even in the period of collaboration with Schelling, Hegel was a co-laborer, not a follower. Since Schelling left Jena early in 1803, it is not surprising that Hegel takes the works of 1802, *Bruno* and *Further Expositions of My System*, as typical of Schelling's philosophy. A similar lag in historical awareness is evident in Hegel's "Difference" essay, where his picture of Schelling's system is more often drawn from the 1800 *System of Transcendental Idealism* than from the more recent *Exposition of My System*.

For the limited purpose of seeing Schelling's influence, positive and negative, on the *Phenomenology*, we can confine our attention to the latter's Introduction, a passage that has the clarity and generality of the Preface, but without its polemics. From the first words, Hegel resolves to disregard the uneasiness about human cognition which characterizes most modern philosophy and thus to evade the whole lot of Kantian epistemological quandaries that are commonly taken to be the necessary starting point for philosophy. Fear of error ranks as fear of truth when the subject is human cognition, so Hegel resolves to take up the stance of natural consciousness from the very first. The first question for philosophy is not whether human cognition is an adequate medium for reaching the absolute, for cognition is no medium for viewing anything; it is consciousness itself. "For it is not the refraction of the ray, but the ray itself whereby the truth reaches us, that is cognition; and if this were removed, all that would be indicated would be a pure direction or a blank space."[77] Kant's mistake was to ask after some fundamental presupposition for adequate knowledge, one unchanging and unchangeable criterion. Conformity to possible experience was his candidate for the criterion, and one which radically altered the territory of what was to count as valid knowledge. But in Hegel's eyes, Kant neglected to make clear that our knowing and our comparison of our knowing to the supposed criterion are both moments *inside* our knowing, or rather, he neglected to pose the crucial question, 'What or whose is the reason that would attempt a critique of pure reason?'[78] Since knowing is comparing, and applying the criterion is an ordinary case of knowing, either the quest for the criterion is futile, hopelessly infested as we are with subjectivity, or, the alternative Hegel seizes upon, the criterion is simply consciousness itself comparing itself with itself in the course of experience. Hegel puts it this way:

Now, if we inquire into the truth of knowledge, it seems that we are asking what knowledge is *in itself*. Yet in this inquiry knowledge is *our* object, something that exists *for us*. . . . What we asserted to be its essence would be not so much its truth but rather just our knowledge of it. The essence or criterion would lie within ourself, and that which was to be compared with it and about which a decision would be reached through this comparison would not necessarily have to recognize the validity of such a standard.

But the dissociation, or this semblance of dissociation and presupposition, is overcome by the nature of the object we are investigating. Consciousness provides its criterion from within itself, so that the investigation becomes a comparison of consciousness with itself; for the distinction made above falls within it.[79]

Now what experience reveals is not an already achieved certainty, but a great diversity of states of consciousness, each apparently certain and adequate when it comes on the scene, but ultimately seen to be flawed and deficient in certain definite respects. Experience must teach itself what it can trust, or rather, it must itself become experienced in the ways of the world, and come to trust nothing that it has not tested. The course of experience thus forms a highway of doubt and despair on which the innocence of initial certainties must inevitably perish, but whose positive meaning is a mature and worldly recognition of untruth as untruth. Experience is trial by error, we might say, frustrating in its individual moments, but of positive general significance if it serves as a process of education. In the *Phenomenology,* the experience of natural consciousness is both the experience of untruth and the education into what is to rank as philosophic truth; the criterion is established by maturation. Here is how Hegel depicts the end-point of the process:

The experience of itself which consciousness goes through can, in accordance with its concept, comprehend nothing less than the entire system consciousness. . . . Thus the moments of the whole are *patterns of consciousness.* In pressing forward to its true existence, consciousness will arrive at a point at which it gets rid of its semblance of being burdened with something alien, with what is only for it, and some sort of 'other,' at a point where appearance becomes identical with essence . . . And finally, when consciousness itself grasps this its own essence, it will signify the nature of absolute knowledge itself.[80]

In these brief remarks, we can begin to discern the shape of Hegel's mature thought, and can appreciate the differences between the *Phenomenology* and the sort of identity-philosophy the *Bruno* advances. Hegel's Introduction puts forth three fundamental claims, each of which must be explored at some length. (1) The first claim is that there is no sense to the criterion quest that has dominated modern philosophy since Descartes. It is not that there is no criterion for distinguishing truth from falsity; there is no one absolute standard. Now when a philosopher makes doubt into a method or attempts to haul reason to court to justify itself and subsequently manufactures one single and absolute criterion for truth— whether it be indubitability, adequacy of idea, direct acquaintance with the given, or conformity to possible experience—he is simply abstracting from the normal process of trusting, doubting, testing and setting provisional standards that experience necessitates. Setting the standard is not something that can be done once and for all. A philosopher cannot replace the richness of life with one argument, or with a book full of them. What an adequate philosophy can do is to distill the learning which a person, his culture, his community's history has accumulated, but abstraction can never be the dominant technique in such a process, for it provides no index for achieving a balance between appropriate generality and appropriate discrimination and detail. Just such a balance is what I take to be the goal of Hegel's philosophic endeavor and, forgetting for a moment the grandness of its final claims, its greatest virtue seems to be the modesty and integrity of its procedure.

(2) Hegel's second claim is that experience as a whole provides the philosopher his subject matter, and that it contains not just a range of objective contents, but the knowing agent's dispositions toward and activities upon the former. As knowers we continually encounter opinion, ideology and superstition as well as truths that will stand the test of criticism and communal acceptance. As agents we find ourselves pulled by self-interest, convention, chimerical notions of piety and sentimentality as well as by genuine moral interest. Experience, taken not as bare occupancy of a span of personal consciousness, but as a process of learning what is true and what ought to be done, is a process of sorting out options, and a process of self-transformation or self-purification as well. And the process is not a strictly individual affair. At every stage, the improvement of our knowledge and the rectification of our society depends on the struggles of others, and on the collective lapses and achievements handed down to us by our history. No one of us leads a life so rich, so varied, and so tortured as the consciousness whose life and history the *Phenomenology* represents, but it might be said that what Hegel depicts is the history of our collective consciousness. And it is from our achieved, corrected, collective rationality, seen as the experience of life in all its dimensions, that an 'absolute' or 'scientific' stance is to be achieved, if it is to be attained at all.

(3) The third fundamental feature of the *Phenomenology*'s stance is Hegel's belief, for reasons some of which are substantial and some of which are articles of faith, that conscious experience is not only self-correcting but self-perfecting. It is one thing to believe, as all educators, parents and moralists implicitly do, that truth can emerge from a process of testing half-truths, but it is something quite different to maintain that it must necessarily result from this process. Here we encounter Hegel's enigmatic metaphysical and psychological concept of *negativity*, the postulate that the self is the sort of thing that becomes itself only by dispersing itself into otherness and returning to itself by negating that otherness. The self is at every moment the identity of the for-itself and the in-itself, of appearance and essential being, but in experience, at least initially, the self apprehends itself as the antithesis of the former to the latter. As experience develops and transforms its initial attitude of self-certainty, the self sees its life as a progressive loss of everything individualistic and subjective; it sees its very life dissolved into an objective world confronting it and sees

its endeavors limited by the conditions of that world. Yet the more it apprehends itself as lost in the world it experiences, the richer that world becomes and the more vigorous the self's contribution to it, not qua individual indeed, but qua universal subject—the knower in science, the agent in morality, the laborer in the economic sphere, the citizen in the polity.

These are striking psychological observations, to be sure, but when Hegel fuses them together into a 'principle of perfection,' when he maps the dynamics of self and world onto an abstract scheme of logical 'movement' governed by an ultimate *telos*, the self is seen to be necessarily self-universalizing and to have for its end-state the absolute identity of subjectivity and objectivity. The destiny of the self is to be the harmonization of appearance and reality, the achievement of the absolute stance. To be sure, Hegel limits this grand claim to 'World-Spirit' or what I have called collective consciousness; an individual consciousness can approximate this final state only partially, depending on the richness or poverty of its world. Nonetheless, many today who agree with Hegel that our rationality is achieved communally and historically fear that it is headed for a denouement considerably less tidy in its logic and more fiery in its appearance than Hegel anticipated.

What in the end accounts for Hegel's optimistic teleology, for his belief that the negativity of the self is infinite, that experience is the certain path to the universal stance of 'science' or absolute knowledge? The clue is to be found, I think, in the many Christological metaphors scattered throughout the *Phenomenology;* it is not just literary cuteness nor a self-aggrandizing attitude on the part of the author that moves Hegel to consistently compare the self's career with the *via dolorosa*. It is the Christian myth of death and resurrection that imparts the *telos* to Hegel's self, for just as the Gospels depict Jesus becoming the Christ through the abolition and ultimate annihilation of his individual will, so self-consciousness attains to universality to the degree it undergoes the loss of its 'mineness.' Only if there is some sense, and Hegel would insist on logical or 'conceptual' sense, in the story of new life obtained by suffering and submission to death can the history of self-consciousness attain to the absolute stance, and what counts as truth for arbitrary individuals be refined into philosophical science. Spirit must evidently perish upon the crossbeams of historical contingency and rational necessity before it can live again, one, whole and of sound mind. Hegel puts it this way at the book's conclusion:

> The *goal*, Absolute Knowing, or Spirit that knows itself as Spirit, has for its path the recollection of the Spirits as they are in themselves and as they accomplish the organization of their realm. Their preservation, regarded from the side of their free existence appearing in

the form of contingency, is History; but regarded from the side of their [philosophically] comprehended organization, it is the Science of Knowing in the sphere of appearance: the two together, comprehended History, form alike the inwardizing and the Calvary of absolute Spirit, the actuality, truth, and certainty of his throne, without which he would be lifeless and alone.[81]

Difficult as it is to obtain any succinct characterization of the *Phenomenology*, we have had to discuss at length the three crucial points Hegel advances in the Introduction: (1) There is no one abstract criterion for adequate knowledge. (2) Experience furnishes the philosopher his initial content, both the structure of consciousness itself and the wealth of 'forms of life' which are the raw material for systematic philosophy. (3) Negativity lends a teleological structure to selfhood and thus opens up access to an absolute or completely universal stance. It is time we look back to the *Bruno* and see how the *Phenomenology* represents an advance beyond Schelling's philosophy of identity, or at least a liberation for Hegel from the obvious drawbacks of Schelling's concepts.

The *Phenomenology*'s success on the first score is obvious, for Hegel wrests the richness of the life-world from the reductive doubt of epistemologists and makes it the proper content of systematic philosophy, making any flight to an otherworldly absolute, whether its content be logical or substantive, irrelevant. Just as Schelling's real quarrel lay not with Fichte himself, but with Kant, so Hegel contests Schelling's metaphysics not by direct dispute, but by going back to Kant. He may well have been moved to do so by observing at close quarters the very limited success Schelling had in attempting to refute Kant on Kantian grounds.

Recall that Schelling wanted to ground systematic philosophy in a metaphysics that was Kantian in tenor but which strictly observed Kant's injunction against employing categorial concepts outside the context of experience and his injunction against hypostatizing logical or psychological states into pure ideas. Schelling was thus forced to postulate an absolute beyond the phenomenal world, disconnected from finite cognition, and as his only evidence to point to certain nonapparent correlations (or 'indifference points') which obtain between opposite orders and aspects of phenomena. The metaphysics of indifference is, accordingly, otherworldly in its direction, weak in evidence, and wholly bound up with a dubious attempt to reify logical connections. And, as the *Bruno* clearly shows, Schelling is forced into these less than happy positions *because he is still Kantian.* Succumbing to the temptation to play the criterion-game with Kant, Schelling rejects as the standard of certitude not only the deliverances of the senses, but conceptual cognition as well. The eternal, the postulated realm of the idea, is the only thing left as the touchstone of truth, but it is accessible only through 'intellectual intuition,' insight so holistic it transcends the subject-object divide and thus escapes notice in any possible state of ordinary consciousness.

In contrast, Hegel's initial move in the *Phenomenology* is both simple and brilliant, namely, to refuse to play the criterion-game, to refuse to let philosophy be encumbered at the start with epistemological problems that, at that stage, are both premature and inappropriately abstract. Hegel decides to focus his description on how experiential consciousness actually learns to discriminate relative truths from partial and dubious information as it is educated into full grip upon its rationality. The basis for systematic philosophy is thus constructed in familiar territory and with familiar tools. The *Phenomenology*, read as an attempt to evoke fundamental logical features of the world from the study of experience, is far from otherworldly. Hegel's absolute would indeed be empty and alone (as is Schelling's) if it were not bound up with the disorderly array of riches, both of content and of psychic states, which experience offers.

On the second score too, it is obvious that Hegel makes an advance upon Schelling's identity-philosophy. Other than to intone sonorous but improbable Platonic generalities about the organic interrelatedness of everything in the absolute, the actual work of Schelling's philosophy is to systematize reality as we know it, abolish the apparent heterogeneity of mind and matter, nature and spirit, and to correlate the various orders and aspects into a coherent account of the whole. But Schelling's sole tool is the indifference relation, and to reduce the differences of various apparently independent orders of phenomena to a calculus of identity and difference is to strip phenomena of their individual qualitative textures, to impose a single quantitative grid upon a rich and multiform universe. A certain systematization is achieved by the imposition of the scheme of the potencies, but it is an abstract and formalistic one; it issues not in a vivid picture of the universe, but in a flat table of contents. Hegel was keenly aware of his former colleague's shortcoming in this respect, as this passage from the Preface testifies:

> The instrument of this monotonous formalism is no more difficult to handle than a painter's palette having only two colours, say red and green, the one for colouring the surface when a historical scene is wanted, the other for landscapes. It would be hard to decide which is greater in all this, the casual ease with which everything in heaven and on earth is coated with this broth of colour, or the conceit regarding the excellence of this universal recipe; each supports the other. What results from this method of labelling all that is in heaven and earth with the few determinations of the general schema, and pigeonholing everything in this way, is nothing less than a 'report

clear as noonday' on the universe as an organism, viz. a synoptic table like a skeleton with scraps of paper stuck all over it, or like the rows of closed and labelled boxes in a grocer's stall. . . . This monochromatic character of the schema and its lifeless determinations, this absolute identity, and the transition from one to the other, are all equally products of the lifeless Understanding and external cognition.[82]

We shall later have occasion to comment on the tone of these and similar remarks. For now, we must note that things stand quite otherwise with the author of the *Phenomenology*, whose conceptual palette is almost as broad as his canvas. To pursue Hegel's metaphor a bit further, to turn one's mind from the *Bruno*'s version of absolute philosophy to the *Phenomenology*'s is like turning one's gaze in a gallery from a Mondrian to a Seurat, both purporting to be portraits of the same subject, the former an exercise in pure geometry, with representation all but effaced and color muted, the latter a sheer explosion of minute packets of experience, a multitude of colored points which only gradually, and with much effort, organize themselves into a meaningful pattern. Hegel himself conceded that in writing the *Phenomenology* he got lost in details—presumably details of historical epochs and literary works such as *Antigone* and *Don Quixote* which he took to illustrate stages in the life of spirit—and failed to make clear the organization of the whole. He further confessed that to achieve clarity on this matter would have cost him more time and effort than he could muster.[83] Perhaps Hegel was too modest, however, for despite its unexpungeable obscurities, the *Phenomenology* does embody what its author was fond of calling "the work of the concept." To a considerable degree, Hegel's work of maturation lives up to the 'conceptual' standard announced in its Preface:

> The formal Understanding leaves it to others to add this principal feature [specificity]. Instead of entering into the immanent content of the thing, it is forever surveying the whole and standing above the particular existence of which it is speaking, i.e. it does not see it at all. Scientific cognition, on the contrary, demands surrender to the life of the object, or, what amounts to the same thing, confronting and expressing its inner necessity. Thus, absorbed in its object, scientific cognition forgets about that general survey, which is merely the reflection of the cognitive process away from the content and back into itself. Yet, immersed in the material, and advancing with its movement, scientific cognition does come back to itself, but not before its filling or content is taken back into itself. . . . Through this process the simple, self-surveying whole itself emerges from the wealth in which its reflection seemed to be lost.[84]

It is obvious that Hegel means the contrast between formal understanding and scientific cognition to be read as a contrast between Schelling's method and his own.

On the third score, however, Hegel's claim that the teleological structure of self-consciousness provides a standpoint for absolute philosophy, it seems that Hegel stands on ground no firmer than Schelling does with his mysterious, uninspectable intellectual intuition. Now Hegel's picture of self-consciousness is multilayered. Much of it is drawn from indisputably brilliant insights into the psychology of the ego and into the dialectics of appropriation and self-surrender inside key human experiences, deplorably termed 'peak moments' by some today; it is the wealth of such insights that made thinkers such as Sartre disciples of the *Phenomenology*. But these insights are wedded to a picture of consciousness inherited from Fichte and Schelling; Fichte produced a theoretical construct of the self as an oscilating energy system, a field of energy both self-limiting and self-transcending, whose ultimate result is the relative stability of appearances, and Schelling translated this construct from pure epistemology to the terrain of social and historical phenomena for the first time in the 1800 *System of Transcendental Idealism*. But to fully understand what is unique in Hegel's picture of self-consciousness, namely the equation of selfhood and negativity, and to come to believe with Hegel that self-negation equals self-perfection and thus furnishes a ladder to the absolute, one must finally come to the foot of the Cross. There, either through the eyes of a naive faith which takes stories to be truths, or through the more 'Königsbergian' eyes of nineteenth and twentieth century liberal theologians who tend to see in the Faith a repository of more general metaphysical and psychological truths, one must try to intuit what Hegel did, the paradigm of *rational existence* in the corpse of a defeated prophet!

What is the philosopher to make of this today? Minds as eminent and diverse as Aristotle and Whitehead, Peirce and Plato have seen no intrinsic reason for the disparity of the viewpoints of religion, philosophy, and science. St. Paul, however, found by experience that the Cross was a folly to the Greeks and a stumbling block to the Jews, and our philosophy has been predominantly Greek in tone.[85] Paul's listeners in Athens may well have had a hard time deciding between their city's ancient wisdom and the folly of the Crucified, but it is striking that in a way, living in a secularized world, Hegel presents his readers the same difficult choice, precisely in the name of wisdom. We can at any rate relish the irony that Marx's vision of the triumph of the proletariat, the class that is no class and so is destined to overcome all fixity of social and economic interests, leads ultimately back to Golgotha and to what there is to be seen through the eyes of faith.[86]

Space will not permit a discussion of all those passages of the *Phenom-enology* where Hegel is either substantially or polemically critical of Schelling's identity-philosophy.[87] What is of more interest is the harshly polemical tone of the whole of the Preface. Though Hegel there achieves a clear presentation of his method in outline, it is hardly comparable to the carefully delineated and soberly argued overview of his dialectical method which comprises the first eighty-three paragraphs of the *Encyclopaedia*. In the Preface, Hegel chooses to use the philosophy of identity as his foil, and he adumbrates piecemeal what he means by 'scientific cognition' through a relatively disorganized series of sharp-eyed and sharp-tongued criticisms of Schelling. In its own way, the Preface is brilliant and entertaining; it contains the clearest sentences ever penned by Hegel, and as satire it ranks alongside some of the deliverances of Mencken and Twain. But it is undeniably rude and ill mannered as well, especially when viewed against the background of the personal relations between the two philos-ophers.

Hegel and Schelling had communicated infrequently, but cordially, since Schelling left Jena in 1803. Hegel broke off the correspondence late in 1804, but after the completion of the *Phenomenology,* breaking a silence of some two and one-half years, Hegel resumed contact with Schelling in January of 1807. The pen that seemed to etch the Preface on copper with acid is deferential and cordial; Hegel evidently looks to Schelling for a warm reception of his long-delayed philosophy:

> I had hoped to send you something of my work, since last Easter in fact, and this too is to blame for prolonging my silence. But I finally see the end of the printing process approaching and this Easter I will be able to send you the first part, voluminous enough, to be sure, for a beginning. I shall be especially interested to see if you do not object to my thoughts and my manner of expression.[88]

Early in 1807, two sets of friendly letters are exchanged. On 1 May, 1807, Hegel again mentions his work; his tone is friendly, candid, and personal:

> My book is finally finished, but the same wretched confusion that dominated the whole editorial and printing process, and even the book's composition in parts, besets even the distribution of exemplars to my friends. For this reason, you as yet have no copy from me in your hands, but I hope to soon bring it to pass that you have one. I am curious to see what you will say about the idea of the first part, which is really the introduction [to the system]—for as yet I have not gone beyond the task of introducing [the system] and gotten into the thick of it.[89]

After commenting on the faults of various sections, Hegel continues:

> In the Preface you will not find that I have concerned myself over-much with the stale gossip that your formulas are so much nonsense and which degrades your science to an empty formalism. Otherwise, I hardly need to say that if you approve some aspects of the whole work, this will mean more to me than if others are pleased or displeased with the whole of it. To the same degree, I know of no one I would rather have introduce this book to the public or to furnish a judgment on it to me personally.
>
> Farewell. Greet the Niethammers for me, who I hope have happily arrived at your place, and especially Madame Schelling.[90]

It is difficult to imagine a culture in which it would be proper to ask someone you had vilified in a book to furnish its first review! Or did Hegel not intend the remarks in the Preface to point to Schelling? He was obviously aware they could be read that way.

Schelling's reply, after he had received the *Phenomenology*, is much delayed; its tone is a bit cold and injured, at least at first:

> You have not had a letter from me for a long time. In your last one you spoke of your book. When I received it, I wanted to read it before I wrote you again. But the many duties and distractions of this summer left me neither the time nor the peace of mind requisite for the study of such a work. So as yet I have read only the Preface. Inasmuch as you yourself mentioned the polemical part of it, decent self-respect forbids me to think so little of myself as to judge that this polemic refers to me. It may therefore only pertain to those who abuse my ideas and to the gossips, as you said in your letter to me, although this distinction is not made in the book itself. You can easily imagine how happy I would be to get this matter cleared up. Where we might really have different convictions or points of view could be clearly and briefly discovered and resolved between us without any shame, for all these points are capable of reconciliation, with one exception. I admit that as yet I do not comprehend the sense in which you oppose 'concept' to intuition. By concept you can mean nothing other than what you and I have called 'idea,' whose nature it precisely is to have one aspect whereby it is concept and another whereby it is intuition. . . .
>
> Farewell; write to me soon again and continue to think of me as your sincere friend.[91]

Hegel never answered the letter, nor its request for a clarification on the polemical comments of the Preface, and so an awkward moment between the two philosophers widened into a breach. Schelling and Hegel never communicated again, except for an unexpected afternoon of pleasant conversation that followed on a chance meeting at a resort spa, late in Hegel's life. The bitter remarks on Schelling's philosophy in the *Phenomenology*'s Preface, the cordial letters between the two in the course of 1807, the dignified but injured tone of Schelling's reaction to the Preface, Hegel's failure to reply—all these add up to a mystery. What is clear is that the cycle of events that had occasioned the *Bruno* had happened once again. Philosophy marched on, over the bones of broken friendships; Plato, at least, would be saddened at the sight.[92]

Notes

1. Johann Michael Salier to Konrad Schmid, December 1803, SPIEGEL, 117.

2. Fichte to Schelling, 31 May 1801, BRIEFE 2, 341.

3. Schelling's writings during this period may generally be divided into works expounding Fichte's transcendental idealism and works exploring the new direction of a transcendental philosophy of nature. In the first class are:

> *On the Possibility of a Form of All Philosophy* (1794)
> *On the Self as the Principle of Philosophy* (1795)
> *Philosophical Letters on Dogmatism and Criticism* (1795)
> *New Deduction of Natural Right* (1796)
> *Essays Expounding the Idealism of the Science of Knowledge* (1796)
> *System of Transcendental Idealism* (1800)

In the second class are:

> *Ideas Toward a Philosophy of Nature* (1797)
> *The World-Soul* (1798)
> *First Outline of a System of Nature-Philosophy* (1799)
> *The Concept of Speculative Physics* (1799)
> *General Deduction of Dynamic Processes* (1800)
> *The True Concept of Philosophy of Nature* (1801)

In 1801 Schelling signaled the new and systematic direction of his thought with the first presentation of identity-philosophy, *Exposition of My System of Philosophy.*

4. Schelling to Fichte, 10 March 1801, BRIEFE 2, 354.

5. Ibid., 355.

6. For an account of the abortive project, see Fuhrmans' note in BRIEFE 2, 229–231.

7. In 1804 Schelling prefaced his lectures entitled *The Complete System of Philosophy* with a 'Propaedeutic' on the history of philosophy. In 1805 Fichte authored *Characteristics of the Present Age,* a study which situated the nineteenth century in a succession of five world-historical epochs. Also in 1805, Hegel began lecturing on the history of philosophy while he was at work on the *Phenomenology of Spirit;* during this period he was finally able to break free from Schelling's logic of indifference and formulate his mature concept of dialectical methodology.

8. *Munich Lectures on the History of Philosophy,* WERKE 10:121–122.

9. A paraphrase of *Timaeus* 68E–69A, which Schelling quotes in explanation of the *Bruno*'s subtitle.

10. Johann Jacob Wagner to Andreas Adam, 6 January 1803, SPIEGEL, 108–109. In full the letter reads,

> I can well believe that M. did not understand the *Bruno* either. I am more than a bit flattered to be one of the two or three in Germany who is roughly qualified to judge the work. Perhaps it is my intimate knowledge of Plato which helps me, to no small extent, to understand this second Plato. *Bruno* is really the authentic Platonism of modern philosophy. I am actually at work on a review of this masterpiece, one that is worthy of it.

See pp. 38–39 for excerpts from Wagner's review.

11. K. Chr. Fr. Kraus to his father, 6 March 1802, SPIEGEL, 93.

12. Friedrich Schlegel to August Wilhelm Schlegel, Paris, 16 September 1802, SPIEGEL, 99.

13. Dated 16 March 1802, SPIEGEL, 91.

14. SPIEGEL, 99–100.

15. See *De mundi sensibilis atque intelligibilis forma et principiis,* section 10, in *Kant Werke* 5 (Darmstadt, 1958), 40–43.

16. WERKE 7:146. Compare Hegel's remarks on the instinct of reason in PHENOMENOLOGY, pars. 257–258.

17. CRITIQUE, A 313/B 370.

18. Ibid., A 327–328/B 384.

19. *Wissenschaft der Logik,* Teil 2, (Meiner, Hamburg, 1966) 407–409. My translation. In 1807, however, Hegel is highly critical of Schelling's use of the term:

> Those who came after him [Anaxagoras] grasped the nature of existence more definitely as *Eidos* or *Idea,* determinate Universality, Species or Kind. It might seem as if the term *Species* or *Kind* is too commonplace, too inadequate, for Ideas such as the Beautiful, the Holy, and the Eternal that are currently in fashion. But nowadays an expression which exactly designates a concept is often spurned in favor of one which, if only because of its foreign extraction, shrouds the concept in a fog, and hence sounds more edifying. (PHENOMENOLOGY, par. 54; translation altered)

20. *Critique of Judgment,* section 77, tr. J. H. Bernard (Hafner, New York, 1974) 256–257.

21. Spinoza defines eternity as follows: "By eternity I understand existence itself, so far as it is conceived necessarily to follow from the definition alone of the eternal thing." ETHICS 1, def. 8.

22. Compare Bradley's suggestive remark: "Nothing in the whole and in the end can be external and everything less than the Universe is an abstraction from the whole, an abstraction more or less empty, and the more empty, the less self-dependent." Cited in Harold H. Oliver, *A Relational Metaphysic* (Nijhoff, The Hague, 1981) 104. Oliver provides a brief history of post-Leibnizean philosophies of relation on 101–151, but omits mention of Schelling or of Hegel.

23. See *World as Will and Representation,* Book 1, sections 3–5.

24. WERKE 4:387.

25. Achim von Arnim to Clemens Brentano, 18 November 1802, SPIEGEL, 103.

26. See below, 4:267–279. All references enclosed in parentheses or brackets in this section are to the *Bruno;* they are cited according to the pagination of WERKE 4, which is indicated within brackets in the translation. See the "Synopsis of Contents" for the correlation between WERKE 4 and the present translation.

27. Schelling's term *Indifferenz* might be translated more clearly as 'nondifference,' but since Schelling meant the term to stand out as a foreign borrowing, I have typically rendered it as 'indifference.' The term carries no psychological connotations; Schelling uses it synonymously with *Gleichgewicht,* balance or equilibrium, but not with *Gleichgültigkeit,* apathy or lack of concern. For Schelling there is but one case of strict identity or monolithic self-identity and that is the absolute's essence. Every other case of identity, for example the identity of the absolute's form and essence, or that of soul and body, is a case of indifference. Indifference is the ultimate nondifference or togetherness of irreducibly different aspects of one and the same thing. The relation between object and mirror image or that of the two sides of a coin provides the simplest example of indifference.

28. Johann Jacob Wagner, "Ueber Schellings Bruno," *Kleine Schriften* 1 (Ulm, 1839) 363.

29. *The Complete System of Philosophy,* 1804, WERKE 6:137.

30. Ibid., WERKE 6:143.

31. See below 4:312 and note 99, p. 256ff.

32. Harold H. Joachim, *The Nature of Truth* (Clarendon Press, Oxford, 1906), 48–49.

33. See CRITIQUE A 71–73/B 97–98.

34. Consult DIFFERENCE, 180 and 185.

35. SYSTEM, 136.

36. In 1794, Fichte had described intuition as follows:
The mind lingers in this conflict and wavers between the two [opposites]—wavers between the requirement [of synthesizing them] and the impossibility of carrying it out. And in this condition, but only therein, it lays hold of both at once, or what comes to the same thing, makes them such that they can simultaneously be grasped and held firm; in touching them and being repulsed, and touching them again, it gives them, in *relation to itself,* a certain content and a certain extension (which will reveal itself in due course as a manifold in time and space). This condition is called the state of *intuition.* (SCIENCE, 201, interpolations mine)

37. Schelling criticizes Spinoza for making thought and extension the immediate attributes of God or nature (see 4:323–324). His own statements, here and elsewhere in the *Bruno,* suggest that thought and material reality can only be attributed to the absolute's form or the absolute idea *analogically,* as an extension of the strictly coordinated but different mental and material orders of phenomena. Neither thinking as such nor materiality can be ascribed to the absolute itself.

38. Compare Hegel's description of the spurious infinite in the *Encyclopaedia:*
But such a progression to infinity is not the real infinite. That consists in being at home with itself in the other, or, if enunciated as a process, in coming to itself in its other. Much depends on rightly apprehending the notion of infinity, and not stopping short at the wrong infinity of endless progression. When time and space, for example, are spoken of as infinite, it is in the first place the infinite progression on which our thoughts fasten. We say, Now, This time, and then we keep continually going forwards and backwards beyond this limit. The case is the same with space. (*The Logic of Hegel,* Wallace trans. [Oxford, 1968], 175)

39. In the *Bruno* Schelling generally does not distinguish the logical possibility of separated existence and its actuality. His statement that "each thing takes from the absolute its own proper life and ideally goes over into a separated existence" (4:258) is typical. But from late 1802 through 1804, he sharply distinguished the two, expressing the finite's actual separation as a "fall" from the absolute, as in the following passage:
In short, there is no gradual transition from the absolute to the actual. The origin of the sensible world is thinkable only as a breaking away from the absolute through a leap. . . . The absolute is uniquely real. In contrast to it, finite things are not real, so their origin cannot consist in a *communication* of reality to them or to their substrate, . . . but only in a *distancing,* in a *fall* from the absolute. (WERKE 6:38)

40. Johann Jacob Wagner, "Ueber Schellings Bruno," *Kleine Schriften* 1 (Ulm, 1839) 363.

41. Ibid., 364.

42. Ibid., 365.

43. In his 1809 *Essay on Human Freedom* Schelling makes the volitonal perspective central to his whole concept of being. "In the final and highest instance there is no other Being than Will. Will is primordial Being, and all predicates apply to it alone—groundlessness, eternity, independence of time, self-affirmation. All philosophy strives only to find this highest expression." *Of Human Freedom,* tr. J. Gutmann (Open Court, Chicago, 1936), 24. In the same essay in which Schelling ties together the ideas of creation, divine revelation, and the human attainment of the moral stance, it is the creature's *self-will,* the creation of good and evil, which effects the definitive separation of the natural and the spiritual. "Just this inner necessity is itself freedom, man's being is essentially *his own deed.*" Op. cit., 63.

44. Consult the "Deduction of Presentation," section III, SCIENCE, 206–208.

45. For a general account of Schelling's philosophy of nature in the years 1797–1806, consult J. Esposito, *Schelling's Idealism and Philosophy of Nature* (Bucknell University Press, Lewisburg, 1977), 47–124.

46. SYSTEM, 227–228.

47. CRITIQUE A 158/B 197.

48. G. Schweighauser, "On the Present State of Philosophy in Germany," *The Monthly Magazine* (London) Vol. 18, no. 2, 1804.

49. In the *First Critique* Kant merely remarks that the modality of judgments does not affect their content: "The modality of judgments is a quite peculiar function. Its distinguishing characteristic is that it contributes nothing to the content of the judgment . . . but concerns only the value of the copula in relation to thought in general." CRITIQUE A 74/B 99. But in the *Prolegomena to Any Future Metaphysics* he succinctly observes, "As modality in a judgment is not a distinct predicate, so by the modal concepts a determination is not superadded to things." Carus/Ellington trans. (Hackett, Indianapolis, 1977), 325n.

50. Johann Jacob Wagner to Andreas Adam, 17 December 1802, SPIEGEL, 198.

51. See SYSTEM, 217–222, 229–232.

52. *De anima* 431^b20–23, trans. D. W. Hamlyn (Oxford, 1968).

53. *Munich Lectures on the History of Philosophy,* 1827, WERKE 10:125.

54. Consult Gabriel Marcel, *Coleridge et Schelling* (Paris, Aubier-Montaigne, 1971); Martin Heidegger, *What Is Called Thinking,* tr. Wieck and Gray (Harper & Row, New York, 1968) and *Schellings Abhandlung über das Wesen der menschlichen Freiheit* (Tübingen, 1971); Paul Tillich, *Mysticism and Guilt-Consciousness in Schelling's Philosophical Development,* tr. V. Nuovo (Bucknell University Press, Lewisburg, 1974) and *The Construction of the History of Religion in Schelling's Positive Philosophy,* tr. Nuovo (Bucknell, Lewisburg, 1974); and

Jürgen Habermas, *Das Absolute und die Geschichte: von der Zweispältigkeit in Schellings Denken,* dissertation, Bonn, 1954.

55. WERKE 10:119–120.

56. WERKE 10:106–107.

57. In a letter to Brinkman of 26 November 1803, Schleiermacher writes: Due to the youthful enthusiasm of the authors, I too have been unable to find any difference between these [polemical] discussions. The slavery on both sides seems equally distasteful to me. One only sees how Schelling adorns himself with a Hegel, A. W. Schlegel with a Bernhardi, Jacobi with a Köppen. Really, all desire fades to capture such a slave or to become entangled with one. (SPIEGEL, 128)

58. *Prolegomena to Any Future Metaphysics,* Ak. 278, tr. Ellington/Carus (Hackett, Indianapolis, 1977).

59. WERKE 10:120–121.

60. WERKE 10:123–125.

61. Jacobi to Reinhold, 10 August 1802, SPIEGEL, 97.

62. See Xavier Tilliette, "Hegel et Schelling à Jena," *Revue de metaphysique et de morale,* 73 (1968), 149–166.

63. Consult Klaus Düsing, "Spekulation und Refelxion: Zur Zusammenarbeit Schellings und Hegels in Jena," *Hegel-Studien,* 5 (1969), 113–114.

64. See Düsing, 117; Tilliette, 162; and Reinhard Lauth, *Die Entstehung von Schellings Identitätsphilosophie in der Auseinandersetzung mit Fichte's Wissenschaftslehre* (Alber, Freiburg/Munich, 1975) 193.

65. Lauth, 160.

66. Hermann Schmitz, *Hegel als Denker der Individualität* (Meisenheim, 1957), 119.

67. Karl Rosenkranz, *Hegels Leben* (Darmstadt, 1963), 159.

68. Ibid., 201.

69. Otto Pöggeler, "Hegels Jenaer Systemkonzeption," in *Hegels Idee einer Phänomenologie des Geistes* (Alber, Freiburg/Munich, 1973), 119.

70. See WERKE 5:267, 269.

71. G. W. F. Hegel, *System of Ethical Life* and *First Philosophy of Spirit,* tr. H. S. Harris (State University of New York Press, Albany, 1979), 99–100.

72. Ibid., 206.

73. See the treatment of infinity in the Jena *Logik, Metaphysik und Naturphilosophie* and in *Faith and Knowledge,* 112–114. Also consult Hermann Schmitz, *Hegel als Denker der Individualität* (Meisenheim, 1957) 104–125.

74. See Schmitz, 119. The notions of infinity as immediate and absolute antithesis and of the infinite or self-cancelling judgment as the appearance of the rational in propositional form continue to play an important role in Hegel's mature thought, but in the *Phenomenology* these are viewed as but tokens of a more fundamental process, negativity or self-supersession as such. See PHENOMENOLOGY, pars. 162, 344.

75. G. W. F. Hegel, *Jenenser Logik, Metaphysik und Naturphilosophie,* ed. G. Lasson (Meiner, Hamburg, 1967), 69.

76. Ibid., 12–13.

77. PHENOMENOLOGY, par. 73.

78. I am indebted to Prof. John E. Smith for the latter formulation.

79. PHENOMENOLOGY, pars. 83, 84.

80. PHENOMENOLOGY, par. 89.

81. PHENOMENOLOGY, par. 808.

82. PHENOMENOLOGY, par. 51.

83. Hegel to Schelling, 1 May 1807, in BRIEFE 3, 431–432.

84. PHENOMENOLOGY, par. 53.

85. See 1 Corinthians 1:18–23.

86. In a fragment penned in 1844, Marx describes the proletariat as "this poverty conscious of its own spiritual and physical poverty, this dehumanization which is conscious of itself as a dehumanization and hence abolishes itself." In the same note he makes clear that the revolutionary programme is soteriological in character: "When the proletariat wins victory, it by no means becomes the absolute side of society, for it wins victory only by abolishing itself and its opposite. Both the proletariat itself and its conditioning opposite—private property—disappear with the victory of the proletariat." *Marx-Engels Reader,* 2nd edition, ed. R.C. Tucker (Norton, New York, 1978), 134.

87. The following paragraphs of the *Phenomenology* are implicitly or directly critical of Schelling's concepts and methods. In some passages, Hegel may well have Kant and Fichte in mind as well, for his treatment of historical matters is fluid, to say the least, and he names no names.

Paragraphs 73–76 and 84–87 of the Introduction criticize the mentality Anselm represents within the *Bruno,* one which, motivated by an abstract scepticism, rejects all empirical truths as untruths and posits an absolute truth beyond experience.

Though the chapter "Force and the Understanding" seems primarily to be a critique of Kant and Fichte, along with Newton, paragraphs 149–150, 155, and 157 may have Schelling in view as well. Throughout this chapter Hegel employs concepts similar to Schelling's 'indifference' and 'essence'-'form' distinction.

The first part of the chapter "Observing Reason" is devoted to an explicit critique of Schelling's philosophy of nature, to his analysis of organism in particular, and to his attempt to make the organism a model of the idea (the last especially visible in *Bruno*). Paragraphs 242–269 seem to positively develop a Schellingian analysis of animate life, while paragraphs 270–300 ruthlessly critique the sort of reason that seeks static laws instead of fluid interrelations. Among the most notable comments: Organism does provide an image of the universe, but as a process, not as a thing (277). Hegel contrasts the living, fluid nature of the concept, which is the dissolution of all law-like structure, and the inert indifference of law, which merely universalizes simple differences (279–280). The quantitative nature of 'indifference' or of any attempt to formalize laws for nature is frequently criticized (271, 280, 286, 290). Schelling's phrase "potentiate" is called bad Latin (282). And finally, the whole effort of observing reason (= Schelling's philosophy) is said to consist of nothing but clever remarks, "a genial approach to the Concept" (297).

Paragraphs 803–804 of the final chapter, "Absolute Knowing," are a summary criticism of identity-philosophy. Hegel objects specifically to the exclusion of process or "conceptual time" from the identity of thought and being, and to Schelling's sharp dichotomy between reason and reflection.

Finally, the Preface as a whole has Schelling in view on almost every page, but explicit and significant criticisms of Schelling are voiced in paragraphs 15–21, 24, 31, 40, 46–48, and 50–54. The philosophically important objections are: Identity-philosophy is a shapeless repetition of one and the same idea (15). Philosophy must effect an analysis of terms such as subject and object, God and nature, not just skate between them (31). Schelling's method of potencies is arbitrary, repetitious, and based on shallow analogies between incomparable phenomena (51–53). Charity counsels me to silence on other passages in the Preface, well-known and acerbic in tone.

The Notes to the Translation document passages where the *Phenomenology* positively echoes or employs Schelling's ideas and terminology.

88. Hegel to Schelling, 3 January 1807, BRIEFE 3, 394.

89. Hegel to Schelling, 1 May 1807, BRIEFE 3, 431.

90. Ibid., 432.

91. Schelling to Hegel, 3 November 1807, BRIEFE 3, 471–472.

92. Many more passages in the *Phenomenology* than the polemics of the Preface are directed toward a criticism of Schelling, though his name is never mentioned. Obviously, I believe that most of the Preface has Schelling for its direct target, not overzealous 'disciples' like Wagner and Oken, as some scholars have maintained. Though it was not foreign to Hegel's practice to fire large shells at small targets, for example, the criticism of Reinhold and Bardili in *Faith and Knowledge,* it is virtually inconceivable that in a polemical preface to what Hegel called "the first part," "the introduction to my work," he would waste ammunition on disciples and second-rate imitators. The Preface is, in whole and in part, a direct comparison between the method worked out in the writing

of the *Phenomenology* and Schelling's philosophy of identity, as Hegel knew it. Since some of the Preface's leading themes, for example, that truth is both substance and subject, emerge late in the work itself, in this case in the chapter on religion, I suspect that Hegel was emboldened to take on the reigning philosophy of the day only because of the certainty he had achieved in writing the bulk of the work, certainty about the precise structure and method of systematic philosophy.

Glossary

Abbild	Image
Abdruck	Copy, mark, stamp
Abgesehen	Apart from, in abstraction from
Anfang	Origin, beginning, starting point
Angemessen	Appropriate, adapted to, commensurate with
Anschauen, -ung	Intuit, intuition, sensory intuition
Ansehung	Perspective, context, viewpoint
An sich	In itself, intrinsically, substantial element
Aufheben, -ung	Surpass, cancel, render inoperative
Auflösen, -ung	Reduce, reduction
Bedeutung	Meaning, sense
Bedingen, -ung	Condition, external circumstance
Begreifen	Comprehend, include, grasp, understand

Begriff	Concept
Bestimmen, -d, -ung	Define, determine, determining, determination, specification
Beziehen, -ung	Pertain, relate, refer, relation, connection
Darstellen	Exhibit, display, depict
Daseyn	Existence, temporal existence
Denken	Thought, think, conceive, imagine
Differenz	Difference
Ding	Thing, finite thing
Eigenschaft	Attribute, property
Einheit, -en	Identity, unity, unities, monads
Endlich	Finite
Entgegensetzen, -gesetzt	Oppose, contrast, opposite
Entzweiung	Self-estrangement
Erkennen	Cognize, know, recognize
Erkenntnis	Cognition, act of cognition, knowledge
Ewig, -keit	Eternal, eternity
Form	Form, procedure, shape
Für sich	For itself, essentially, substantially
Ganze	Whole of reality, totality, the universe
Gegenbild	Copy, antitype
Gegensatz	Opposite
Gestalt	Form, shape
Getrübt	Beclouded, distorted, affected

Gewissheit	Certitude, certainty
Gleich	Identical, equal, similar
Gleichgültigkeit	Indifference
Göttlich	Divine, godlike
Grund	Reason, ground of existence, basis
Hervorbringen, -d, -ung	Create, produce, creator, creation, product
Ideal, ideelle	Ideal
Idee	Idea
Indifferenz	Indifference
Körper	Body, chemical substance
Kunst	Artistry, artistic talent, art
Möglichkeit	Possibility
Potenz	Power, potency, potentiality
Real, reelle	Real
Realität	Reality
Schein	Play, reflection, illusion
Schönheit	Beauty
Setzen	Posit, suppose, assume, establish
Seyn	To be, subsist, have being, being
Stoff	Matter, stuff
Trennen, -ung, getrennt	Separate, divide, divorce, division, separate existence
Unendlich	Infinite, endless
Unvergänglich	Unchanging, invariant
Urbild, -lich	Archetype, archetypal
Verbinden, -ung	Bind, tie into, connection

Vereinigen, -ung	Unite, unify, union
Vergänglich	Changing, transitory, varying
Verhalten	Stand to, relate
Verhältnis	Relation, proportion, ratio
Verkehrtheit	Distortion, ruin
Verknüpfen, -ung	Join, connect, connection
Verstand	Understanding
Vorbild, -en	Exemplar, pattern, foretype, exemplify
Vorstellen, -ung	Represent, picture, representation
Wahrheit	Truth
Werth	Value
Wesen	Essence, essential reality, abiding reality, being, a being
Wirklichkeit	Actuality, realization
Wissen	Know, knowing, knowledge
Wissenschaft	Philosophical science, science

F·W·J·SCHELLING

BRUNO

OR

On the Natural and the Divine Principle of Things

1802

Synopsis of Contents
Added by K. F. A. Schelling in 1859.

ANSELM. [217] Lucian, would you repeat what you said yesterday about the relation of truth and beauty, when we discussed the mystery rites?

LUCIAN. It was my opinion that many works of art could embody the highest sort of truth and yet not, for that reason, deserve the prized title 'beauty' too.

ANSELM. But Alexander, you maintained the opposite view, that truth itself satisfies all the demands of art, and that solely through its truth does a work of art become truly beautiful.

ALEXANDER. That is what I claimed.

ANSELM. Would you like to resume our discussion now and settle the issue that remained undecided when time ran out? For happily we are met again, and not by prior arrangement, but by some hidden harmony!

LUCIAN. Welcome is every breath of speech that drives us back into the storm of discussion.

ALEXANDER. Through the rivalry of shared discussion, we penetrate ever more deeply into the heart of the matter; though dialogue begins on a gentle tone and proceeds slowly, finally it swells up like a tidal wave and carries away its participants, filling them all with joy!

ANSELM. Did not this dispute originate in what we had established about the mysteries and mythology, and about the relation of philosophers and poets as well?

LUCIAN. It did.

ANSELM. Do you not think it is fitting that we settle this conflict [218] by turning the discussion back to its origin? Then we can proceed with confidence and build from a secure foundation.

ALEXANDER. Excellent!

ANSELM. So you, Lucian, think it is possible for some work of art to possess the perfection of the highest sort of truth, but still be lacking in beauty. In claiming this, it looks like you are applying the name 'truth' to something we philosophers might be reluctant to call by that name. But you, Alexander, grant that an artwork is beautiful through its truth alone. Thus you raise the question whether there is a point where truth and beauty are identical—where they are equally unconditioned, neither one dependent on the other nor subordinated to it, each one for itself the highest reality. If there were such an [indifference] point, beauty and truth would be absolutely identical; one could be substituted for the other, and a work which exemplified this [indifference] point could be viewed under both attributes, in exactly the same respect.

Gentlemen, do you not think it is most important for us, above all else, to try to reach agreement on what 'truth' means, and then 'beauty' as well? If we do so, we will not make the mistake of equating beauty with something that is considered truth in a trivial sense. Nor shall we lose sight of the sole real truth when we stipulate that the sort of 'truth' that is not substantial and independent is not even comparable to beauty.

LUCIAN. It is an important matter to discuss.

ANSELM. If it is all right with you, my excellent Alexander, I shall direct my questions to you, for you have chosen truth ahead of beauty, untroubled by the thought of how few men can bear truth's gaze, or even the glimpse of its aegis.

ALEXANDER. If I can come to understand the idea of truth, I will happily follow your lead, my friend.

ANSELM. My friend, if you place truth above all else, even above beauty, could you hesitate even for a moment to ascribe the very highest attributes to it? And when applied to truth, would these terms mean what everyone commonly takes them to mean or signify the sort of thing one usually understands by them?

ALEXANDER. Of course not. [219]

ANSELM. And so you would not grant the attribute of truth to the sort of cognition that is accompanied by just a present certitude, would you? Or to any cognition whatsoever that is accompanied by a changeable certitude?

ALEXANDER. Not at all.

ANSELM. And for this reason, you would never ascribe truth to any sort of cognition that is either directly linked to an immediate affection of the body or indirectly facilitated by such an affection.

ALEXANDER. Impossible, since I realize that bodily affections, together with the objects that excite them, are all subject to the conditions of time.

ANSELM. For the same reason, you would never ascribe truth to any cognition that was unclear, indistinct, or not adequate to what knowing really is.

ALEXANDER. Truth belongs to none of these types of knowing, for each is just a sensible form of cognition, facilitated by the affections of the body.

ANSELM. But would you use the sublime name of truth to denote the sort of cognition that indeed has enduring certitude, but of an inferior sort? To a form of cognition valid only for human understanding, for instance, or to some other mode of knowing that is less than the highest?

ALEXANDER. Not to this kind of cognition either, if such a thing exists.

ANSELM. You doubt there is such a certain but inferior cognition? Let us see what you would oppose to what we have termed changeable certitude or where you would locate unchanging certitude!

ALEXANDER. Necessarily in the kind of truth valid not just for individual things, but for all things, and not for one determinate time span alone, but for all time.

ANSELM. Ah, but should you really locate unchanging certitude in that sort of cognition which, if valid for all time, still is valid only in reference to time? Is is not evident that truth which is generally valid for time and for things in time is invariant only in comparison with that which is not eternal, but it is not absolutely unchanging, when regarded in itself? But it is unthinkable that the truth which pertains only to what is finite [220], even if it does so universally, should have a higher value than the finite itself, and it is unthinkable that we grant a status higher than relative truth to this sort of certainty, since it stands and falls with the finite. For what man would deny that a cause precedes every effect, or that this certainty is indubitable, without need of empirical verification? This proposition is immediately certain the moment we relate the data of finite cognition to the concept of cognition. Yet if this same proposition is meaningless outside the context of what is intrinsically finite, then it is impossible to ascribe 'truth' to it. Do you not agree with me then? In the exact sense of the term, we cannot regard as true the kind of cognition that provides certainty for only a subordinate form of understanding.[2]

ALEXANDER. Certainly.

ANSELM. But furthermore, you could not agree with the view that knowledge of the finite and the temporal pertains only to finite cognition, that it does not occur within absolute cognition. For you could not be satisfied with a truth that was useful only for cognizing finite being, could you? With a 'truth' that was not absolutely the truth in the sight of God, and measured against the highest type of cognition? Or is it not rather the case that all our effort is directed toward knowing things as they are exemplified in the archetypal understanding, of which we see only images in our understanding?[3]

ALEXANDER. It would be difficult to deny it.

ANSELM. But can you in any way imagine that this highest or absolute cognition exists under temporal conditions?

ALEXANDER. Impossible!

ANSELM. Or is it conceivable either that this absolute cognition be determined by [categorial] concepts, concepts which, even if they are intrinsically universal and infinite, still refer only to time and to what is finite?

ALEXANDER. That it is determined by such concepts, no indeed. But it is quite conceivable that it determines these concepts itself.

ANSELM. This point is quite important for us, for within finite cognition, we do not seem to be the ones determining these infinite concepts; instead we seem to be determined by them. [221] And if we do appear to be the agent determining them, evidently it is through a higher sort of cognition. In all cases, then, we are forced to accept the following proposition as certain: The sort of cognition that pertains generally to time or the temporal existence of things does not even approach absolute truth, granted that it does not originate in time and that it is valid for infinite time and for all the things within time as well. For this sort of cognition presupposes a higher one, whose nature it is to be independent of all time, without reference to time, self-contained, and hence simply eternal.[4]

ALEXANDER. This conclusion follows inevitably from our first assumptions.

ANSELM. And so we shall not have scaled the summit of truth itself until our thought has reached up to the nontemporal existence of things and to their eternal concepts. Only then shall we recognize things and explain them truly.

ALEXANDER. I cannot deny it, although you have not yet shown how we can attain that region.

ANSELM. Right now that question does not concern us.[5] Our sole concern is the idea of truth, either to exalt it higher than it is currently held or to topple it from its lofty position and devalue it, making it easier for most men to reach. But are you satisfied that our investigation stick to this course?

ALEXANDER. Certainly.

ANSELM. Then let us pay closer attention to the difference between eternal and temporal cognition. Tell me, do you think it is possible that everything we call mistaken or distorted or imperfect is actually and essentially so? Or is it only when they are considered from our perspective that things seem this way?

ALEXANDER. I cannot imagine how the imperfection of some human work of art, for instance, does not actually reside in the work itself, nor that what necessarily strikes us as erroneous is not actually false as well. [222]

ANSELM. Do not let the sense of the question elude you, my friend. I was not speaking about what the artwork is when considered by itself, isolated from the whole of reality. On the correct view, it is not perversion if a man creates a thoroughly disfigured artwork instead of a perfect one, nor is it error if another man makes false statements instead of true ones. On the contrary, it would be a flaw in nature and a perversion of reality if the first man, conditioned the way he is, were able to create something perfect or something different from the insanity and evil his work in fact embodies! Neither distortion nor error are possible in nature, though. Whatever a man creates or produces follows necessarily from who he is, that is, it partially follows from the individuality of his character, and partially it follows from the outside influences to which he has been subjected. And so, in our examples, both men express the supreme truth and perfection of the whole of reality, the one through the falsity of his statements, the other through the imperfection of his creation. Each bears witness, even in his very own case, that no falsehood is possible in nature.

ALEXANDER. You seem to be caught in your own words. That the one man's falsity is really a truth, and the other's imperfection really a perfection, readily follows from what you admit, the ruin and disfigurement of their natures—

ANSELM. —Which again, viewed in itself, is no perversion of reality! For the one man, for instance, will have been begotten by such and such a father, the other determined by such a set of external circumstances. Their current dispositions, therefore, are completely necessary within the rule and general order of things.

ALEXANDER. On this line of explanation, your sole problem will be to provide an account of the origin of imperfection.

ANSELM. Granted, though it is generally impossible for thought to determine the origin of any temporal being. Imperfection occurs solely within the province of reality governed by the law of cause and effect. It does not pertain to that higher region where, since no beginning for finite reality as such is acknowledged, the imperfect eternally dwells alongside the perfect and is itself posited as perfection. Up to now we have confined our thesis to the works of man, [223] but does it not seem necessary that we extend it to the products of nature too, to all things in general? Should we not assert that, considered in itself, nothing whatsoever is lacking or imperfect or unharmonious?

ALEXANDER. It appears we should do so.

ANSELM. And, on the other hand, that things are imperfect only when judged from the perspective of temporality? Is this not so?

ALEXANDER. This too.

ANSELM. Let us go one step farther, then. Tell me, should we not suppose that a type or model is prescribed to productive nature for all its products, and not just for the totality of its creatures, but for particular creatures as well? And that productive nature models both species and individuals upon these types?

ALEXANDER. This is evident, since we see not only different species of plants and animals expressing one and the same fundamental form, some more closely, others more remotely, but we see precisely the same design repeated in the individuals of a species.

ANSELM. Now if we call the living mirror in which all things are exemplified 'archetypal nature,' and the agent that stamps these exemplars upon substances 'productive nature,' tell me, which of these two realms must we think of as subject to the law of time and to mechanics, archetypal or productive nature?

ALEXANDER. Not archetypal nature, it seems to me, for we must think of the archetype of each created being as forever identical and unchangeable, indeed as eternal. Hence archetypes are not in any way subject to time; neither are they generated nor can they be destroyed.

ANSELM. Thus it is that things within productive nature are subject to time and to the laws of mechanics, not voluntarily indeed, but as enslaved to futility.[6] But those eternal archetypes of things are like the immediate offspring or sons of God, and so one of the sacred books says, "Creation anxiously yearns for the glory of the sons of God," that is, the excellence of those eternal archetypes.[7] For within archetypal nature [224] or in God, all things are necessarily more splendid and more excellent than they are in themselves, since they are freed from the conditions of time. The created earth, for instance, is not the true earth, but only an image of the earth which is uncreated, unoriginated, and never to pass away.[8] But the idea of earth also contains the ideas of all things that are included in it or that come into existence in it. So too, there is on earth no man nor beast nor plant nor stone whose likeness does not shine brighter in the living artistry and wisdom of archetypal nature than in its lifeless copy, the created world. Within this exemplary life, things never come into being nor will they ever perish, whereas their imaged life under the rule of time begins and ends, and not voluntarily or from agreement with the things' own natures, but constrained by the violence of external circumstances. We must therefore admit that just as nothing in its eternal existence is in any way flawed or imperfect, so within the bounds of time, no perfection of any sort can come into being. Indeed, in the domain of time, everything is necessarily flawed and imperfect.

ALEXANDER. We have no choice but to affirm all this.

ANSELM. Tell me now, do you think beauty is a perfection? And lack of beauty an imperfection?

ALEXANDER. Of course, and in my opinion, beauty, the outward expression of living perfection, is the most unconditional excellence a thing could have. Any other perfection a thing may have is valued for its suitability for some purpose or end beyond itself. But beauty is what the thing really is, considered purely in itself, without reference to any external situation.[9]

ANSELM. So will you not grant me the next point, that beauty cannot at all come into being within the temporal order, [225] since of all perfections it most demands independence from external conditions? And the converse too, that nothing in the temporal order can rightly be called beautiful?

ALEXANDER. On this view, we would have to confess that our habit of calling certain natural or artistic objects 'beautiful' is quite mistaken.

ANSELM. Yet I do not deny the existence of beauty in general, only its existence in time. On this point, I could answer you the way Socrates does in Plato's *Phaedrus*.[10] A person just recently initiated into the mysteries will not readily be moved to represent beauty in and for itself when he chances on the sight of some sensible beauty, one that borrows its name from the former. But for the one initiated in his youth, if he now beholds a godlike face wherein beauty is pictured, or rather its incorporeal archetype, he experiences wonder and, at first, terror. Fear overcomes him and he greets the beautiful one as a deity. For those who have seen beauty in and for itself are also accustomed to seeing the archetype within its imperfect copy, undaunted by the flaws pressed in upon resisting nature through the force of causes.[11] They love everything they remember from their former state of blessed vision.

In every living form, the elements that contradict the archetype of beauty are to be understood through the natural principle, but those elements in harmony with it, never so, for the harmonious elements are prior in their nature, and the reason for this priority is to be found in ideal nature itself, and in the identity we have to postulate between productive and archetypal nature. And this identity also clearly explains why beauty shines forth wherever the course of nature permits, though it never itself enters existence. In general, wherever beauty appears to come into being (and this is always just a case of appearance), it can come to be only because it [eternally] is. So if you call an artwork or an object beautiful, it is just this work or this object that has come into being, not beauty, which is eternal by its nature, [226] even in the midst of time.[12] Therefore, if we review our conclusions, the result is that the eternal concepts of things are more excellent and more beautiful than things themselves; moreover, they alone are beautiful. Indeed, the eternal concept of a thing is necessarily beautiful.

ALEXANDER. There is nothing objectionable in this conclusion. For if beauty is something atemporal, it is necessary that everything be beautiful through its eternal concept alone. And if beauty can never come into being, it is necessary that it be the primary, positive and substantial element of things themselves. And since the antithesis of beauty is mere negation and limitation, and these cannot enter into the region where nothing other than reality is to be found, it is likewise necessary that the eternal concepts of all things are necessarily and exclusively beautiful.

ANSELM. But did we not agree a bit earlier that these same eternal concepts of things are absolutely and exclusively true, and that all other notions are mistaken or only relatively true? And, further, that to know things with absolute truth means to know them in their eternal concepts?

ALEXANDER. Certainly, we agreed.

ANSELM. Have we not then demonstrated the supreme identity of truth and beauty?

ALEXANDER. I am trapped in your chains of reasoning; I cannot deny it.

ANSELM. So you were in fact perfectly right when you ventured the opinion that a work of art is beautiful solely in virtue of its truth, for I trust you took the word 'truth' to mean nothing of less worth and stature than the truth of the eternal archetypes of things. But outside of this kind of truth we have yet another kind, inferior and deceitful; it borrows its name from the higher sort, though essentially unlike it; oftentimes it consists in unclear and indistinct cognition, though it always involves a merely time-bound cognition. Only the man who has never seen immortal, divine beauty could make this 'truth' into the rule and standard of beauty, [227] for it allies itself with the imperfect, temporal elements of existing forms, with qualities impressed on them from without, rather than with those developed organically from their concepts.

From imitation of this 'truth' stem those works that cause us to remark on the artistic talent which can achieve only the natural, but is unable to unite the natural and the divine. Yet one cannot even say, as Lucian did, that this sort of truth is subordinate to beauty; it simply has nothing in common with it. But the unique and exalted truth is not accidental to beauty, nor is beauty accidental to truth. And just as truth which is not beauty is not properly truth, so beauty that is not truth is not really beauty either. It seems to me we have clear examples of this in the works of art that surround us nowadays. For don't we perceive that the majority of artists swing between two extremes? At one extreme the artist aims merely at producing truth and instead yields to a crude naturalism, for in confining himself to nature, he neglects that element which no experience can provide. At the other extreme the artist totally breaks with truth and creates a weak and empty play of form, which the ignorant admire as beauty.

Since we have demonstrated the supreme identity of beauty and truth, it would appear, my friends, that we proved the identity of philosophy and poetry as well.[13] For what does philosophy strive, other than the eternal truth that is one and the same with beauty? And does not poetry strive for that unborn and undying beauty that is identical to truth? But is it to your liking, my good fellow, that we analyze this relationship a bit further, and so return to our starting point?

ALEXANDER. Of course I want to.

ANSELM. Then the supreme beauty and truth of all things is to be intuited in one and the same idea?

ALEXANDER. We have decided so. [228]

ANSELM. But this is the idea of the eternal?

ALEXANDER. None other.

ANSELM. Now just as truth and beauty are identical in this idea, they will necessarily also be identical in works that resemble this idea.

ALEXANDER. Necessarily.

ANSELM. But who or what do you think is the creator of such works?

ALEXANDER. It is hard to say.

ANSELM. Every work of this sort is necessarily finite, is it not?

ALEXANDER. Naturally.

ANSELM. But we have said the finite is perfected by being joined to the infinite.

ALEXANDER. Correct.

ANSELM. Now how do you think the finite can be joined to the infinite?

ALEXANDER. Evidently, only through something for which the finite is originally identical to the infinite.

ANSELM. Thus only through the eternal itself.

ALEXANDER. That is clear.

ANSELM. Is it clear as well that a work which displays supreme beauty is created only through the eternal?

ALEXANDER. It seems clear.

ANSELM. But is the beautiful artwork created through the eternal, considered in itself, or through the eternal insofar as it directly pertains to the creative individual?

ALEXANDER. The latter.

ANSELM. But how do you think the eternal is related to this individual?

ALEXANDER. Right now, I cannot comprehend it.

ANSELM. Did we not say that all things subsist in God solely through their eternal concepts?

ALEXANDER. Certainly. [229]

ANSELM. So the eternal is related to all things through their eternal concepts. Hence it is related to the creative individual through the concept of that individual. This concept subsists in God, though it is one with the individual's soul, just the way his soul is one with his body.[14]

ALEXANDER. Then we will consider the eternal concept of the individual to be the creator of the artwork that displays supreme beauty.

ANSELM. Assuredly. But what about the beauty which the work expresses? Is this not the eternal again?

ALEXANDER. Without a doubt.

ANSELM. The eternal, regarded simply as eternal?

ALEXANDER. It does not seem to be, for the eternal creates the beauty of the work only insofar as the eternal is the eternal concept of the individual, only insofar as it is directly related to this concept.

ANSELM. And so the eternal is not essentially manifested in the created artwork. It indeed appears, but only insofar as it is related to one single thing or to the concept of such a thing.

ALEXANDER. Necessarily.

ANSELM. But to what sort of thing is the eternal so related? To something united to the eternal concept of the individual, or to something that is not?

ALEXANDER. Necessarily, to something united to the individual's eternal concept.

ANSELM. And will this concept not have an appreciably greater perfection the tighter the concept of all other things is bound into it in God?

ALEXANDER. Certainly.

ANSELM. Do we not then see that the more perfect and, as it were, organic this individual concept is, the more the creator will be apt to depict things other than himself, and, indeed, to totally distance himself from his own individuality? Conversely, the less perfect the concept of the creative individual is, the more particular it is, the less he will be fit to manifest anything other than his own personality, however intricate the forms of his art.

ALEXANDER. That is all clear enough.

ANSELM. But is it not also apparent from this [230] that the work's creator does not reveal beauty in and for itself? He only translates beauty into things, and thus always produces mere concrete beauty.

ALEXANDER. That is evident.

ANSELM. But even in this respect does not the artistic creator also resemble the being whose outflow and expression he is? For this latter, God namely, has to some extent revealed beauty within the sensible world just as it subsists in him. And further, does he not grant a proper and independent life to the ideas of things that he contains and allow them to exist as souls of individual bodies? Indeed, for that very reason, is it not likewise true that every artwork lives a double life, one independent and self-contained, and another in its creator?

ALEXANDER. Necessarily.

ANSELM. Hence an artwork which does not live on its own and endure independent of its creator will not count for us as a truly beautiful work, one whose soul is an eternal concept.

ALEXANDER. It is impossible that we mistake it for one.

ANSELM. Furthermore, we have established that each thing is beautiful in its eternal concept, have we not? So what we have been calling the work's 'creator' and the produced artwork itself are identical, that is, both are beautiful. The beautiful, therefore, produces the beautiful; the divine brings forth the divine.

ALEXANDER. Obviously.

ANSELM. Now within the creative individual, the element of divine beauty is immediately related to just this one individual. Since this is so, is it conceivable that the idea of divine beauty could exist in this [limited] way and at the same time exist fully and essentially as well? Rather, is it not necessarily the case that the idea's full reality lies elsewhere? In the same individual, indeed, but in an absolute mode, and not as the immediate concept of the individual?[15]

ALEXANDER. Certainly.

ANSELM. And does this not help to make one more fact about creativity intelligible? [231] The artists most fit to produce beautiful works are often those least in possession of the idea of absolute truth and beauty. They lack the idea precisely because they are possessed by it.

ALEXANDER. It is quite natural.

ANSELM. Now since the creative artist does not [consciously] recognize the divine, he will necessarily look like one who defiles the mysteries, not their initiate and devotee.[16] And yet by nature he utilizes the divine, even if he does not recognize it; thus his practice shows, even if he is unaware of it, that he understands the most hidden of all mysteries—the identity of divine and natural being, the heart and core of the ever-blessed absolute which contains no opposition. Because of this understanding, from the most ancient of times poets were revered as mouthpieces of the gods, divinely moved and inspired men. But tell me what you think, should we not call every sort of cognition that displays ideas only in things, not in themselves, 'exoteric'? And, on the other hand, should we not call those kinds of cognition that exhibit the archetypes of things in and for themselves 'esoteric'?

ALEXANDER. That seems quite appropriate to me.

ANSELM. Then the artistic creator will never exhibit beauty in and for itself; he will depict beautiful things instead.

ALEXANDER. So we have said.

ANSELM. Then the mark of his artistry will not consist in the presence of the idea of beauty itself. It will instead be his ability to produce so many things that are possibly similar to beauty.

ALEXANDER. Of course.

ANSELM. Necessarily, then, his art is exoteric.

ALEXANDER. That is obvious.

ANSELM. But the philosopher strives to recognize truth and beauty in and for themselves, not the particular truth and the particular beauty.

ALEXANDER. That is the case.

ANSELM. He thus employs, but in an inward way, the same God-given faculty that the artist uses externally and unknowingly.

ALEXANDER. Evidently. [232]

ANSELM. But the principle governing the thought of the man who philosophizes is not the eternal concept insofar as it is immediately related to his individuality, but this same concept considered absolutely and in itself.

ALEXANDER. So we must conclude.

ANSELM. Then philosophy is necessarily esoteric, by its very nature. There is no need to try to keep it secret, for, instead, it is essentially mysterious.[17]

ALEXANDER. That is clear.

ANSELM. And are we not forced to consider this very point as central to the concept of the mystery rites, that their esoteric character is due more to their nature than to external circumstances?

ALEXANDER. The ancients themselves seem to have left us an example of this truth.

ANSELM. Quite right! For even though all of the Greeks could be admitted to the mysteries, they did not cease to be 'secret' rites, or to be honored and carefully observed as such. Taking part in the rites was regarded as a universal blessing. Thus Sophocles introduces one of his characters with the words,[18]

> Oh you happiest of mortal creatures,
> Who first behold this initiation rite
> Before coming to Hades!
> For there alone your lot it is to live yet,
> For others, all there is grief.

And Aristophanes, in *The Frogs,* put the following words in the mouth of the chorus of blessed spirits:

> For us alone is there a sun here,
> And pure light, as many as
> Partaking once in the initiation,
> Lived afterwards with right and justice
> 'Midst foreigners and citizens alike.

Wherefore we have to conclude that there was something in the nature of the mysteries which could not be profaned, even if a great multitude took part in them. [233]

But the purpose of all the mystery rites is none other than to show men the archetypes of all that they are accustomed to seeing in images. Polyhymnus, who was here with us yesterday, argued this point at length. And as we were returning to the city and discussing the content of the mysteries, he claimed it was futile for us to seek to discover teachings more sacred than those imparted by the mysteries, or signs and symbols more meaningful than those represented in the rites.

Regarding their teachings, Polyhymnus said that it was in the mysteries that men first learned that there is something unchanging, uniform, and indivisible beyond the things that ceaselessly change and slide from shape to shape. Also that the soul is most similar to the divine and the immortal, while the body most closely approximates the polymorphous, divisible, and ever changeable.[19] Men learned that the individual things [they see] had cut themselves off from the essentially identical through that element in them which was divisible and particular; nonetheless, in that element whereby they are themselves self-identical and individual, things carried with them into existence a copy, or an imprint, as it were, of the absolutely indivisible. Now we notice that concrete things are similar to the essentially identical; we perceive that they strive to imitate its identity, but never achieve a state of perfect similarity. Since this is so, we must have known the archetype of the essentially identical, the absolutely indivisible, in some nontemporal way, before birth, as it were.[20]

The mysteries portrayed this knowledge of the absolute as a state of soul prior to our present life, a state in which it was able to participate in the immediate intuition of the ideas and archetypes of things; the soul was first torn from this state by its union with the body, that is, its transition over to temporal existence.[21] For this reason, Polyhymnus described the mysteries as an institution which, by purifying the soul, brings its participants to a recollection of the previously intuited ideas of the true itself, the beautiful, and the good, and which thereby brings men supreme happiness.

Now since [234] philosophy's lofty position is based on its cognition of the eternal and the unchangeable, it is evident that the mysteries' teachings are philosophy—the most sublime, sacred, and excellent philosophy, passed down to us from remote antiquity. Thus the mysteries are actually related to mythology in the way we surmised, the very same way philosophy is related to poetry. There was good reason, then, behind our decision that mythology ought to be left to the poets, while philosophers establish and conduct the mystery rites.

Well, since we have brought the discussion back to its starting point, consider whether you wish to continue and how we should conduct any further discussion.

LUCIAN. If you can stay, gentlemen, a fine course of discussion lies ahead.

ALEXANDER. It looks that way to me, too.

ANSELM. Then listen to my proposal. It is my fancy that we continue discussing the conduct of the mystery rites and the nature of mythology. And it seems perfectly appropriate that Bruno, who has been a guest at our discussions up to now, should describe the kind of philosophy he thinks the mysteries must have taught. I mean the philosophy that made them an impulse toward a happy and godly life, a quality we are right in demanding of every sacred teaching. And then take up the threads of Polyhymnus's discourse, sir, just where he left them! Spell out the sensible images and actions that might be used to present a mystery. And finally let one of us, or all of us together, it does not matter, tackle the discussion of poetry and mythology themselves.

BRUNO. I have enjoyed your hospitality so much and so often, I would seem ungrateful if I did not do my best to reciprocate and share my thoughts with you.

I will not refuse what duty commands, and so I turn not to the authorities that govern the earthly mysteries, but to the powers that direct the eternal mysteries instead—the ones celebrated in the light of the stars, in the revolutions of the planets, and in the cycle of death and renewal [235] of life among earthly species—and I implore them for two gifts: First, that I be permitted to achieve insight into what is sacred, simple, wholesome, and holy. Second, that I may escape the evils that afflict most men, to a greater or lesser extent; they are vexed in life as well as in art, troubled in action as well as in thought, for they try to avoid the rule of unrelenting fate, which has ordained that the world consist not in life alone, but in death as well, and not in body alone, but in soul too.[22] And it decreed that the universe be subjected to the very same destiny man is, that it be composed both from the mortal and from the immortal, and belong exclusively neither to the infinite nor to the finite.

But now I must address you, gentlemen, and beg your forgiveness if I expound the one philosophy I know to be true, rather than describe for you the philosophy I think best for the mysteries to have taught. And I shall not explain this philosophy itself, but merely show you the ground or foundation on which it must be built. Then too, if you will permit me, I will not proceed in a set discourse, but will adopt your custom and unfold my heart's thoughts by posing questions or answering them. And in particular, allow me to single out one of you to answer my questions, or to receive my answer to his. So if both you and he are satisfied with this arrangement, I invite our good Lucian to share the discussion with me, and in just the way it suits him.

Now to lay the foundation for our dialogue! What better topic could I, or anyone else in this august company, provide than the one to which you have already led us, Anselm? We can all agree on this fundamental notion: the idea [of the absolute], wherein all opposites are not just united, but are simply identical, wherein all opposites are not just cancelled, but are entirely undivided from one another.[23]

So I begin by praising this principle as first and prior to all else. For if we do not adopt this identity of opposites as our principle, only two other cases are possible. Either we posit as our first principle the kind of identity that is opposed to opposition, [236] or we shall have to suppose that opposites themselves constitute the first principle.[24] In the first case the principle would be posited along with some opposite, [but this is impossible, since our principle would not be primary]. The second case is impossible as well, for every pair of opposites is really and truly an opposition only insofar as its members must be posited in one and the same thing.

LUCIAN. I shall obey your command to question you, and remind you of it early on. Good sir, take care not to entangle yourself in contradiction right at the start! For identity is necessarily opposed to opposition, since it is impossible to conceptualize identity without contrasting it to opposition, or to think of opposition apart from its contrast to identity. It must therefore be impossible to posit the reality of identity without positing some real opposite along with it.

BRUNO. There is just one thing you seem to have overlooked, my worthy fellow, namely this: since we make the identity of all opposites our first principle, 'identity' itself along with 'opposition' will form the highest pair of opposites. To make identity the supreme principle, we must think of it as comprehending even this highest pair of opposites, and the [abstract] identity that is its opposite as well, and we must define this supreme identity as the identity of identity and opposition, or the identity of the self-identical and the nonidentical.[25]

LUCIAN. Quite clever, the way you jump over the trap and postulate an identity which itself connects identity and opposition! But how can you acknowledge the reality of opposition in the latter context [viz. the contrast of identity and opposition] and not be forced, for that very reason, to posit it within the former context too, [or within identity itself]? Thus it seems there is no way you can reach a pure identity, no way you can attain the sort of identity that is not distorted by difference.[26]

BRUNO. It certainly seems, my friend, that you are claiming that opposition distorts identity in both senses of the term, the identity that is opposed to opposition and the supreme identity as well, the one wherein identity itself is identical to difference. Whichever of the two you meant to assert, I intend to talk you into the opposite point of view. [Let us consider the latter case first.] If you maintain that identity and difference are opposites with respect to the supreme identity, and that the supreme identity is thus distorted by some opposition, I deny it; specifically, I deny your premise, that in the context of the supreme identity, identity and difference are opposed to one another. Hence you would be able to predicate [237] being distorted by difference only of the kind of identity that is opposed to difference, the one that is 'identity' only insofar as it is the opposite of 'difference.' But you could not ascribe being affected by difference to that identity which transcends the opposition of identity and difference and in whose sight this opposition itself simply does not exist. Or am I wrong?

LUCIAN. I will agree for now, at least in the case of the supreme identity.

BRUNO. So you still maintain that the inferior kind of identity is affected by its opposition to difference? [This was the first sense of your objection].

LUCIAN. Of course.

BRUNO. But how are identity and difference opposed, absolutely or relatively?

LUCIAN. What do you mean by 'absolute opposition' and 'relative opposition'?

BRUNO. I say that things are relatively opposed if they can cease being opposites and can be united in some third thing. Such an identification is unthinkable for absolute opposites, though. You will have an example of relative opposition if you think of two chemical substances with opposite properties, for they can be combined and so produce a third substance. You will have an example of the other sort of opposition if you think of an object and the mirror image of that object. For can you conceive of any third thing that would allow mirror image to pass over into object or permit the object to be transformed into an image? Aren't they precisely so related that one is object, and the other image, absolutely, necessarily, and eternally distinct from one another?

LUCIAN. Certainly.

BRUNO. So what sort of opposition do you think we have to posit between identity and difference?

LUCIAN. Necessarily an absolute opposition, at least on your understanding of the situation, for you will allow their unification [not in some third, mixed thing, but] only in some higher identity.

BRUNO. Excellent! Except for the fact that you have presumed that this higher identity is cancelled and inoperative! For was it not true that you thought that identity was only distorted or diminished to the extent that it was opposed to difference?

LUCIAN. That is what I said.

BRUNO. But only if you think the higher identity is cancelled and inoperative, [238] will identity and difference be opposed. Therefore the correct way to think of the pair is as merely relatively opposed.

LUCIAN. Certainly.

BRUNO. And since they are merely relatively opposed, so too they can be united only in a relative manner, just like the two chemical substances we discussed earlier, and [if that is the case, each will remain what it is, but] they will reciprocally restrict or limit one another.

LUCIAN. Necessarily.

BRUNO. And only to the extent that they mutually restrict and limit one another will identity be distorted, by which you mean exactly this, that identity comes to participate in difference.

LUCIAN. Quite right!

BRUNO. So when you assume that identity is beclouded by difference, you necessarily posit a relation of cause and effect between the two. It is similar to the practice of armchair philosophers who posit unity here, multiplicity there, unity exerting causal influence upon multiplicity and multiplicity acting upon unity.[27] Yet they concede that the two mutually fit into one another, like bevelled joints of wood.

LUCIAN. God forbid I should seriously maintain such a doctrine of quantity!

BRUNO. Then you cannot seriously maintain [the first sense of your objection] either, that we must suppose that the identity whose opposite is opposition is distorted or diminished by difference.[28]

LUCIAN. Certainly not. But one thing does not follow from your views on relative opposition and relative identity; they imply that only in the unique case of absolute opposition can opposites be absolutely identified, and vice versa! How is this so?

BRUNO. Indeed it follows! Think back for a moment to our previous example. Tell me, can you imagine a perfect identity between an object and its image, granted that it is totally impossible that the two coexist in some third substance? So you will have to suppose that they are identified in some higher sort of entity wherein that which makes an image an image, namely light, is identical with that which makes an object an object, namely body. Now if you posit the kind of world order or constellation of things where, generally speaking, [239] if an object exists, so does an image, and if an image exists, so does an object, then necessarily, for this very reason, image and object would be together everywhere since they nowhere coincide. For things that are absolutely and infinitely opposed can only be united infinitely. And what is infinitely united can never split itself up in any way; therefore what is absolutely self-identical and absolutely indivisible must, for this very reason, be absolutely opposed to itself.[29]

[But let us apply this to your contention that difference beclouds relative identity.] If you wanted to have identity really distorted by difference, you would have to abstract identity from the identity of identity and opposition, then suppose its independent reality; then you would have to contrast difference to it as its relative opposite. But all this is impossible, for this relative identity you have produced by abstraction is nothing outside of absolute identity, and only within the latter is it anything at all. And whatever you assert about this relative identity can be truly predicated of it only in the context of absolute identity. But in the context of absolute identity, we cannot imagine that relative identity is distorted or diminished by difference, for in the absolute perspective identity is simply not opposed to difference at all. In the absolute there is nothing but transparency, pure light. This you understand, for you have already admitted that there are no shadows of obscurity or confusion in the domain of absolute identity, inasmuch as the absolute encompasses the finite as well as the infinite, and not just as united [after the fact], but as indivisibly one.

LUCIAN. But you are certain that you have surpassed all oppositions in the entity you call the identity of identity and opposition? How do other pairs of opposites, any such as you would care to make in working out your philosophy, fit into this absolute identity?

BRUNO. On the first point, why should I not be certain? One of two cases will necessarily be true: All the typical pairs of categories we could fashion must either fall under the principle we call 'opposition' or they must fall under the heading 'identity and opposition.' But you look like you are still in doubt, so why don't you tell us what you believe to be the chief pair of opposites, and I will answer your second question while illustrating my answer to the first.

LUCIAN. I believe there could be no opposition more ultimate than the one we express by the category contrast, 'real' and 'ideal;' and accordingly, it seems to me that the supreme identity must be defined as the identity of the 'ideal ground' and the 'real ground.' [240]

BRUNO. We cannot be content with this sort of answer, at least not yet. We must ask you, then, to explain what you mean by the identity of these real and ideal 'grounds.'

LUCIAN. The identity of thought and intuition.[30]

BRUNO. My friend, I will not pick a fight with you over this definition. Neither shall I ask you whether you might again describe this identity as an ideal one or as a real one—for how could the identity that transcends both opposites itself be opposed to one of them? Nor shall I inquire right now whether [this real ground] that you term 'intuition' might not itself be an identity of real and ideal factors. For now, we will leave all these details up in the air and simply ask you again, what do you mean by this 'identity of thought and intuition'? Indeed, it seems to me to say exactly the same thing that our expressions, 'the identity of identity and opposition' and 'the identity of the finite and the infinite' did! So tell me, my worthy man, are you not claiming that intuition or sensory representation is completely determined in each and every one of its individual occurrences? And did you not assert the identity of thought and intuition in light of this model of completely determined intuition? For this is the only way I can imagine that thought and intuition form an opposition as well as an identity.

LUCIAN. That is actually what I hold.

BRUNO. But you must necessarily think of intuition as determined by something?

LUCIAN. Indeed, one intuition is determined by another intuition, and this latter by yet another, and so on to infinity.[31]

BRUNO. But how can you posit one intuition as determined by another, if you do not also assume that the first intuition can be differentiated from the second, and the second from the first? Will you not have to suppose that difference is coextensive with the whole sphere of intuition, so that each sensory representation would be individual, and no one intuition wholly like another?

LUCIAN. It would be impossible any other way than as you have said.

BRUNO. Now, on the other hand, call to mind some concept, a plant or a figure or whatever you want. Tell me, [241] is this concept ever altered in its details or specified the way the series of your sensory representations is, when you look at several plants or several figures in succession? Or is it not rather the case that this concept remains one and unchanged, appropriate in the same way to plants or figures that are quite different, or indifferent toward them all?[32]

LUCIAN. The latter case.

BRUNO. So you have defined the series of intuitions as that which is necessarily subject to difference, but concepts as that which is indifferent?

LUCIAN. Yes.

BRUNO. And further, you have conceived intuition under the attribute of particularity, but the concept under that of universality?

LUCIAN. It is clear that this is the case.

BRUNO. What a splendid and lofty idea you have expressed in this identity of thought and intuition![33] Could thought comprehend anything more excellent or more magnificent than the nature of that sphere wherein not only is the particular posited by and determined through the universal, but objects are posited by the concept as well, with the result that both factors are intrinsically inseparable within it? Ah, with this idea you have far outstripped finite cognition, which keeps object and concept, particular and universal distinct from one another. Even more so, how far you have surpassed the fuzzy thinking of those self-proclaimed philosophers who first posit unity, then multiplicity, and leave them simply opposed.[34]

Let us concentrate on this idea, then, and not adulterate it with anything foreign or dilute it from full strength, the way we first conceived it. Let us posit such an identity between thought and intuition that what is expressed in the one is also necessarily expressed in the other. Then the two will be intrinsically identical, united prior to all distinction, not just put together in some third thing, and each will then have all the attributes of the other, not just at the same time, but in exactly the same respect. All this is implied by the excellence of that [absolute] nature which in itself is neither thought nor intuition, nor even both at the same time, but is simply their identity. [242] Do you not see now that the identity of the finite and the infinite is contained in what we call the 'identity of thought and intuition,' and vice versa? And hence that, using different terminologies, we have chosen the very same thing as our ultimate principle?

LUCIAN. I think I see it quite clearly.[35] For every concept essentially involves an infinitude in that it is equally appropriate to one individual or to an endless series of things. On the other hand, the particular thing which is the object of sensory intuition is necessarily both an individual and a finite entity. Therefore, when we posit the identity of concept and intuition as our first principle, necessarily we also posit the identity of the finite and the infinite. But this identity looks to me to be an especially worthwhile subject of inquiry. So continue please, and pursue this investigation further, paying special attention to the manner in which the real and the ideal, the finite and the infinite, are united in the same principle.

BRUNO. You are correct in saying this question of the absolute's identification of opposites is especially worth our effort, though perhaps you would have been more accurate if you had said it was the only subject worth philosophical investigation and that philosophy is concerned with this topic alone. For is it not clear that what dominates all philosophical talk or investigation is the [dialectical] impulse, the tendency to either posit the infinite within the finite, or the reverse, to set the finite within the infinite?[36] This thought-process is eternal, just like the absolute's reality which it expresses, and neither has it just come into being nor will it ever cease to be; it is, as Plato has Socrates say, the immortal and inalterable feature of every inquiry.[37] The young man who first tastes of it rejoices as if he had found a treasury of wisdom; bolstered by his joy, he eagerly attacks every inquiry, at one moment gathering everything he encounters into a unity, and the next moment dissolving all unities back into multiplicity. This method is a gift of the gods to mankind, akin to that purest heavenly fire that Prometheus brought to earth. By this [dialectical] arrangement of things which will eternally obtain, and whereby everything stems from both the infinite and the finite [243], while everything we correctly distinguish must be either the one or the other of the pair, it is necessary that there be one idea of all things, and hence that all things subsist in one idea, too.

Now we differentiate 'idea' and 'concept' as follows.[38] The concept is mere infinitude, and for precisely this reason, it is directly opposed to multiplicity; and this is why the concept possesses only a portion of the idea's reality. The idea, on the other hand, inasmuch as it unites multiplicity and unity or finitude and infinity, is identically related to both factors, [that is, it includes both and excludes neither]. Since we learned earlier that philosophy is concerned solely with the eternal concepts of things, we now realize that philosophy has but one sole object of study, the idea of all ideas. And this one idea is exactly what we conveyed in our formulas for the supreme principle, 'the indivisible unity of the identical and the differentiated' and 'the inseparability of thought and intuition.'

The nature of this idea's identity is that of truth itself, and beauty. For the beautiful is what absolutely identifies the universal and the particular, or unites the species and the individual, as in the [ideal human] forms of the gods. But this same identity is truth too, and the sole truth. And since we regard this idea as the best criterion of truth available, we will accept only what conforms to this idea as absolutely true, but what does not measure up to the idea's truth, we will account merely relative and unreliable truths.

All the more reason, then, to intensify our investigation into the way the supreme principle unites the finite with the infinite! First, we should remind ourselves that we have adopted as our principle the indivisible unity of the two factors, so that the absolute's essence is indeed neither the finite nor the infinite, and that is precisely why it is absolute. But for everything that subsists in the domain of this absolute, inasmuch as it is ideal it is immediately also real, and inasmuch as it is real it is directly also ideal. It is evident this is not the case within our cognition, since for us, on the contrary, the concept or the ideal element seems to be a bare possibility, while the thing or real factor seems to be what is real. And wouldn't this analysis apply to all possible concepts whereby we express the opposition of the ideal and the real? [244] Are we not forced to say, for example, that unity and multiplicity, or boundary and unbounded [reality] are absolutely identified in one and the same absolute, wherein the ideal and the real are indivisibly one?

LUCIAN. That is completely true.

BRUNO. But, on the other hand, is it not evident that to finite cognition, unity means only endless possibility, while multiplicity comprises the actuality of things? And further, that in unbounded reality we see only the infinite possibility of all actuality, while we perceive its actualization in the limit or boundary? Within the sphere of finite cognition, therefore, negation turns into positing and positing becomes negation! This happens to such an extent that finite cognition takes 'substance,' that which is believed to be the essential element of all things, to mean the bare possibility of a being, while it accepts what is incidental, what is termed 'the accidents,' as the being's realized actuality. In short, if we compare finite understanding to the supreme idea and to the way that all things have their being therein, it looks like everything is upside down, almost like the things you see reflected in a pool of water.[39]

LUCIAN. It would be difficult to cast doubt on anything you have said.

BRUNO. Since with the positing of the opposition of the ideal and the real, the opposition of possibility and actuality is posited throughout all our concepts as well, would it not be reasonable for us to conclude straightaway that all concepts based on or derived from the contrast of possibility and actuality are just as false as those derived from the contrast of the real and the ideal? With respect to the supreme idea, are not all such concepts meaningless?

LUCIAN. We are forced to conclude they are.

BRUNO. What about our ability to think of something that does not exist? Can we consider this a perfection of our nature or must we account it an imperfection? And what about the fact that we have the concept of nonbeing alongside that of being, that we can as easily judge that something is unreal as we can judge that it is real?

LUCIAN. Well, if we compare this ability of ours to the supreme idea, [245] we cannot possibly call it a perfection. For the concept of nonbeing involves a thought that cannot be expressed in sensory intuition. But in the absolute, it is not possible to have any such divorce of thought and intuition, since in its domain, what is expressed in the one must immediately be expressed in the other as well.

BRUNO. With respect to the supreme idea, then, we will find that the distinction of being and nonbeing makes as little sense as does the concept of impossibility.

LUCIAN. No, we cannot allow impossibility to be a concept valid for the absolute either, for impossibility presupposes there is a contradiction between concept and intuition, [that what can be validly thought can never be intuited]. In the context of the absolute, this is unthinkable.

BRUNO. But have we not already established that the ideal, as ideal, is incapable of limitation? And thus that every single concept is intrinsically infinite? But now, what sense do you make of the concept's infinitude? Is it the sort of infinity that is generated within time, and so is by its nature impossible to complete? Or is it an absolutely present infinitude, completed and self-contained?

LUCIAN. The latter, if a concept is infinite by its nature.

BRUNO. So is it not understandable the way inexperienced minds congratulate themselves as if they had made the greatest discovery when they realize that their concept of a triangle, a space enclosed by three lines, may be considered infinite. For they do not require the intuition of all triangles that ever were or ever will be, nor even the intuition of all the various types of triangles, the equilateral and those with unequal sides, the equiangular and those with unequal angles, and so on. Without further ado, they can be certain that the concept includes all possible triangles, past, present and future; regardless of differences in type, the concept is appropriate for all triangles in the same way. As we know, the concept intrinsically and essentially includes the infinite possibility of all the things that correspond to it over the endless stretch of time, yet it includes it only as possibility, so that, even if the concept possessed a nature totally independent of time, it still could not be considered absolute. [246]

LUCIAN. That is true.

BRUNO. Now we have defined the absolute as that which in essence is neither ideal nor real, in essence neither thought nor being. But in relation to things, the absolute will necessarily be both one and the other, with equal infinitude, [and this is the absolute's 'form']. For we have said that everything in the absolute's domain is ideal inasmuch as it is real, and is real inasmuch as it is ideal.

LUCIAN. You are perfectly right.

BRUNO. So we are now able to determine the infinite ideality [of the absolute's form] as 'infinite thought,' in contrast to what you have called intuition.

LUCIAN. I fully agree.

BRUNO. Won't we now have to posit the concept of each and every finite thing inside this infinite thought? And, since every concept is infinite by its nature, must we not posit these concepts as simply infinite and without any relation to time at all?

LUCIAN. Indeed we must.

BRUNO. Then we shall consider infinite thought, in contrast to intuition, as the ever-identical infinite possibility of all things, wholly unrelated to time.

LUCIAN. Necessarily.

BRUNO. But in the absolute, thought and intuition are simply identical. Since this is so, finite things will not merely be expressed in an infinite way in the order of concepts, they will be expressed in an eternal way as well, in virtue of their ideas; hence they will be without any relation to temporality, not even that of opposition to time. Within the absolute, that supreme identity of thought and intuition, they will be expressed as simple identities of possibility and actuality.

Now, Lucian, since you ascribe the same relationship to intuition and thought that others attribute to 'being' or 'reality' and thought, we will regard intuition as [the real side of the absolute's form or] 'infinite reality,' and say that it furnishes the possibility of all things for infinite thought, with this single qualification: Because of the absolute identity of thought and intuition, if we posit the possibility of things, immediately we establish their actuality as well, and therefore, since concepts are infinite, in the absolute nothing intervenes between concept and intuition. Nothing divides them or causes [247] the intuitions of things to be located outside of their concepts; rather, intuition is perfectly matched to the nature of the concept. Therefore, in the ideas, intuition must be expressed as an infinity.

LUCIAN. Ah, but did we not decide for ourselves earlier that each act of sensory intuition is determined by another intuition, which in turn is determined by another, and so on endlessly?

BRUNO. You are perfectly right. Here is why we did so. Since we have posited the finite as the sphere of sensory intuition, we had to assume that causal connection could link together only acts of intuition, [and not intuition and something else.]

LUCIAN. How in the world can you reconcile this endless serial determination of things, which seems to pertain merely to existence within time, with the eternal being of things in their ideas?

BRUNO. We shall soon see how. [But first let us review our conclusions]. You have established, have you not, that the concept is infinite, that intuition is finite, and the two are completely identical and indivisible in the idea?

LUCIAN. I have.

BRUNO. And you did adopt the view that the idea was the sole intrinsically real entity?

LUCIAN. This too.

BRUNO. Then from the idea's perspective, which is to say, in truth, neither the infinite nor the finite is anything essentially real or anything independent of the distinctions which our understanding makes. Now since neither element is intrinsically real, since each of them is what it is only through its contrast to the other, we can never subordinate one to the other, nor can we favor one [in our philosophy] at the expense of the other.

LUCIAN. That would be impossible.

BRUNO. Necessarily, then, if the infinite has being, the finite subsists in and with it; the two subsist inseparably together in what we have posited as the eternal.

LUCIAN. Evidently, for otherwise we would be forced to adopt the infinite alone as our first principle; but the infinite is itself infinite only in virtue of its opposition to the finite.

BRUNO. Yet you claimed that what is finite is, as finite, necessarily always a determinate being. One determinate finite being is determined by another finite being, which in turn is determined by another, and so on without end. [248]

LUCIAN. Right.

BRUNO. And yet this endlessly finite sort of being is immediately joined to the essentially infinite and posited as identical with it in the idea?

LUCIAN. We suppose this is the case.

BRUNO. And this independent and essentially infinite sort of being is the concept?

LUCIAN. I grant it.

BRUNO. Now in general there cannot be any finitude that is identical with the infinite or suited to the intrinsically infinite nature of the concept except an infinite sort of finitude.

LUCIAN. That is clearly the case.

BRUNO. But is this infinite finitude infinite according to time?

LUCIAN. That seems impossible, for whatever is nontemporally infinite takes up no time, not even infinite time, and no time-dependent infinity can be similar to what is intrinsically infinite, or commensurate with its nature.

BRUNO. [So if the finite is identical with the infinite in the idea] it must have the sort of finitude that is nontemporally infinite if it is to be commensurate with the concept's nature?

LUCIAN. That indeed follows.

BRUNO. But only the concept is nontemporally infinite?

LUCIAN. We agree.

BRUNO. Therefore a nontemporally infinite finitude would have to be infinite in and for itself, or infinite by its very essence.

LUCIAN. I agree to this, too.

BRUNO. But a finitude that is infinite in its very essence could never in any way cease being finite, could it?

LUCIAN. Never.

BRUNO. And furthermore, since [the finite within the absolute] is essentially infinite and not infinite in reference to time, the absence of time [that obtains in the absolute] could not make it cease being infinitely finite.

LUCIAN. This too could not be.

BRUNO. Nor could it ever stop being intrinsically finite either, since it subsists in the absolute, and is timelessly present therein.

LUCIAN. I agree. Yet this notion of an infinite finitude puzzles me, even if it is not totally obscure. [249] So please explain it further, for it is one of the darkest matters there are, and not easily understood at first glance!

BRUNO. Now we have divided infinite thought from the idea, though only in our conceptual distinctions, for in the idea it is immediately one with the finite. Now considered from the side of possibility, all things are identical in infinite thought, with no distinction of times or kinds of objects; but considered from the side of actuality, they are not all one, but are many, and necessarily and endlessly finite. But what is essentially and substantially finite transcends all time, just the way the essentially infinite does; and if the finite cannot achieve infinitude within time—its concept excludes this serial infinitude—neither can it lose its finitude through the negation of time. Therefore we do not require any time-concept at all in order to think of an infinitely finite element included in the absolute.[40] Indeed we will be forced to represent the finite as spread out over endless time once we conceive it abstractly, outside the context of the absolute. Within this endless span of time, however, the finite will not be infinitely finite. If, as befits its nature, it subsisted solely within the momentary 'now,' and if in the sight of the absolute it subsisted in no other way than in this momentary 'now,' then it would be infinitely finite.

Perhaps you will understand this point more intuitively in this way. Every finite entity necessarily has the ground and reason for its existence not in itself, but in something external to it; a finite being is thus an actuality whose possibility is located elsewhere, in another finite being. Conversely, the finite being contains the possibility of infinitely many other finite beings, but only as unactualized possibility;[41] for this very reason the finite being is necessarily, even infinitely, imperfect. In the domain of the absolute, however, this divorce of possibility and actuality is unthinkable. For in that absolute, [although we distinguish its 'form' from its 'essence',] form is identical with essence; if we confine our consideration to form [the expression of the absolute's reality in both the infinite and the finite], the finite or the real factor is necessarily and eternally opposed to the ideal factor, just the way a copy is opposed to its original. In its concept, then, what is real is necessarily finite; really, however, or viewed in the order of essence, the real is absolutely identical to the ideal.

[Thus there are two ways of viewing finite entities]. If you consider the finite solely in its concept, it will be necessarily and infinitely individual; and since the finite individual is itself an actuality whose possibility is located in another individual, [250] it will contain the endless possibility of other individuals, which, for the same reason, will contain the boundless possibility of still other individuals, and so on without end. But if you consider the real situation and view the finite in the context of its absolute identity with the infinite, [this divorce of possibility and actuality disappears, and] the boundless possibility of other individuals that one given individual contains is immediately joined to its realized actuality;[42] in the same way, the given individual's actuality is directly united to its possibility; everything, therefore, is absolute insofar as it is in God, and it lies outside of all time, and lives an eternal life.

Now it is for this very reason that the finite individual is individual and cuts itself off from community with the absolute: Either it is merely the possibility of other finite beings, but not their actuality as well, or it embraces some actualized reality in itself whose possibility it does not contain. Whatever kind of finite entity you would care to posit, whatever the degree of divergence of possibility and actuality its existence implies, insofar as it subsists in the absolute neither is its actuality divorced from its possibility, nor its possibility from it actualized reality; within the absolute it subsists as in an organic body. The infinite potentiality of the whole organism is contained in every part of the animate body; this is what directly establishes the organism's actuality, not temporal [or causal] interrelations among individual parts. The finite's being within the absolute is like the organic body in another way as well; no individual living part of the body possesses its peculiar function in virtue of some other part or organ, or in virtue of its own prior states; it possesses its capacities immediately in the way it is bound into the other parts. And so the best example we can find among familiar sensible things of the way the finite inheres in the infinite is the way individual parts of the animate body are tied into the whole organism, for neither is one individual living part posited as an individual in the animate body, nor is the finite individual posited as an individual within the absolute. And though the living part of the whole organism is not really an individual, yet [sustained by the whole] it continues to be ideally individual or individual in its own sight; the same holds for the finite entity inasmuch as it inheres in the absolute. Within the absolute, therefore, the relation of one finite being to another is not that of cause and effect, but the correlation of one part of a living body to the other individual parts; of course in the absolute this union of the finite and the infinite is infinitely more perfect than the living union of the parts of the body, for every organism as a whole still includes some possibilities whose actuality is located in some other entity beyond itself, and it is related to this external [251] reality as cause is to effect. Then too, an organism is merely an image of an archetype within the absolute, wherein every possibility is united with its actualization, and every actuality with its possibility.

Now precisely because the true universe is an infinite fullness where nothing is divorced or excluded from anything else, where everything is absolutely integrated into one, in the image world it is forced to spread itself out over a boundless expanse of time. Similarly, reflection [or finite cognition] dismembers the absolute unity of possibility and actuality which is expressed nontemporally in the organic body, and then this unity seems to require for its development a time span so great that it could have neither a beginning nor an end.

[The upshot is this:] Outside the absolute, there is no intrinsically finite entity; only within its own perspective is a finite entity an individual. How is this so? In the absolute, ideal and nontemporal aspects of a finite being are real as well as ideal, but if the finite being interprets the relation of possibility [and actuality] as one of cause and effect, it posits and realizes the relation this way for itself. And if it gives a temporal interpretation to the relation of possibility and actuality [and makes cause necessarily precede effect], then it must posit and realize its own time. Thus the finite entity realizes all the finite beings whose actuality it contains, but not their possibility, as the past; and it realizes all those whose possibility it contains, but not their actuality, as the future. Thus what constitutes the finite individual's time is its concept, the determinate possibility it contains by virtue of its relation to an individual real entity; it is the determinate nature of the individual's concept [specified by its reference to a body] that excludes the past and the future as well [and establishes the present. Thus we see how the finite individual individuates itself by temporalizing its existence].

But it is just the opposite with the absolute, where being and nonbeing are directly joined together. Even things that do not now exist and the concepts of these things subsist within the eternal the same way existing things and their concepts do;[43] both are equally included in the absolute, in an eternal manner. Conversely, things that exist and the concepts of these things do not subsist within the absolute any differently than do nonexistent things and their concepts, namely within their ideas. Any other sort of existence is illusion, mere appearance.

In God, no concept of any individual is excluded from the concept of all things that are, or were, or will be, for these temporal distinctions we make have no intrinsic meaning. To give an example, the boundless potentiality included in the concept of one human person is united to the infinite actuality of all other men; [252] and not only are his possibilities so linked up with the rest, but everything that actually follows [from his works and deeds] too. For this reason, the exemplary life of the individual person in the absolute is pure, free of confusion, more blessed than his real life; for even that which appears impure and disorderly in the individual and in his life yet serves to advance the splendor and the godliness of the universe, when it is viewed as a part of eternal reality.

Therefore, my friend, if we understand this identity of thought and intuition you asserted in its true and most profound sense, we will admit that we never truly encounter it within finite cognition. We will have to confess, instead, that it is elevated far beyond [the powers of our under-standing]. If we do this, then we shall discern in the essence of that identity which is the neither-nor of all opposites the eternal and indivisible Father of all things; He never steps forth from his eternity, yet in one and the same act of divine intellection He comprehends and contains both the finite and the infinite: And in the infinite [potency] we shall recognize the Spirit, the unity of all things, but the finite [potency], though in itself equal to the infinite, is yet by its own accord subjected to time and made into a suffering God.[44] I think by now I have adequately shown how these three could be united in one single being, and how the finite is finite, yet timelessly inheres in the infinite as well.

LUCIAN. Well, my friend, you have managed to delve pretty deeply into the nature of the incomprehensible! But I am curious to see how you will get us back to the plane of consciousness, once you have soared so grandly beyond it.

BRUNO. I cannot tell whether or not you are objecting to this oversoaring of consciousness, as you call it, but I must say, my good man, that I do not think it is objectionable. So tell me, have I done anything else than expound, in its most profound sense, the idea you advanced as the first principle?

LUCIAN. You have done just that, nothing more. And yet you have interpreted this identity in such a way that it ceases to be the principle of knowledge; and if it is no longer the principle governing how and what we know, it seems to me that this identity is no longer the first principle of philosophy, for philosophy is the science of knowledge.

BRUNO. We are probably of one mind on this last point, [253] yet I am afraid that you might mean by the term 'knowledge' just some subordinate kind of knowing, one that would call for a mere subordinate principle too. So, before anything else, let us get to know just where you are hunting for this 'knowledge.'

LUCIAN. But I locate knowing in precisely that identity of thought and intuition that was our starting point!

BRUNO. But, on the other hand, you describe this identity as the principle governing knowing?

LUCIAN. Yes.

BRUNO. Let us take a closer look, my friend, at how you conceive this identity, insofar as it is both the principle governing knowing and knowing itself. So tell me, first of all, do you mean to say that the real and the ideal are identified in the principle of knowing in just the same way we decided they were identified in the absolute? Or do you think they are identified in some other way in the principle of knowing? If you reply, "In the same way," then we do not disagree, and so you will assert everything we said about the absolute of this principle governing knowing. But in that case, you may well be agreeing with me, though not with yourself! For if you find the same absolute identity expressed in this principle of knowing that we found in the absolute itself, you will overleap the territory of knowing and consciousness with this 'knowing' of yours.[45]

LUCIAN. You overlook one fact. We indeed acknowledge that this identity is absolute insofar as it is the principle governing knowing, yet we know it is absolute only in the unique case of its reference to the territory of knowing. Therefore, we recognize it as the principle of knowing, [no more].[46]

BRUNO. I don't really know if I understand you! Knowing, by which we mean the identity of thought and sensory intuition, is consciousness, right? And yet the principle governing consciousness is supposed to be this very same identity, but now conceived as pure or absolute; the principle of consciousness thus turns out to be 'absolute consciousness,' while the factual identity of thought and intuition is 'derivative' or 'grounded consciousness.' Now is this your contention, that in doing philosophy we have no warrant to step beyond the [appearance] of pure consciousness which is given [to us] inside grounded consciousness? That, in general, we have no way to investigate pure consciousness other than in connection to the derivate consciousness whose governing principle it is? [254]

LUCIAN. That is precisely my point.

BRUNO. Then you would also be forced to say that the identity found within grounded consciousness is different from the identity of absolute consciousness!

LUCIAN. Necessarily, since it is necessary that, in general, the principle's identity be different from identity in things governed by the principle.

BRUNO. Yet we found that the identity of absolute consciousness was the same as the identity of the absolute, considered simply in itself, did we not?

LUCIAN. Correct.

BRUNO. And we thought that the absolute's identity was absolute?

LUCIAN. By all means.

BRUNO. So inside knowing, the identity is not absolute?

LUCIAN. Of course.

BRUNO. Hence it is a relative identity?

LUCIAN. You are quite right.

BRUNO. But if knowing's identity is a relative one, necessarily both its elements, the ideal and the real, will be distinguishable from one another, will they not?

LUCIAN. Necessarily.

BRUNO. But did we not think they were indistinguishable or completely indifferent in the absolute?

LUCIAN. We did.

BRUNO. But if they are indistinguishable or absolutely identical, is there any possible determination under which one could be posited without the other factor being posited under the same determination too? For example, could we posit the ideal as ideal and not have to posit the reality of the real as well? And does not the reverse hold true too?

LUCIAN. It cannot be denied.

BRUNO. So we could never assert that a purely ideal being existed, nor a purely real one either?

LUCIAN. Never.

BRUNO. But always and only a certain relative identity of the real and the ideal?

LUCIAN. Indisputably.

BRUNO. And just as the two are identical within the eternal, in the same way they will remain together if they detach themselves from the absolute identity; one will subsist in the other, the real subsisting only in the ideal, and the ideal only within the real. [255] And where this is not the case, neither the one nor the other is posited, but the absolute identity of the two. Do you agree?

LUCIAN. Completely.

BRUNO. Then you will appreciate the inevitability of this consequence: As soon as any relative identity is posited as real, immediately and necessarily so is its opposite. So, for example, if the real detaches itself from absolute identity and subsists within the ideal, so too the ideal detaches itself by reason of its connection to the real. The upshot, viewed from the perspective of absolute identity, is this general rule: Absolute identity must necessarily appear as two distinct though correlated points, one of which actualizes the ideal through the real [and this is nature], the other of which actualizes the real as such by means of the ideal [and this is the domain of consciousness].

LUCIAN. All this is undeniable. And it also allows us to directly conclude that as soon as one instance of consciousness is posited, even that of my own self-consciousness, this division of absolute identity into two points or relative identities is necessary, just the way you described it.

BRUNO. But knowing is one relative identity, is it not?

LUCIAN. I think it is.

BRUNO. Hence there is another relative identity opposed to it?

LUCIAN. This too I will grant you.

BRUNO. What do you call this relative identity opposed to knowing, the identity which, as the opposite of knowing, is that which I do not know?[47]

LUCIAN. Being.

BRUNO. Being is therefore a relative identity of the real and the ideal, just as knowing is?

LUCIAN. Yes, it follows.

BRUNO. Then neither is knowing a pure case of ideality, nor is being a pure instance of reality!

LUCIAN. You are right.

BRUNO. And neither of the two relative identities is anything real in itself, since each has its being only through the other.

LUCIAN. It would seem so.

BRUNO. No, it is evident! Neither can you have a real instance of knowing without supposing some instance of being realized along with it, nor can you have a real instance of being without a corresponding instance of knowing. [256]

LUCIAN. That is clearly the case.

BRUNO. Neither one of the two relative identities, therefore, can be the governing principle of the other.

LUCIAN. Neither.

BRUNO. So the relative identity of knowing is not the governing principle of being, nor is the relative identity of being the principle of knowing.

LUCIAN. Granted.

BRUNO. In that case, then, you cannot reduce one of these determinate orders of identity to the other, for the one stands and falls with the other, and if you eliminate the one, the other disappears as well.

LUCIAN. Certainly. But such a reduction of being to knowing is not what I intend!

BRUNO. Instead, you want to reduce both being and knowing back to absolute consciousness. Am I correct?

LUCIAN. You have hit on it exactly.

BRUNO. And yet you maintain that absolute consciousness is [absolute] identity only insofar as you consider it to be the principle of one specified relative identity, namely knowing.

LUCIAN. Of course.

BRUNO. But you have no compelling reason to consider absolute identity chiefly as the principle of one of the two relative identities, specifically that of knowing; in doing so, you abolish the relative opposition of being and knowing within absolute identity, which is equally the principle of both orders. Now either you are considering what identity intrinsically is, even in the special case of its reference to knowing, or you are viewing it extrinsically. If the first alternative is the case, there is no reason to restrict absolute identity to the context of knowing. If the second is the case, then, if you are considering it in the context of knowing, you can with equally good reason view it the context of the opposite relative identity; being is just as real as knowing, and equally primary too! Instead of making identity your principle only in the case of knowing, why don't you acknowledge that this identity is universal, all-pervasive and all-encompassing? Why do you not extend it to everything? For I will not believe you truly understand the real nature of absolute identity or that you possess intellectual intuition of it until you free it from this exclusive reference to consciousness.[48] For in finite things you do not really see anything else. [257] but displaced and disorganized images of absolute identity, and even within the other relative identity of knowing, you do not perceive anything but an image of absolute cognition, displaced in a different direction. But in absolute cognition itself, neither is being determined by thought, nor is thought determined by being.

LUCIAN. I think we may well agree on this point, my friend. For we have restricted philosophy to the domain of consciousness only to express the insight that you too maintain: The opposition of being and knowing, or however else you would express it, has no truth outside of consciousness; apart from consciousness, there is no being as such nor knowing as such.[49] Everything that is commonly called real depends, as you yourself said, on a displacement or distortion of absolute identity, that is, on a relative division together with a restoration of identity. Now since this division of the real and the ideal is purely ideal, made only within consciousness, you can easily see why this teaching is called 'idealism,' not because it determines the real by the ideal, but because it refuses to grant more than an ideal status to the opposition of the real and the ideal.

BRUNO. Certainly I understand that is why it is called idealism.

LUCIAN. So, my friend, we are really in agreement on the central issue. Considered in the light of the supreme idea, the distinction of knowledge and being is untrue. Yet there is one question you have left unanswered; in fact you have not even touched on it. How can we come to understand not just the possibility, but the necessity of the finite's departure from the eternal? Consciousness is bound up with just such a departure, so must we not finally comprehend its necessity?

BRUNO. You are right in asking me to address this issue. You first raised the question yourself when you wanted to adopt the primitive and absolute identity as your first principle, but only in reference to the relative identity of knowing; for this was just one particular case of the general problem of the origin of the finite from the eternal. And so, worthy fellow, it looks like you are suggesting the following path: You want me to deduce the origin of actual consciousness, as well as the exclusion [of relative being] from the absolute and its division [into opposite independent spheres], for all this is implied by the actual existence of consciousness. And you want me to argue from the standpoint of the eternal itself, not assuming anything else than the supreme idea. [258] [In fact no other assumptions are required,] for the supreme idea comprehends even this division of opposites, together with the things and concepts posited by this division. However much an individual being enlarges the sphere of its existence, eternity still holds it fast; no individual oversteps the brazen band that circumscribes all things.

Recall then [that we anchor our philosophy in] the supreme identity wherein essence is also form and form is also essence; we view it as the sacred abyss from which everything springs forth and to which everything returns. First we establish that absolute infinity inheres in this identity, and then timelessly present and infinite finitude as well. The finite is not opposed to the infinite within this absolute identity; rather, it is absolutely conformed to its nature, absolutely sufficient. And neither is the infinite itself limited, nor does it restrict the finite; both are one thing. Only within the things that belong to appearance are they distinguishable and in fact distinguished; the finite and the infinite are completely identical in reality, even though they are conceptually different and are eternally opposed to one another as thought and being, or as the ideal and the real. But within absolute identity, neither factor is distinguishable from the other, since, as we have shown, everything is perfect and itself absolute within the absolute; things can be distinguished solely through their imperfections or limitations, and these limitations are established in things because of the difference between their essence and their process of development. But form is always adequate to the essential and abiding reality in the absolute, that most perfect of natures.[50] And the reason is this: It is the inclusion of the finite in the absolute that is solely responsible for the difference between the absolute's essence and its form; yet the absolute includes the finite not as finite, but as infinite, and hence there is no difference between the absolute's abiding identical reality and its form; [they are simply indifferent.]

But even if this is so, even if the finite is in reality perfectly identical with the infinite, ideally it never stops being finite; thus the absolute identity of all things also contains within itself the difference of all forms [of appearance]. Yet, since in the domain of the absolute, difference and indifference are indistinguishable, it includes the difference of all things in an indivisible unity with their indifference; thus it contains things in such a way that each thing takes from the absolute its own proper life and ideally goes over into a separated existence. In this way, the universe sleeps in an infinitely fruitful womb, as it were, along with the profusion of its shapes and forms, the kingdom of life, and the totality of its developments; all its forms, inexhaustible within time, [259] are here simply present in the eternal identity; the past and the future, each one an infinity for finite [consciousness], are not separated, but lie together under a common cloak. Now, my friend, I think my previous remarks adequately clarified how this absolute eternity (which we could term a 'rational eternity,' following others' usage) comprehends the finite and how the finite, for all that, does not cease to be finite.[51] For if the finite subsists in and with the infinite while remaining finite in its own sight, then for itself the finite is the relative difference of the ideal and the real, even though it does not look that way from the point of view of the infinite. And the finite first posits itself and its temporality as real by actualizing this difference; hereby it also establishes the actuality of everything contained in its own proper concept as mere possibility.

Yet you will grasp this point more intuitively if you recall your previous admission that the identity of thought and intuition is omnipresent and universal; from this it follows that no thing or being of any sort could have being apart from this indivisible identity, and that no being could be the determinate being it is, if it were not a determinate identity of thought and intuition. Since you classified intuition under 'difference' and thought under 'indifference,' there is no finite being in which difference is not encountered as the expression of intuition, and indifference as the expression of thought. And difference indeed corresponds to what we call 'body,' while indifference corresponds to 'soul.'[52]

Therefore all the things eternally comprehended in the nontemporal finitude that inheres in the infinite are directly animated through the being they possess within the ideas, and it is their life in the ideas that makes them capable, to varying degrees, of the state in which for themselves, but not for the eternal, they withdraw from the absolute and achieve existence within time. Hence you should not believe that particular things or the manifold shapes of living substance you usually distinguish are actually contained in the real, essential universe in the divided manner that you perceive; instead you should believe they are individuated just for you, for in reality each and every being discloses the identity of all things, and precisely to the extent that it has separated itself from that identity [and achieved individuality]. The stone that you see, for example, is in absolute identity with all things; [260] hence for it, nothing is distinguished from anything else, nothing steps forth from self-enclosed night. But in the finite entity that possesses its own life, the animal for instance, the totality of things more or less manifests itself, and it does so to the degree that the animal's life is individual. And finally, before man the universe pours out all of its treasures. But take away this relative identity [and difference] of all beings, and you see all return to identity once more.

But does it not strike you, from this very observation, that we can be certain that there is but one and the same reason that makes the existence of all beings intelligible? And thus that there is but one formula necessary for the cognition of all finite things? This one, namely: Each thing separates itself from the totality of things by actualizing the relative opposition of the finite and the infinite. [The separation is merely apparent] though, for in that aspect whereby it identifies the two, the thing carries within itself the stamp of the eternal, an image of eternity, as it were. The reason is this: Since, in the fullness of its perfection, the identity of the finite and the infinite, of the real and the ideal, is the eternal form, and since this form is at the same time the absolute's abiding essence, the finite thing, or that aspect of it whereby it is a relative identity, receives the reflected light of the absolute's identity, wherein idea is substance too and form is what is absolutely real.

And so we can formulate completely general laws for all finite existence from this relative identity and opposition of the finite and the infinite. Where it is found to be living, this identity and opposition is called knowing; its expression in the order of things, however, is the very same as its expression in the order of knowledge.[53] But I have stated this only generally, and it would not surprise me very much if someone found it unclear, since we have not yet applied this general scheme to particular cases. So it looks like we should now turn our thought to the visible universe and the process of the idea's embodiment.

Difference does not intrinsically reside in the factor you have called intuition; it is there only insofar as intuition is set opposite to thought. Now intuition is by its very nature passive with respect to every form or shape, and receptive of them all; from all eternity, infinite thought impregnates it with all the forms and varieties of things, yet it is infinitely adapted to infinite thought, [261] linked to it in an absolute identity that extinguishes all multiplicity. And since intuition contains everything, for this very reason it cannot contain anything that is discriminable. Hence it is only in the perspective of the particular thing itself that intuition separates itself from thought and becomes opposed to it; this does not happen in the absolute, where, as you remarked, thought and intuitioin are identical, for only within the finite thing is intuition inadequately conformed to the nature of thought. But inasmuch as it distinguishes itself from thought, intuition draws that which identifies the two, namely the idea, over into temporal existence, and within time the idea appears as the real substance of the thing. But whereas the idea is first in eternity, here it is third instead.

Neither thought nor intuition is intrinsically subject to temporality; each becomes subject to time only through its relative division from the other and through their relative reunification [in the finite individual]. For, as the tradition handed down from the ancients informs us, what is responsible for the element in all things that is receptive of difference is the maternal principle, while the concept or infinite thought is the paternal principle; but the third which issues from these two is a generated being, one that has the character of a creature.[54] The generated entity partakes equally in the nature of both principles and in a transitory way it reunites thought and being within itself, thus imperfectly imitating the absolute reality whence it took its origin. But for itself the generated being is necessarily individual, even though it is individual, and in fact this determinate individual, only in virtue of the way it establishes the opposition of the real and the ideal. Neither the real nor the ideal aspect of a thing is essentially mortal, yet in being relatively opposed to one another, each is made mortal through the other, and, in addition, the thing itself, or what is real in the thing, [the image of the idea,] is delivered over to temporal existence.

Therefore the generated being is necessarily and endlessly finite, although it is so only relatively. For in truth the finite never exists on its own; only the identity of the finite and the infinite exists. Hence if we consider the finite by itself, its real element consists solely in this very identity, though in its formal aspect [that is, the manner in which it comes to be within appearance,] it is a relative identity of the finite and the infinite, [and thus their relative opposition as well]. Now the more perfect a thing is, the more it endeavors to show forth the infinite, even within its finite elements; in this way, [262] it strives to make what is intrinsically finite equal to the substantial and independent infinite. Now the more the finite dimension of a being possesses the nature of the infinite, the more it takes on the imperishable character of the totality, the more it appears to be stable, enduring, and intrinsically perfect, and the less it seems to need anything outside of itself. The stars and all the heavenly bodies are finite beings of this sort; their ideas are the most perfect of all those that are in God, since they best express this subsistence of the finite in and with the infinite in God.

But understand that the heavenly bodies are the primary unities of every type of finite being; the multiplicity of individual things and their condition of being divided from one another proceeds from these unities, just the way the endless multiplicity of all types of things issues from absolute identity. Thus each heavenly body endeavors to display the whole universe within itself, and it not only endeavors, but actually does so. Since this is so, they are all capable of endless changes and adaptations, like an organic body, but they are essentially indestructible and immortal, free, independent the way that the ideas of things are, carefree and self-sufficient. In short, they are blessed animals and, compared to mortal men, undying gods.[55] But to understand how this is so, pay attention to what follows.

The idea of every heavenly body is absolute, freed from time, and truly perfect. Within appearance, however, what unites its finite and infinite factors, what produces the derivative reality we spoke of earlier, is the immediate image of the idea itself; this image is incapable of difference, as is the idea itself, [so it imitates the idea] and eternally establishes the universal within the particular and the particular within the universal. In itself this image is identity pure and simple, identity ungenerated and unconditioned, although in connection with the opposition [that governs the world of appearance] its function is to produce identity. The opposition we are talking about, as you know, is that of the finite and the infinite. And the finite is related to the infinite just the way difference is related to indifference. [263]

But no share of reality falls to what is essentially finite. Instead the finite is related to substantial reality in such a way that only when it is multiplied by its square [or the infinite potency] is it equal to substance. You will be able to figure out what I mean by its 'square' from what I said earlier, at least in part; at any rate it will become clearer as we proceed.

In things, that aspect we have called 'the finite' is set opposite to the infinite. Now this infinite aspect, insofar as it is directly related to the finite element of a thing, is merely the infinite aspect of this finite thing; it is not the infinite identity of all finite entities, but only the relative identity of this finite being; it is the concept directly referred to just this one thing, and so it functions as its soul.

In each and every concrete thing, this relative identity [or infinite, conceptual factor] is joined to the finite, and it is related to the latter as the universal is to the particular; it is united with the finite through the image of the idea, that wherein identity and opposition are indivisibly one. It is this soul or infinite aspect that enables the thing to separate itself from the totality of things and to continue existing in this separated condition, eternally the same, differentiated from other things, identical to itself alone. [In general, therefore, the positing of the finite is responsible for the thing's separated existence, while the infinite is responsible for the thing's individuality.]

Now the primary condition for the intrinsically and substantially infinite becoming the infinite aspect or soul of this finite thing, to the exclusion of all others, is that the finite aspect itself be simply finite, and not infinitely finite [as it is in the absolute. In this process of ensouling the finite] not only is the infinite posited in relation to the finite, but also that third element which joins the other two, the one that we decided was an image of the eternal. [The individual thing, therefore, involves all three potencies—the finite, the infinite, and the eternal—all of them directly referred to what is finite].

Absolute space arises from this relation of the finite, the infinite, and the eternal to the finite potency, if, that is, the two terms of the relation become absolutely equal; space is thus the eternally resting and unmoved image of eternity. But the concept which directly binds itself to the finite thing as its soul, expresses itself in the thing through pure length, the first dimension. For, from the following two facts, you will readily see that the line's place in the domain of extension corresponds to the concept's place in the domain of thought: First, the line is essentially endless; it contains in itself no reason for finitude [or limitation]. [264] Secondly, since the line involves the highest and purest act of abstraction from the totality of spatial relations, it is the soul of all figures; for this reason, geometricians, unable to generate the line or to derive it from the totality of spatial relations, postulate the line, perhaps to indicate the line is more an activity than it is an entity.[56]

[Now when the infinite establishes its existence as the soul of this one finite being and expresses itself as length, something analogous to the geometer's initial postulation takes place.] This act that sunders length from the spatial totality is the disruption, as it were, of universal identity, and with this act, everything particular is precipitated out of the indifferent absolute, wherein nothing is distinguishable; for since identity in this first dimension is a relative identity, and one which will become opposed to particularity, an absolute identity of subject and object cannot be established within it, but only a relative one.

Now in things, what expresses this relative identity of subject and object [that is established in the dimension of length] is the things' capacity to coincide with themselves and be self-identical. Similarly, we see in nature that iron adheres to a magnet and that each thing clings to the element of its closest affinity or greatest natural similarity; this is due to the relative identity of nature as a whole. But since relative identity can exist in no other way than as bound to an individual finite being or as related to difference, a second dimension, [namely breadth] is necessarily united to the first, [and it is the expression of difference].

So you see that just as the eternal is the absolute identity of identity and opposition, the generated being is the place where identity, opposition, and the third element which unites the two all come to be differentiated. And so the external and dispersed image of the absolute's unitary internal relations is the framework of the three dimensions; and if these dimensions are absolutely equal to one another, the image of the eternal is space itself. I trust this will become clearer in what follows.

Now we said that the concept, insofar as it is directly tied to this determinate finite entity, is itself finite too; thus it functions as the soul of this individual. But the concept is intrinsically infinite. Now a thing's finite aspect stands related to the infinite concept the way that, [in the domain of real numbers,] the root [or first power] is related to its square [or second power. And so we call the finite the first power or 'potency' and the infinite the second potency]. Now insofar as the concept's proper infinitude lies outside the thing that it ensouls, the concept is necessarily subject to time; for the thing does not contain time within itself. [265]

For time is a continuously moved, eternally novel, harmoniously flowing image of infinite thought.[57] And that relative identity [of subject and object] in a thing, the identity established by the first dimension or length, is itself the expression of time. Hence in the sort of thing where this identity is living, infinite, active, and manifest, it is time itself, and in us, indeed, this living time is what we call self-consciousness. In the bare thing, however, there is but a lifeless expression of this living line of thought, for the infinite concept is not absolutely linked to the thing. And where this is so, the act of time's production, expressed in the thing's inherent self-identity, remains hidden in infinity.

Through this sort of identity, then, the thing is self-identical, and in this way it is both its own subject and its own object. [This identity results from the connection of the infinite concept to the finite thing as its soul.] Thus it is that things are subject to rectilinear extension in space and to [life and development in] time as well.

[By now it should be evident that] the thing is individual and located outside the concept only ideally, or for itself. Really it has its being only through the [third power, the image of the idea,] whereby it is bound to the infinite and assimilated into the totality of things.

Now if the thing were capable of maintaining its self-identity, the universal and the particular would be linked in it the way lines and angles are linked in the triangle. [They would coincide, in that they would simply be different aspects of one and the same thing. But the thing possesses its self-identity through being ensouled by the concept]. And insofar as the thing is bound to the infinite concept of all things, the universal and the particular in it can be joined in it only the way a square and its root [or original power] can be joined, for the infinite is related to the finite as the square is related to its root. [But how can two and the square root of two, for instance, be united? It is not a case of simple coincidence, as happened in our example of lines and angles.]

But the thing can be bound to the infinite concept only through something which is the identity of the universal and the particular, something which is, as you know, essentially incapable of difference. [This something, then, must have the nature of the idea.] Yet since the thing is the sort of being that exists only in virtue of the opposition of the universal and the particular, it is unlike this unity which is without opposition, or rather, it is separated from this unity, and so stands to it in a relation of difference. Accordingly, from the viewpoint of the thing, this unity appears not to exist, but to be the ground of existence instead.

[What is this unity that binds thing and concept and is capable of linking the square to its original power?] Well, if you multiply the square or second power by that whereof it is the square, you generate the cube or the third power, which is the sensible image of the idea, [266] or of the absolute identity of opposition and of identity itself. [The third potency corresponds to the eternal, just as the second potency corresponds to the infinite, and the first to the finite.] Yet you will come to understand this more fully in the following way.

What is real within appearance must be just like that which is true; it must be the sort of thing that connects the infinite and the finite. For identity as such and difference as such are both mere ideal determinations, and only those aspects of things which express the identity of the two factors are real. Now since identity is exhibited in things through the first dimension, and difference through the second, their identity must be perfectly expressed in the dimension wherein the other two are [united and] extinguished [in their independent existence], namely thickness or depth. [And this third spatial dimension of things is established by the third or eternal potency, which appears in the whole system of things as gravity.]

Now that principle which joins soul or the expression of infinite thought in things to body is gravity, although inanimate things indeed appear to stand over against it in a relation of difference; it is only insofar as time does not fall within things and become animate in them that things are subject to the rule of gravity. But if they contain their own time, things are independent, living, free, and themselves absolute, just as the heavenly bodies are.

First we must realize that gravity's function is to ceaselessly assimilate difference into universal indifference. Gravity is intrinsically indivisible, and, accordingly, while a sensible thing may be divided, gravity is not divided, nor is its intrinsic force either increased or diminished by the sensible's partition. And further, since its nature is to be the indifference of space and time, it cannot be opposed to either of them; neither is gravity's force decreased if [the distance in] space [between two things] is increased (this increase in distance is the expression of difference), nor is its force increased if the spatial distance between things is decreased. However much a thing separates itself off from the totality of things, however much, ideally considered, its desire or endeavor to return to the identity of all things weakens, the force of gravity is not altered on that account. It remains unchanged, with the identical force exerted over and against all things.

[We have said that all three potencies are involved in the thing's existence.] Now it is the thing's inorganic aspect [or its finite element] that determines the thing's existence as extended in three-dimensional space and which makes its concept finite. But what gives it form and determines it for judgment is its organic [or infinite] aspect, [267] whereby the thing's particularity is assimilated into universality. But the feature whereby the thing expresses the absolute identity of the universal and the particular is its rational part.

All that we require for explaining the actuality of each and every thing can be expressed in terms of these three levels or potencies [—the inorganic, the organic, and the rational, or, as we previously called them, the finite, the infinite, and the eternal. All three are involved in every thing. And each of the three expresses one and the same absolute identity as a relative identity and opposition]. Thus every single thing exhibits the whole universe, each in its own way.[58]

Earlier we established the fact that the level that is third in individual things is essentially the first. This third level of being is in essence supreme purity and undistorted clarity, which in things is distorted by what we called 'identity' and 'opposition.' When the thing in question is animate, however, we can say it is the opposition of self-consciousness and sensation that disturbs the indifference of reason.

Nevertheless, the real and substantial dimension of a thing is reason alone, the immediate image of the eternal; it is only in relation to difference that reason constitutes absolute space. And although we have said that the relative identity and opposition that characterize finite being are merely formal determinations, their opposition nevertheless affects the pure equality of dimensions in absolute space, disturbs its purity, and so fills space.

Up to this point I have mostly discussed the less perfect sorts of things, the ones that have the infinite concept outside themselves. But now I shall direct your attention toward the more perfect sorts, called 'heavenly bodies' by others, but which we will call 'sensitive and intelligent animals.'[59] For it is evident that time is innate in them, that the infinite concept is granted to them as their soul to direct and regulate their movements. They express the idea fully and directly, since they display the infinite within their finite dimensions; and they live an absolute and godlike life as well, unlike the conditioned and dependent life lived by things externally subject to the concept.

From what we have previously established, you will not find it incomprehensible that the finite which eternally subsists in and with the substantially infinite can contain an innumerable multiplicity or an infinite fullness of things, and can still be a unity itself, one which gathers and joins the power of innumerable things. For according to the same law whereby one of these intelligent animals withdraws from the supreme identity, [268] it shatters the perfection of that first unity, and, recovering for itself infinitely many things, it breathes forth what it took from above in innumerably many individual beings.

In this way, everything that exists originates from an [animate] unity, though it is separated from it by the relative opposition of the finite and the infinite within itself. Yet this unity itself is sprung from a higher one, [the idea] which indifferently contains all the things comprehended within it.

Now either a thing includes its own being and is therefore a substance, or it is not itself substance. A thing will be a substance only if its finite aspect is identical to its infinite aspect, that is, only if it can exhibit the whole universe within itself, even in its state of separated existence. But if it is not a substance, a thing is continually driven to exist [in isolation and to inhabit the place] where it alone can exist, and then to return to the unity which is its origin. [Thus it is that the heavenly bodies move in orbits rather than existing in one place.]

Now generally it is pure finitude or the element of pure difference in a thing that causes the reflection of its idea to fall within space, but such a small portion of the true idea's reality is reflected in the thing's [body] that it must be [raised to the third power or] triply multiplied by itself before it is equal to the idea. And further, since the magnitude of the thing's difference also determines its spatial distance from the image of its identity, this distance stands related to the true space-filling image of the idea in the same proportion that pure difference stands to the idea itself, [namely as the first power stands to its cube].

But the distance of a thing from its center of gravity is either a real factor or merely an ideal one. Where a thing is not a substance in its own right, it is always an ideal factor, [for gravity's force is not affected by distance]. Even when you see a manifold of things bound together into a system, like the earth, the system as a whole stands over against the individual thing and behaves likes one body. Thus each thing within the system is heavy because it is located a certain definite distance from the center; the magnitude of this distance determines the thing's particular weight.

Now in gravity, as you know, the living identity of time is bound up with difference, and from this connection of identity to difference arises motion, the measure of time. Thus when a thing does not possess substance in its own right, [269] it necessarily moves away from its origin or center of being. And it moves in such a way that the time of its motion is not equal to the distance it travels but, since distance is the sensible expression of difference [while time is the expression of identity], its time is equal to the square of the distance instead. Conversely, if it moves towards its center of being, the time of its motion diminishes and the distance covered becomes equal to the square of the time.

[In imperfect things, then, the distance moved and the time of their motion stand related as the first power does to the second.] Now in those more perfect things that possess being and life in their own right, even if the element of difference or pure finitude in them is really and substantially in a perfect identity with the infinite, it does not cease to be opposed to the infinite in concept. Now insofar as it is ideally opposed to the infinite, the finite is related to the infinite as its square or second power; and this opposition, occasioned by the star's finite dimension, also determines its path of motion away from [the system's center,] the image of identity. [In these respects the more perfect thing does not seem to differ from the less perfect.]

But in the domain of beings that have life in their own right, the finite is really joined to the infinite in such a way that it is not related to the latter as its square or second power, but as perfect equal to perfect equal. Again, an individual thing can itself be substance only if its path of motion away from the center is endowed with life, but its path can become animate only if the star's difference or pure finitude becomes equal to the infinite concept. Since the concept is time, when identical with the finite, it equalizes the time and distance, and transforms the star's path of motion away from the center into a circular revolution.

In this way, time is implanted in the heavenly spheres as their own possession, and because of their heavenly nature, they are appointed to be sensible images of the whole real universe, for especially in their circular motion, they imitate the idea which extends itself through all types of being and yet continually reverts back into its identity. For, unlike what happens in the things of earth, in the heavenly bodies, the element whereby things separate themselves and distance themselves from the image of identity is not divorced from the element whereby they are assimilated into the infinite concept, and they are not split up into contending forces. Instead their elements are harmoniously yoked, and just as they alone are truly immortal, so these heavenly beings alone enjoy the blessed condition of reality as a whole, even in the state of separated existence. And in the course of their revolution, [270] which is pure identity and the destruction of all oppositions, and absolute independence as well, they breathe in the divine peace of the true world and behold the majesty of the first mover.

Take note, then, my friend, of the significance of the laws [of planetary motion]; they seem to have been disclosed to us by a divine intelligence:[60]

A being that is godlike and independent is not subject to time; rather, it compels time to submit to itself and to depend upon it. Furthermore, by bringing its finite and infinite aspects to a state of equality, it restrains overpowering time. When this happens, time is no longer multiplied by distance, that whose square or second power it is; it is multiplied by itself instead, and becomes equal to the true idea. From this tempering of time's pace arises the standard or measure of time, the [circular] motion wherein [identical arcs are traversed in identical times and] space and time themselves are established as perfectly equal magnitudes; this motion, multiplied by itself, generates these godlike beings.

You should therefore think of the planets' course of motion as something perfectly whole and simple, not a composite of forces, but an absolute identity thereof. One of the factors of this identity, [centripedal force,] causes a thing to inhere within the identity of all things; it is commonly called gravity. The other is [centrifugal force] which causes a thing to reside in itself [and maintain its individuality over against the whole system's identity]; we commonly view it as the opposite of gravity. But these are absolutely equivalent forms of the identity that constitutes the planet's motion; both are the same totality, one thing in fact.[61] For neither can a thing residing inside the identity of all things possess its being independently if it is removed from the center of identity, nor can a thing that has its being in itself reside within the identity of all things, unless its finite dimension is absolutely joined to its infinite one [the way the magnitudes of distance and time are integrated in circular motion]. But once these factors are integrated so absolutely, they can never be divided, and what we distinguish in the moved heavenly body, [for example, the time of its motion or the arc it has moved through] is due neither to the one factor nor the other, but always and necessarily to the very identity of the finite and the infinite.

None of the heavenly spheres, then, is [moved] by anything other than its own inborn excellence. And this excellence consists in its ability to transform its principle of individuation into absolute identity itself and, conversely, its ability to make the identity of all things into the principle of its individual existence. Thus the planets are neither removed from the center of their identity nor are they integrated into it, [but they inhere both in themselves and in the center of identity by continually revolving about it]. Now when a self-moved thing like a heavenly body [271] can assimilate difference within itself into indifference and can, conversely, establish indifference within its dimension of difference, and in such a perfectly identical manner, its motions generate the circle, for the circle is the figure that is the most perfect expression of reason, which is the identity of the universal and the particular.[62]

[We have shown the reason for the circular motion of the heavenly bodies. Yet in their sensible appearance, not all of them appear to describe a perfect circle in their orbits. Nor do they all seem to move at the same speed. How is this so?]

If this perfect form of circular motion obtained universally, these heavenly animals would all describe the same arc of their respective orbits within the same period of time. But if that were the case, the difference you have observed in the movements of the individual [planets] around the image of their identity would be completely abolished, namely the variations in length of arc [for the same time period] and in the time [it takes various planets to move through the same arc]. They would all be equally perfect then. But the unborn beauty that discloses itself within them willed generally that a trace of particularity should remain in their sensible appearance, and that the sensible eye should perceive them this way too, for the sensible eye delights in recognizing beauty within particular things; but it willed that the nonsensible eye abstain from the beauty and indestructible identity expressed even in this medium of difference, that it attain instead to the intuition of absolute beauty and of its intrinsic and substantial reality.

So for sensible eyes, absolute beauty has veiled its starry countenance, and for this reason it also decreed that the absolute identity which directs the motions of the heavenly spheres should appear divided into two points. Indeed each of the two points expresses the very same identity of difference and indifference, except that in one, difference is identified with indifference, while in the other, indifference is identified with difference; the true identity is thus really and essentially present in each of them, though not, indeed, in the order of appearance.

In this way it happens that the heavenly bodies move themselves in self-reverting lines or orbits that are similar to circles, but unlike the circle, which is an arc described about one point or origin, the planets describe arcs around two separate foci that are mutually balanced [and that together determine the planets' path of motion]. One focus coincides with the sun, the luminous image of that absolute identity that is the origin of all the stars; the other focus expresses the idea of the individual heavenly body insofar as it is the universe itself, absolute and independent. Things were so arranged so that we might recognize identity within difference itself and appreciate the peculiar destiny of each of the heavenly bodies, as particular beings to be absolute, and as absolute to be particular things. [This is the significance of Kepler's first law, which tells us that the planets traverse elliptical orbits, with the sun as one of the focal points determining the ellipse]. [272]

But since difference exists solely for the sake of appearance, since it is intrinsically and truly the sort of thing that ought not exist, a genuinely divine artistry taught these heavenly creatures at one moment to check and restrain their movements, and at others to freely follow their impulses; the aim of this instruction was to restore to identity once again the ratios between the time-periods and distances covered [for all of the arcs on a planet's elliptical path]. It was also meant to insure that [the planet's finite dimension of] distance, animated solely through its identity with the planet's native time, would not cease to be living [if the time it takes to move through a given arc were altered]; thus at a greater distance [from one focus, the sun], they were to traverse a smaller arc in the same amount of time it takes them to move through a greater arc, when closer [to the sun. The result is that the planets seem to move at a constant rate, as if they were describing circles. This is the significance of Kepler's second law of planetary motion, which states that the ratio between the time of motion and the distance covered in an arc is constant, although times, distances, and velocity vary throughout the elliptical orbit.]

Instructed, therefore, by this supernatural intelligence which preserves identity even within difference itself, the stars, though they seem to travel paths that are distorted circles, truly describe circular orbits, in conformity with the idea.

And yet, my friend, everything I have said to this point about the order of the heavenly motions is insufficient. To explain all these things in a manner worthy of their subject-matter would take us farther than the purpose of our investigation permits, though perhaps we can discuss these matters among others in what follows. No mortal discourse, however, is capable of adequately praising this heavenly wisdom, or of measuring the profundity of the intelligence that is perceived in these motions.

But if you want me to tell you what laws determine the arrangement, number, size and other knowable properties of the stars, I shall oblige you, my friend. As concerns their arrangement, I would say that the whole universe is divided into two regions. The very same matter exists in all regions, though variously transformed. The one region is inhabited by those heavenly spheres to whom time is more perfectly married than it is to the rest; their identity closely approximates the absolute's identity. In the other region live those stars that possess time in a less perfect way and are less self-sufficient.[63]

Everything to which time is united in a living manner also bears the external expression of time, the line [273] (which in connection with matter constitutes cohesion and resistance). Since this is so, the line or mark of time is implanted within each individual in that region of the more perfect stars; we call this line the star's 'axis,' and designate its extremes as 'north' and 'south.' But time is also expressed within the universe as a whole, so all the stars together constitute a line, common to them all.[64] According to the position they occupy on this line, the stars exhibit a greater or a lesser degree of cohesion and self-identity. But the extremes of the whole universe are again related as south and north.

And so those heavenly spheres that display the connection of south and north within the universe as a whole are made of sterner, more enduring stuff than the others are; in connecting these polar extremes, they interconnect all the regions of the heavens. But it takes [a constellation of] three stars to exhibit the connection [of polar extremes]. The first and third star stand related as opposites, the first one being the least distant from the sun or image of identity, and the third the most distant. But the middle star exhibits the indifference of both of the others in the group, so that no one of them is essentially different from the others. However the number of stars in such a constellation may be as high as twelve.

This type of star is endowed with the most perfect motion. And just as these stars, taken as a whole, exhibit the connection of south and north, so the stars that dwell in the second region display the connection of east and west; within this latter opposition itself, all the regions of the heavens are once again intertwined and interconnected. And in each corporeal thing, too, there is necessarily an expression of each one of the heavenly regions.

These stars of the second region more or less deviate from the perfect motion [of a circular orbit], for they possess a self-identity that is far from absolute, precisely because they have separated themselves from absolute identity least of all. But to find the formula for the number of these inferior stars might well be impossible, for it increases in great proportions.

And you could comprehend the law according to which distances increase among the stars that possess life more perfectly [274] if you give some further thought to what we have already discussed. But you would understand it more readily if you were aware of the mysteries of the triangle.

But as concerns the mass and density of the stars, the divine artistry so shaped things that, taken as a whole, stars of the greatest mass occupy the middle of the heavenly regions, while the densest stars are closest to the identity of all, or to the image of identity. And the same holds true for the groups of three stars that form a constellation; the one closest to the sun will be the one most characterized by density, the next one will have the greatest mass, while the orbit of the outermost one will deviate most from the circle.

But concerning this last topic, there is the following general law: Things in the universe are more or less perfect, the more or less they embody time. But all the things of the preeminent sort incorporate time.

For we said that the line or pure length is the expression of time within individual things, and thus that things which perfectly express the dimension of length have a greater share of time within them than do other individual corporeal things. But if time is actively united to a thing as living time [it will be conscious to some degree, that is,] the thing's concept will necessarily include the possibility of other things. And so we observe that the stone which the ancients called 'the stone of Heracles' and which later ages named 'the magnet,' though it appears to be isolated from other things, nonetheless has a cognizance or a feeling of things and moves them, either by attracting them to itself or by repelling them. We see, further, that the succession of seasons is not alien to things that actively contain time, things such as migratory birds that steer their flight toward another climate and thus act as an indicator of time. Individual things too have their years and their days and so are like the stars, only less perfect and more subject to the identity that is external to them. But if a thing does not embody time to a very great degree, [275] the reason lies in the imperfection of its body, or its dimension of pure difference.

The more tightly time is bound into a thing, then, the less it will stand in need of the identity of all things which is external to it, [in the system's center], for such a thing establishes its own identity; this also explains why time cannot belong to the things most subject to gravity. On the other hand, the way the densest of things imperfectly possess time is the reason that they are less subject to gravity as well, for since things with the least share of time are the least individual, and are separated from the external identity of the whole system the least of all, and since gravity demands that things be distinguished and differentiated from one another, the densest things will not be greatly subject to gravity's force.

Now apply this to the stars and you will comprehend why those that incorporate time to the fullest extent and which are thus the most excellent are classed among the less dense heavenly bodies, and why their motions perfectly express the identity they contain, too. And, on the other hand, you will understand why the densest stars deviate far more from the most beautiful pattern of motion. Finally you will understand why the stars that least show the stamp of time, namely shape and form, and that deviate the most from the beautiful pattern of motion, are classed among the least dense stars. It is not because their need for identity is less than others', but because they have separated themselves from it the least. And in these formulae lies the secret of the variations we perceive in the motions of the heavenly bodies, and in the perfection of their imitation of the most beautiful figure.

In this way, everything was arranged according to proportion and number, so that beauty would prevail.[65] And each heavenly sphere was endowed with a double center of unity. By means of the first, the star would itself be absolute and would approximate the most perfect union of the finite with the infinite in God; we could call the idea of this absolute union 'the absolute animal.' It is in virtue of this first center of unity that the star is organic, free and animate. By means of the other center of unity the star would exist within the absolute and be absorbed as a whole into the identity of all things, along with its dimension of difference. [276] And the heavenly wisdom further ordained that only within the domain of difference would these two centers of unity remain in a state of equality. But with this decision that difference was to be the enduring condition for the existence of things, a division between classes of individual things was decreed as well. Things whose difference could be annulled only by being assimilated into indifference, and which are completely subject to gravity on account of the imperfect way they contain time, would appear to be dead and lifeless. But those things in which difference already was itself indifference and which possessed time and life more completely were to be living and organic. It was decreed that these latter would be the most perfect individual beings, since they would most perfectly exemplify the identity the heavenly spheres possess, the identity whereby the stars are themselves all things and free and rational.

In this way the heavenly spheres were populated with living creatures of every sort and of every grade of perfection, when they separated themselves from their identity.[66] These creatures were contained in the primal identity, before the separation of the individual stars forced them to live within an other. But the stars are thus populated through the same decree that made their orbital paths more or less deviate from the circle. Now the more perfectly one of the heavenly spheres unites the center of unity whereby it is organic with the second whereby it is inorganic, the more its motion necessarily approximates the archetype of motion. [For, if the foci of an ellipse are brought closer together until they finally coincide, the figure described about them will no longer be an ellipse, but a circle.]

But in the middle of all the stars, in the image of their identity, flared up immortal light, the idea of all things. For at that point where all the things of the universe are one in substance, the idea of all things must be expressed too, since the idea is the [absolute's] form, and is equal to, and in fact identical with, [the absolute's] essence. Therefore, in order to make this identity of form and essence manifest and evident, the divine artistry shaped this one star so that it would be totally mass and totally light, the hearth of the world, or, as others say, the blessed sentinel of Zeus. But since the sun is itself derived from a higher identity and is thus still an individual, the divine artist symbolized the trace of difference that still resides in it by scattering dark spots over the brightness of its face.

But since light, as the expression of the idea, is at the same time the indifference of space and time, it was further decreed that, first, [277] it would cover all the dimensions of space without filling space, next, that it would illuminate all things, and finally that it would be the torch and indicator of time, the measure of the year and of the day as well.

For not only is the sun the indifference of all the things contained in the universe, but, over and above this, it continuously endeavors to gather together the element of difference in the other spheres that revolve around it and unite it to itself. It seeks to extend its own relative identity throughout them all and so to augment itself through them; in short, it strives to become one with its satellites, just the way an individual thing is one with itself.

But any individual thing is more self-identical the more perfectly it incorporates time, [and the earth is one of those things that embodies time to a great degree,] for we see that the earth impresses the stamp of living time even on that which is lifeless in it, unifying difference through the identity of the concept and of the line, which is the expression of self-consciousness. The earth displays this union in appearances as its axis, whose extremes we designate south and north.

Since in this way the earth integrates what is particular in itself into the universal, it strives against the sun. The sun, however, endeavors to posit the particular as particular, and to unite it with its own innate expression of time. Now since the earth and every other heavenly sphere as well establishes its own relative self-identity in the dimension of length by uniting its element of difference to its concept, the sun endeavors to create an equal relative identity in the dimension of breadth insofar as it seeks to unite its own concept to the particular elements of each sphere. But since every sphere resists the sun's efforts through its own native life, the alteration of day and night was first created, (for the sun's effort makes every sphere revolve around itself). The year was divided from the day, however, and its motion was retarded, so that the living and innate time of each of the planets [expressed in its yearly revolution around the sun] would not be set equal to that of an inferior motion.

For if the sun became identical with a heavenly sphere [278] the way a thing is identical with itself, this sphere would complete its revolution about the sun in the same time it takes to complete its daily revolution about its axis. If this happened, the year would be equal to the day, and half the earth would neither see the sight of the sun, nor perceive, as we do now, the serene light of that lesser sphere we call the moon; this satellite would always turn the same side toward us, and it would have one and the same time-period for its revolution about its axis and for its circuit around the earth.

But if the earth's difference were bound into the sun's relative identity, it would suffer complete death; as it is, this difference is animate and besouled, but solely through its union with the concept and the soul of the earth.

In this way, then, just as we have described it, the universe is intertwined with itself, and it forever strives to be more like itself and to become one body and one soul.[67]

But within the universe, things stand the same way they do within the living organism, for in the animal, the soul portions itself out over the many and various members, and each part takes its particular soul from the whole; all the individual members, even though they are bound together into a whole, still live for themselves. Accordingly, in order that the universe be one in its multiplicity and finite in its infinitude, although a particular time span is allotted to each individual, the universe as a whole is so shaped in the divine imagination that it contains absolute time within itself as its possession. And so the universe itself is contained in no period of time, and is such a well-organized animal that it can never die.

Now, my friend, have we not called the eternal idea of all corporeal things light? But where the finite is identical to the infinite in a thing, the idea is also expressed as absolute cognition, that cognition in which there is no opposition between thought and being. Moreover, in such an absolute cognition, form is substance, substance is form, and the two factors are indivisibly one. But the more a thing is individual and persists in its individuality, the more it divorces itself from the eternal concept of all things, which then falls outside the thing as light, just as infinitude falls outside it as time. And the thing itself then pertains to that which does not exist, but is the ground of existence—primordial night, the mother of all things. [279]

Now the light that is seen by the sensible eye is not itself the indifference of thought and being, absolutely considered, but it is this indifference modified by its relation to a quantum of difference, that of the earth, for instance, or of some other heavenly body. Now if an earthly body separates itself from the totality of [the things of] earth, it necessarily becomes opaque, but if the degree of separation is lesser, the body will necessarily be more transparent. [And so external light distinguishes things more marked by individuality and difference.]

But concerning the degree to which things are animated, I would say that a thing has life and soul in proportion to its internal possession of time and light. Now what ensouls individual things is not form as such; the more perfect form is, the more it is simply identical to substance, [as it is in the absolute]. Soul, on the other hand, is the concept of a thing, and so, from the viewpoint of the finite, it is also determined to be the soul of an individual existing thing.[68] Hence it follows that only so much of the universe falls within the soul of an individual thing as is actually expressed in the thing. Now the bare corporeal thing is, as we know, necessarily and to infinity individual and isolated from others.

The organic being, however, wherein light and form are themselves substance, contains within its concept the possibility of infinitely many things that lie outside of its individual state; it may contain its own possibility in the guise of an infinite number of offspring that may arise from propagation; or it may contain the possibility of other beings different from itself, related to it through motion. Finally it may contain the possibility of other individual things that are different from it but are at the same time within it [as objects of its cognition]. And this last case is possible because the organic being embodies the idea itself, and in relation to difference, the idea indeed functions as the intuiting agent [or knower].[69]

Yet since organic beings do contain the infinite concept and life within themselves, they must admit an element of difference from outside, though such beings always adapt difference to the concept's infinitude; in this way, they are forced to accept the conditions of their life from without, and in doing so they are first made dependent and needy, and then are subjected to disease, aging, and death. Thus they in no way approach the excellence of the things in the heavens. [280]

But the earth more or less imperfectly sustains the identity whereby it is itself a substantial reality, yet organic beings stand related to this identity as the ground of their existence, without being identical with it. And their actions are indeed rational, though not through any power dwelling in them, but through the reason that inhabits the universe as a whole; this power manifests itself in organic beings as their own principle of gravity [and it is the principle of their perception and appetition].

But since organic entities are individual and are necessarily imperfect, because the real and the ideal, or soul and body, are opposed in them, so all their actions are indeed ordered toward the identity of all things, not by their own power, but by the divine principle that guides them. And the divine principle has given them a sense of identity with all things, intrinsic to their very existence, so that they sense themselves in other things and in every way endeavor to unite with them. And they are also endowed with one spark of the living artistry that fashions all things, and it instructs them to achieve, through more or less coherent actions, the indifference of thought and being they do not intrinsically contain; they achieve this indifference in external deeds, and thus their works and actions appear purposive, for the concept that ensouls them is more or less integrated into the concept of other things. Even a small bit of the divine artistry implants in them the heavenly music which subsists in the universe as a whole, and in light and in the heavenly spheres, and it teaches those that are accustomed to dwell in the air to forget themselves in song and so revert to the identity of all things.

The earth's identity has left other organic beings more freedom, and allowed them more to internally include its [rational] power than externally possess it. The earth is thus like a fruitful and talented mother, who gives of herself to all her children, but more to one and less to another, while she fully shares herself with one alone.

But in positing the indifference it natively contains alongside difference in every one of these organic beings, the identity of all things has made what is indivisibly one in itself divisible. For every particular attribute and function of a living organism arises because no one attribute or function in isolation can convey the full indifference of identity itself, and since this latter is the sum and content of all forms, it cannot itself be identified with any particular attribute.

And yet a being which does not completely possess substance in its own right [281] cannot completely separate itself from the identity of all things; it has being only within it. Indeed we know that the mere corporeal thing contains just a lifeless expression of the concept, that the living concept is located above and beyond it in the infinite, and that it has merely an external life inside the absolute. But within the universe, for every passive mode of being there is a corresponding active one, and each animal, over and above the fact that it is a particular mode of being, participates in the living concept too, and has an inward mode of being in the absolute. Yet it has this being only by way of participation, and since its finite dimensions express the infinite only imperfectly, the animal is not itself [reason or] the principle of intuition, but stands in a relation of difference to it.

But inasmuch as a soul has the nature of the intrinsically and substantially infinite, while the body is finite (though infinitely finite and capable of depicting the entire universe), the individual entity that exists in time reveals the mystery hidden away in God—the absolute identity of the infinite, which is the pattern or foretype, and the finite, which is the antitype. And so the element in a thing that is responsible for the absolute union of soul and body, or of thought and being, will intrinsically convey the essence of the absolutely eternal, the indivisible identity wherein idea is also substance.

But the soul, although it is indeed absolute cognition in itself, is, as the soul of this existent individual, the infinite possibility of everything that is actually expressed in the thing. Now we defined the latter as the body, and even though the body is an infinite-and-finite sort of thing, capable of exhibiting the whole universe, it is still ideally individual, and necessarily so. Thus it is necessarily opposed to other things, and capable of being determined by them, whether they express an infinite mode of being or a finite one; and the body's concept includes these external determinants as well, either as unactualized possibilities or as actualities lacking possibility.[70]

When it has become identical with being, infinite thought manifests itself within the domain of the finite as infinite cognition. Hence, if we think of infinite thought as functioning as the soul of some body, since that body is necessarily individual, thought will necessarily seem to be infinite only within the context of the finite; it will appear to be an individual concept of infinite cognition, [282] and, though it will belong to the most perfect class of concepts, still it will be individual. But, on the other hand, if we consider what it is in itself, this concept is not the soul of this particular thing; it is the infinite concept of soul itself, that which is common to all souls.

Therefore when you suppose that infinite cognition, the infinite and immortal idea of all things, actually exists, you directly posit once again the opposition of difference and indifference, for actual existence cannot be established except in connection to an individual thing; if you posit the existence of infinite cognition as the soul of one particular body, then you are positing a double soul, as it were, one soul embracing the [limited] actuality of infinite thought, the other soul its infinite possibility.

Now I have almost reached that goal you proposed, namely the deduction of consciousness from the idea of the eternal itself and from its internal identity, and I have not been forced to admit or introduce any kind of transition from the infinite to the finite. I shall finally attain that goal when I am able to demonstrate that with this division of the actuality of infinite thought from its possibility, consciousness and the temporal being of things as well are simultaneously posited, the whole world of appearances in fact. Indeed consciousness has no reality in the sight of the absolute, but, just like everything else that pertains to the image world, consciousness is real for itself and in its own perspective.[71]

But before [we complete our task of deducing the origin of consciousness,] let us hold fast to what is abidingly real, to that which we must suppose is immovable when we also assume the existence of what is movable and changeable, for the soul never tires of returning again and again to the contemplation of what is most excellent.[72] Accordingly, let us recall how all the beings that seem to issue from absolute identity or to depart from it, have their possibility of existing for themselves predetermined in this very identity. The actuality of separated existence resides only in the things themselves; separated existence is merely an ideal condition, but even as an ideal condition, it occurs only to the degree that the thing's mode of being inside the absolute makes it capable of being an identity in its own right.

Thus a thing cannot be determined by temporal duration unless it is the object associated with a soul which is finite and has its existence determined by temporal duration, nor, on the other hand, can the soul's existence be determined as a duration in time, [283] unless it is determined to be the soul of an individual existing thing. Hence the soul is nothing intrinsically real, nor is the body either; each of them exists in time only in and through the other. The only element of an individual thing that is intrinsically real is the identity of soul and body, and it subsists within that ever-blessed nature that is not subject to duration. What is real subsists [in the absolute,] where possibility is not divorced from actuality, nor thought divorced from being, in the archetype, therefore, which is uncreated and truly indestructible. For neither is the soul that is immediately joined to the body immortal—since the body is not immortal, and since, in general, the soul's existence is determinable and in fact determined through duration only insofar as the body endures—nor is even that soul of souls itself, [the infinite concept of soul,] for it is related to the individual's soul the same way the individual's soul is related to its body.[73]

Furthermore, the soul is not anything that is intrinsically real, since it exists only through its relative opposition to the body; it is only in virtue of this opposition that it seems to be determined to exist in time, that is, only insofar as it is the concept of an individual being. But it is not its condition of being joined to a thing that makes the soul individual; rather, it is a function of its own intrinsic finitude, the fact that, from the soul's point of view, the possibility [of its existence] and the actuality [of the possibilities it contains] are located outside itself, whereas in God, possibility is linked to actuality and actuality to possibility.[74] For concepts that are the immediate concepts of finite things act like finite things, and they are opposed to the infinite concept, just the way things are, and only insofar as they are infinite in their finitude are they adapted to the concept's nature.

And just as the thing constitutes its time by containing an actuality whose possibility lies outside of it or a possibility whose actuality lies beyond it, so too does the concept insofar as it is simply finite. For reflection is operative in the domain of the immediate concepts of things, just as it is in the domain of things themselves; it tears apart the infinite identity [of the idea,] wherein every possibility immediately includes its actuality and every actuality its possibility, and puts the separated factors into a relation of cause and effect, so that each individual concept seems to have its existence determined by another concept that is viewed as its possibility, and this latter concept is in turn determined through another of the same sort, and so on without end. [284]

Accordingly, since the finite concept is the finite thing itself and is absolutely identical with it, we can generally express the opposition of the finite and the infinite as the opposition that obtains between the finite concept and the infinite concept of all concepts. And since the finite concept stands to the infinite concept itself as the real does to the ideal, the difference of the ideal and the real is itself a difference within the order of concepts.

Although considered in its separation from the infinite concept, the concept seems to be determined to exist in time, considered in its union with the infinite concept, that is, in its idea, it exists in eternal communion with God.[75] But only so much of what is eternal and timeless in God falls to the concept's share in its finite, separated condition as withdraws itself from the absolute totality at the same time the concept does. And this, the concept's share in the eternal communion of things, is again determined by the way the possibility of other things is linked to the concept in God.

But there is a rule according to which the soul separates itself from the identity of all things, though only for itself, and seems to be determined to exist in time. Since every soul is a member of the infinite organic body that exists in the idea, if we understood this rule, we would be permitted a fleeting glimpse, at least, into the harmony of that luminous world, a world we now dimly perceive, as if looking through a mirror.[76] But to find this precise rule is a task so difficult that, for all practical purposes, it is impossible, [Not that we should despair!] For it is one of thought's exalted goals to discover the most general laws whereby the absolute world maps itself onto finite cognition.

Accordingly, let us try to attain this goal and proceed in our argument from the point we indicated earlier, where, within cognition itself, the relative opposition of the finite and the infinite is directly posited, for it is the connection of infinite cognition to an individual thing that necessitates the positing of this opposition. Now all the oppositions that determine finite things and differentiate them from one another [285] are established in this one act of separation [whereby the concept divorces itself from the totality and relates itself to an existing individual]; this separation happens only within the eternal, though it is real only for the concept that is itself separated from the totality, but not for the absolute. Once we have demonstrated all of this, we will be perfectly certain that we have arrived back at the first principle and origin of all things.

But since we are certain about the task ahead of us, don't you think it would be a good idea to once again briefly rehearse the points we are agreed upon?

LUCIAN. By all means.

BRUNO. So infinite cognition can only exist as the soul of a thing that endlessly displays what is finite, one, therefore, which portrays the whole universe in itself?

LUCIAN. That is right, for we have said that only by being the concept of an existing thing can any concept exist.

BRUNO. But this thing is still necessarily individual, and inasmuch as it exists as an individual, it is subject to temporality and to duration.

LUCIAN. Of course.

BRUNO. So is the soul which has the thing as its immediate object any less subject to time?

LUCIAN. No, soul and body are equally subject to time.

BRUNO. Hence the soul that is the concept of this thing—later on we will discuss the thing itself—this soul is but one portion of the infinite possibility that is timelessly actualized in God. Within the individual soul, however, falls only the actuality of the things whose possibility it contains.

LUCIAN. Necessarily.

BRUNO. But do we not assume that soul is itself infinite cognition?

LUCIAN. Of course we suppose it is, when we regard it in itself, but when we consider it as the soul of this individual thing, we posit it as necessarily finite and subject to duration within time.

BRUNO. Hence we necessarily have a double view of the soul?

LUCIAN. Naturally, for if we posited it merely in relation [286] to this individual thing whose concept it is, we would not posit it as infinite cognition, and if we were to posit it as simply infinite, we would not be positing it as the concept of an existing thing; in fact, we would not be positing it as existent at all. Necessarily, then, we posit the soul's existence as simultaneously finite and infinite.

BRUNO. And so infinite cognition exists or enters appearance only under the form of difference and indifference.[77]

LUCIAN. That is true.

BRUNO. But do we necessarily assume that the two souls are united, the one that is soul properly speaking inasmuch as it is one with the body, and the soul insofar as it is infinite cognition?

LUCIAN. Yes, they are united through the eternal concept, wherein the finite is identical with the infinite.

BRUNO. Except that this idea subsists in God alone, while the opposition of difference and indifference holds good only in the soul insofar as it exists.

LUCIAN. That is also true.

BRUNO. But did you not say that the soul, considered in a certain respect, is one with the body, indeed that it is itself the body?

LUCIAN. So I said.

BRUNO. In that case, how will you define the relation between the soul considered as infinite and the soul viewed as finite?

LUCIAN. Necessarily it is the same as the relationship between soul and body in the individual.

BRUNO. So we have now transposed the opposition between soul and body over to the different aspects of soul itself?

LUCIAN. It seems that we have.

BRUNO. Then we have to ascribe all the conditions we necessarily attribute to the body to the soul insofar as it is finite.

LUCIAN. There is no alternative.

BRUNO. But we defined soul, insofar as it is related to the body, as the possibility of all that is expressed in the body as actuality.

LUCIAN. Quite right.

BRUNO. But since we have established that the soul [287] or the immediate concept of the body and the body itself are one thing, are we not forced to contrast the former, inasmuch as it is immediately related to the body, to the soul that is infinite the way we contrast actuality to possibility? And does not the infinite soul stand to the body-related soul as possibility stands to actuality?

LUCIAN. Without a doubt.

BRUNO. And we necessarily posit this possibility as infinite, but its actuality as finite instead?

LUCIAN. How else?

BRUNO. Then you would also be satisfied if we designate the former possibility 'the infinite concept of cognition,' while we call the latter 'cognition itself,' or rather 'objective, existing cognition,' since it is an instance of thought that is related to an instance of being?

LUCIAN. Why not?

BRUNO. But since it is finite, identical with the body, and subject to interconnection with other finites according to cause and effect, this objective cognition is necessarily and endlessly a determined and individuated sort of thing.

LUCIAN. That cannot be denied.

BRUNO. But what do you think determines objective cognition? Is it determined from without, or is it self-determined?

LUCIAN. It must be the latter case.

BRUNO. So you assume that determination by way of the interconnection of causes and effects is intrinsic to objective cognition, so that one individual act of cognition is determined by another such individual cognition, and this latter is again determined by another, and so on without end.

LUCIAN. In fact, that is how things stand.

BRUNO. And for the very same reason, you suppose that each act of cognition in this series is distinct from the cognition that determines it, and that acts of cognition differ in endless variety.

LUCIAN. That is exactly what I hold.

BRUNO. But, [on the other hand,] you think the infinite concept of cognition is self-identical and incapable of change, independent of temporality, and not determined by the sort of causal interconnection that we just now agreed obtains between acts of objective cognition.

LUCIAN. Necessarily. [288]

BRUNO. Then you ascribe the very same relation to objective cognition and the infinite concept of cognition that, earlier in the discussion, you attributed to intuition and thought.

LUCIAN. It would seem so.

BRUNO. But, back then, you located the identity of the real and the ideal in this very same identity of thought and intuition.

LUCIAN. Of course I did.

BRUNO. You see, then, that you picked your terminology for expressing this identity of the real and the ideal from quite a particular location, as if that identity were confined to that perspective. The particularity of your stance furnishes us good reason to trouble ourselves about defining this perspective more sharply, so that we can assess its value. Thus, if you posit the identity of intuition and thought, you are necessarily identifying objective cognition and the infinite concept of cognition, are you not?

LUCIAN. That is what I do.

BRUNO. But objective cognition is finite only insofar as it is related to the body, its immediate object; hence, insofar as it is related to the concept of cognition, it is infinite, is it not?

LUCIAN. That follows, I suppose.

BRUNO. And this latter, the concept of cognition, it too is infinite?

LUCIAN. You are correct.

BRUNO. [Now if you posit the identity of existing or objective cognition and the concept of cognition,] what is related and what it is related to are indistinguishably one.

LUCIAN. Necessarily.

BRUNO. And thus the infinite, [objective cognition as thought, not as related to the body,] attains to the infinite, [that is, the proper infinitude of the concept]. But tell me how you would express this, the infinite's coming to itself? What term do we have for it?

LUCIAN. 'The self.'

BRUNO. You have named the one concept that makes the world disclose its riches, as if responding to some magic blow.[78]

LUCIAN. Certainly, the name expresses the greatest possible separation of the finite from the finite, [that is, the separation of objective cognition from its immediate object, the body, which is its coming to itself as infinite, or what we call consciousness].

BRUNO. Would you care to elaborate upon this concept of the self? [289]

LUCIAN. What we call the self is just that identity of the ideal and the real, or of the finite and the infinite; this identity, however, is its own proper deed, and its alone. The act that constitutes the self is, at the same time, its very self; accordingly, it is nothing independent of this act of constituting itself, nothing outside of its own deed; rather, it exists only for itself and through itself.[79] And the self's nature also explains why things that are intrinsically eternal end up located in objective, temporal cognition, where they are determined by time; this happens only because, [in consciousness,] infinite thought becomes its own object within the finite.[80]

BRUNO. But is not this objectification of infinite thought exactly what we have been calling the identity of the finite and the infinite?

LUCIAN. Necessarily, for we posit one and the same reality within finite cognition or in things and in the infinite concept of cognition; what we posit in each order is the same, only viewed from different sides, there objectively, here subjectively.

BRUNO. And the self consists in this way of being, at one and the same time, subjective and objective, or infinite and finite.

LUCIAN. Certainly.

BRUNO. Therefore the finite things of appearance exist only for the self and through the self, for you said they enter into temporal cognition only through the infinite being objectified within the finite.

LUCIAN. That is exactly what I maintain.

BRUNO. You see how closely we agree! The greatest division of the finite from the whole order of finitude occurs when the finite enters into union with the infinite, when finite [objective cognition] lives in direct fellowship, as it were, with the infinite [concept of cognition]. Since objective cognition is finite, the infinite can only actualize the infinite possibility contained in its thought in a finite manner, and what is infinitely exemplified in the infinite can be reflected only in a finite way within the finite. Hence what exists as a perfect identity of possibility and actuality in the eternal divides itself up and appears within the objective aspect of the self as actuality, [290] and in the subjective aspect as possibility, whereas in the self itself, the identity of the subjective and the objective is reflected as necessity, the abiding image of the divine harmony of things, and, as it were, the immovable reflection of the identity from which all things are derived.— Are you in agreement with me on this last point?

LUCIAN. Completely.

BRUNO. And for this very reason, must not all things known in finite cognition bear the stamp of the infinite, the region whence they are reflected? And shall we not recognize as well the mark of the finite, the [medium] in which they are reflected, along with that of the third [potency, the eternal]? For, as we said earlier, what is first in the absolute necessarily becomes third in the derivative image world.

LUCIAN. Your conclusions seem indisputable.

BRUNO. We can, therefore, comprehend the laws and conditions for finite things, without having to extend our investigation beyond the question of the nature of knowing.[81] For do you not also share my conviction that we cannot rightly call either objective cognition or its counterpart 'knowing'?

LUCIAN. Rather, knowing consists in the identity of objective cognition and the concept of cognition.

BRUNO. Necessarily it does, for in every occurrence of knowing there are two components, an actual act of cognition and then the concept of this knowledge-act, to which the first is united; whoever knows also immediately knows that he knows, and this knowing that he knows and knowing about knowing that he knows are one, and they are directly united to the first act of knowing.[82] But the danger of infinite regress is eliminated, for the concept of knowing that is united to the first act of knowing is itself what is intrinsically and substantially infinite, and this concept of knowing is the governing principle of consciousness.

It would be worthwhile at this point, though, to examine each of the components of consciousness in itself, so that we can untangle these complicated relationships by developing them from within. So knowing, you said, consists in the identity of objective cognition with its infinite concept. But previously you equated objective cognition with intuition, and claimed it was necessarily finite, determined by time, and, in contrast to thought, [291] different [rather than indifferent. Well, this is all fine,] except that you can hardly posit sheer finitude or pure difference; when you do posit a finite entity, it is posited merely in contrast to another one. But the only man capable of unravelling the web of reality woven from the finite and the infinite is the one who comprehends the fact that everything is contained in everything, and who realizes how the abundance of the whole universe is stored in individual beings too.

[Since everything expresses the reality of the absolute in all its modes or under all three powers] intuition is all at once the finite, the infinite, and the eternal, except that they are subordinated to the finite as a whole. Now the finite aspect of intuition is that which corresponds to sensation, while the infinite aspect is the expression of self-consciousness inherent in it. Sensation as contrasted to awareness is necessarily difference; awareness as contrasted to sensation, indifference; sensation is the real element of intuition, awareness the ideal. But the aspect that identifies the real and the ideal, or unites difference and indifference, is what imitates the nature of the absolutely real or the eternal; [hence it is what is real and abiding in the act of intuition.] Now do you still believe you could oppose this eternal element in intuition to thought, as you did before, [when you defined absolute consciousness as the identity of thought and intuition]?

LUCIAN. I really do not see how that would be possible.

BRUNO. You did define intuition as difference, and thought as indifference, did you not?

LUCIAN. Certainly.

BRUNO. But that which does the intuiting in the act of intuition is neither difference nor indifference, [neither the sensation nor the bare awareness,] but rather the factor that identifies the two. How did it come about, then, that you were led to contrast intuition to thought, that you could suppose intuition was the real factor in the identity of the ideal and the real?

LUCIAN. [I do not quite understand your objection.] Explain it to me, would you please?

BRUNO. As I pointed out just now, you wanted to confine the identity of the ideal and the real to a single determinate point, [namely, consciousness,] and to make the real into the true opposite of the ideal. But this opposition of the real and the ideal is always and everywhere merely ideal, and intuition, which you defined as the real factor, is itself an identity of the real and the ideal; now what is truly real within intuition is just this identity itself, while what corresponds to the opposition of the real and the ideal in it is only an ideal determination of this truly real factor. [292] Thus you will never encounter anything purely real, as opposed to something purely ideal.

But in regard to intuition in particular, if you want to discover for yourself that you posit an identity of thought and being with each and every intuition, whatever it be, you need only ask yourself what you really intuit when you say you perceive a triangle or a circle or a plant. Without a doubt, what you intuit is the concept of a triangle, or the concept of a circle, or the concept of a plant, and you never intuit anything other than concepts. The reason that you call what is intrinsically a concept or mode of thought an intuition is that [when you are perceiving] you posit a thought within a being; but the intuiting agent whereby you posit some thought within some being cannot itself be either a thought or a being; it can only be that truly real element wherein thought and being are forever undistinguished.

Now it is the absolute identity of thought and being inside intuition that is the reason for the certainty of geometrical intuition. But in all types of intuition, the intuiting agent is in itself absolute reason, that which is incapable of any opposition between the universal and the particular, and apart from the distortion that is attached to it when it is reflected in the finite, reason is undisturbed identity, the highest possible clarity and perfection.

But what reflection adds to reason that distorts it when it functions as intuition is the relative opposition of the finite and the infinite, as we have already shown. When reason operates as intuition, the infinite factor is identity, the finite one, difference; the former is the expression of the concept in intuition, the latter the expression of the judgment. The infinite factor in intuition posits the first dimension of space; the finite one establishes [the difference] of the first and second dimensions. And it is the relative opposition between the infinite and the finite aspects in intuition that is responsible for what is opaque, empirical, and not pure space—for space itself is the pure identity of thought and being.

Yet the reason that the finite, the infinite, and the eternal are all subordinated to the finite in intuition lies solely in the soul's immediate relation to the body as an individual thing. For body and soul form one thing, and it is only in and through one another that they are separated from the totality of things; since this is so, from the viewpoint [293] of the infinite concept, it is all one and the same whether you define the body as a finite being or as the concept of a finite being. But since the concept of the body necessarily contains the concept of other things, this concept too, that is, the soul itself insofar as it is the concept of this individual existing thing, is determined by the concepts of other such things, and for this reason, the indivisible unity of the finite, the infinite, and the eternal in the soul is subordinated to the finite. And it is this intuition, subject to time and necessarily individual and divided from itself, that you opposed to thought.

Yet intuition, determined in this manner, is not truly intuition, but only a distorted and confused reflection thereof. Since this is so, it follows that the identity of thought and intuition you posited as your first principle is a particular and subordinate principle, one borrowed from mere experience. So, come now, abandon that narrow strand that you clung to before, when you tried to confine the supreme identity to the domain of consciousness! Venture with me upon the free ocean of the absolute, where we shall move with greater freedom, the more we come to directly know the heights and the depths of reason!

But for now we still have to discuss how the trinity of the finite, the infinite, and the eternal, which in intuition is subordinated to the finite power, is subordinated to the infinite in thought, but to the eternal within reason.

In each moment, only a portion of the entire universe falls within the scope of intuition, even though the concept of soul that is directly and organically joined to the soul is the infinite concept of all things. It is the separation of objective cognition [or representation of the body's states] from this infinite concept that establishes the individual's temporality. On the other hand, it is the relation of objective cognition to the infinite [concept or self-awareness] that produces knowing—not an absolutely timeless cognition, but a cognition that is valid for all time. Through being related to the concept, the act of intuition, including its finite, infinite, and eternal aspects, becomes infinite as well, and is transformed into an infinite capacity for acts of cognition. [But we distinguish three functions within this capacity, specified by the three potencies.] The infinite that is posited as infinite we call 'the concept,' [294] while the finite subsumed under the infinite generates the judgment, just as the eternal posited as infinite generates the syllogism.

Everything within this sphere of infinite cognition possesses infinitude, even if only the infinitude of the understanding. The concept is infinite, judgment is infinite, the syllogism is infinite. For all of these forms of thought are valid for all objects and for all time. But each of them must be examined more closely.

Now in intuition, the infinite aspect [or self-awareness] is the expression of the infinite concept of soul, and it is identical with the soul itself; in the concept it is once more posited as infinite. But the finite aspect of intuition, [namely sensation,] is the expression of the soul as the immediate concept of the body and as united to the body. And the eternal aspect of intuition is what identifies the two. Now, as we know, the infinite concept of soul comprises the endless possibility of all acts of intuition, the soul whose immediate object is the body comprises the finite and infinite actuality of those acts, while the eternal aspect that unites and identifies soul and the concept of soul comprises the infinite necessity of those acts of intuition. [Therefore, even on the level of intuition, the three potencies are expressed as possibility, actuality, and necessity, which Kant called the categories of modality. But these basic logical concepts are expressed on the level of the concept as well.]

Now since the concept is the infinitely posited infinite, it is the infinite possibility of discrete, differentiated acts of intuition, posited as *infinite.* The judgment, however, is the infinite determining of their actuality, since it infinitely posits the finite, while the syllogism is the infinite necessity of the different acts of intuition, since it infinitely posits the eternal.

But the concept is itself again a concept, [or a concept of a concept,] and thus it is the infinite possibility not just of the powers of the infinite, the finite, and the eternal as such, but of the infinite, the finite, and the eternal subordinated in turn to the infinite, the finite, and the eternal. Thus the three powers, permeating one another and multiplied by one another, determine the number of concepts.[83] [The powers themselves furnish the so-called categories of possibility, actuality, and necessity. When they modify one another, for example, when the infinite, the finite, and the eternal are all expressed in the finite power, they generate three others. The total number of concepts is nine.] Here is a web of concepts that is tightly woven and difficult to unravel, but if you will join forces with me in trying to disentangle it, I think we will reach our goal.

Now the concept's infinitude is merely an infinitude of reflection, although the schema of reflection is the line that implants time within the things that express it, and makes them animate and active; in objective cognition, this schema is time itself. [295] Since this is so, what kind of concepts do you think express the infinite, the finite, and the eternal when they are subordinated to the infinite?

LUCIAN. Temporal concepts, necessarily. And it seems to me they are determined in this way: The bare infinite possibility of time constitutes pure unity itself; the infinite and finite actuality of time is difference or plurality, while the whole actuality of time as determined by its infinite possibility is totality. [Thus the temporal concepts furnish us the categories of quantity, namely unity, plurality, and totality.]

BRUNO. Excellent! I don't suppose I need to make explicit to you that the first of these concepts corresponds to the concept itself or to quantitative indifference. The second corresponds to the judgment, since plurality involves the subsumption of what is differentiated under a unity, or the positing of indifference within difference. And the third, totality, stands related to the other two the same way the syllogism stands related to the concept and the judgment.

But it is obvious that unity is not unity, and plurality is not plurality, unless unity is posited within plurality, and plurality is assimilated to unity. And so totality, which unites the other two, is necessarily the first concept in this group, although it appears within reflection as the third. But if you remove the relativity that attaches to all things in reflection, you have the supreme concepts of reason—absolute identity, absolute opposition, and the absolute identity of identity and opposition which subsists in the totality of things.

Now if you subordinate the powers of the infinite, the finite, and the eternal to the finite potency, you generate the following concepts:

For reflection, [the sphere of the concept subordinated to finitude,] the endless possibility of all actuality comprises limitless reality, while the actuality of what is actual is located in something absolutely unreal, the mere limit or boundary, [which is pure negation]. But the actuality of what is actual as determined by its total possibility is that which unites boundless reality and the boundary [and gives rise to limited reality or determination]. This third concept, considered absolutely, is again the first; within intuition, it constitutes absolute space. But it is evident that, just as things were mainly determined for the concept by means of temporal concepts, [296] they are chiefly determined for judgment by means of spatial concepts. [The former furnish the categories of quantity: unity, plurality, and totality. The latter furnish those of quality: reality, negation, and determination.]

But the infinite and the finite bound together in the eternal must generate kindred pairs of concepts [when the three potencies are subordinated to the eternal], since the finite and the infinite are already united in the nature of the intrinsically and substantially eternal. This happens in such a way that, of the two concepts forming the pair, one necessarily partakes in the nature of the finite, and the other in that of the infinite.

So the form of the eternal expresses itself in the infinite potency through two concepts which we call 'substance and accident;' reflection understands them to be related in such a way that the first concept again expresses possibility, while the second expresses actuality; but both substance and accident taken together, as they in fact exist together, generate necessity.

But the eternal mirrors itself within the finite potency by means of the concepts of cause and effect; reflection interprets the first as the bare possibility of causal efficacy, the second as the actuality thereof, and the two united as the necessity of causal connection. But in reflection, time intervenes between possibility and actuality, and it is solely in virtue of the concepts of cause and effect that things endure. Finally, the eternal expresses itself as necessity [in the third or eternal power] in the concept of a universal reciprocal determination of things, and this concept is the highest sort of totality that can be recognized within the domain of reflection. [And thus the eternal, or reason itself, grasped imperfectly within reflection, furnishes the categories of relation: substance and accident, cause and effect, and community or reciprocal determination.]

It has become clear, now, that the infinite, the finite, and the eternal as subordinated to difference, that is, to the finite potency, appear as space. In the same way, as subordinated to relative identity or to the infinite potency, they appear as time. And it is just as evident that the same unity when intuited under the form of the eternal, constitutes reason itself, and that the three powers manifest themselves as reason within the sphere of concepts. And from these facts too, we can readily discern both the identity and the difference of the three sciences of arithmetic, geometry, and philosophy.

Now it would be useless labor to elaborate the organic life of reason as it is reflected in the judgment, for it is the very same as it is in the concept, given our previous definition of the difference between concept and judgment.

But concerning the syllogism, the form of thought that infinitely posits the eternal, [297] just a few words will suffice. Since possibility, actuality, and necessity are already substantially identified within every syllogism, all further specification of the syllogism is limited to this: In every syllogism, the identity of possibility, actuality, and necessity is expressed either under the form of the infinite, or under that of the finite, or that of the eternal. The infinite form is the categorical syllogism, the finite is the hypothetical syllogism [which reasons from condition to conditioned], while the disjunctive syllogism best expresses the nature of the eternal [since it reasons from a totality of conditions, which, though they exclude one another, indeed do form a logical totality]. Despite all these differences, the major premise of every syllogism is categorical or infinite in comparison with the minor, the minor premise is hypothetical and finite, while the conclusion is disjunctive, since it unites both the major and the minor in itself [and thus forms a totality].

LUCIAN. How admirable are the workings of the understanding! And what a joy to explore with you the relationships between the three potencies and to recognize the stamp of the eternal in everything from the structure of corporeal things up to the forms of the syllogism! A pupil would lose himself in your course of study, since he would perceive in you the image of the most splendid and ever-blessed identity, in whose reflections the stars move themselves and run their prescribed course. Within this identity, all things are just what they appear to be, and necessarily so. And this necessity is not founded on appearance; its ground lies in the true nature of things, whose secret no one other than God possesses, and those among men who know him.

BRUNO. But in order to recognize the principles that govern things, those laws that are in God and that determine how things behave within appearance, it is important, above all, to know what belongs to reflection. If you know this, you will not act like those people who philosophize haphazardly, who randomly reject some features that belong to appearance, while accepting others as true; such a procedure disfigures philosophy, and the divine reality as well.

For some philosophers postulate the absolute, though they do not clearly apprehend its nature; they then make many other assumptions which they use to establish what they fondly call their 'philosophy,' but they fail to separate and distinguish what is true merely for appearances from what is true in the sight of God. Some even dig down underneath appearances [298] and postulate some primitive 'stuff,' to which they ascribe infinite multiplicity and the form of externality.[84] But absolutely, in the perspective of divine nature, nothing is external, either to itself or to that identity whence it derives its perfection, for this latter is the absolute identity of identity and opposition. Indeed, it encompasses opposition as well as identity, but an opposition that is absolutely identical to identity and is totally without time, so that in the domain of the absolute, there is never any division or separation, never any reflection.

Since the world of appearances is simply nothing in the sight of the absolute, other philosophers define this world as if it were opposed to the divine nature. [And herein they are closer to the truth,] for what we call the world of appearances is not the finite that is joined in a perfectly nonsensible way to the infinite within the idea; instead, it is a mere reflection of the finite as it subsists within the idea. For alongside the intelligible things, the true and substantial universe also includes the idea of the sort of being that was destined to perceive the universe through visible images. Thus the idea is indeed prior to the appearance world, though it does not precede it in time; it is similar to the universal light which is prior in nature, not in time, to the individual things it illuminates; though it be reflected by innumerably many things, each of which casts back its light according to its specific nature, light does not thereby become multiple; it gathers all these reflections together into its undistorted clarity. In the same way, the true world is not the world that the individual constructs for himself in reflection, having taken its idea from that which is above. The true world is the immovable and harmonious fire-heaven, suspended over everything and embracing everything.[85]

Well, my friend, at this point we have succeeded in showing how the finite, the infinite, and the eternal function within intuition, when subordinated to the finite potency, and how they function as thought, when subordinated to the infinite. And we have seen how all those concepts whereby things are universally and necessarily determined, and which therefore seem to precede their objects, arise from the connection of objective cognition to the infinite concept. But I don't suppose you would believe any more that things are determined apart from these concepts, would you? [299]

LUCIAN. I would never think that.

BRUNO. And since things cannot be separated from these conceptual determinations, in general, they are nothing apart from these concepts.

LUCIAN. Absolutely nothing.

BRUNO. And what did you call the identity of objective cognition and the infinite concept of cognition?

LUCIAN. Knowing.

BRUNO. And so these things would turn into nothing, if they were independent of this knowing?

LUCIAN. Utterly nothing. Things come to be only through knowing, and they are themselves this knowing.

BRUNO. Excellent! You see how we agree on all points. The whole world of appearances, therefore, is to be understood purely through knowing, considered for itself.

LUCIAN. That is true.

BRUNO. But from what sort of knowing are we to comprehend the world of appearances, from the type that is intrinsically real, or from the sort of knowing that pertains merely to appearances?

LUCIAN. Necessarily the latter, if, in general, both the opposition of finite and infinite cognition and their identification [in self-consciousness] pertain to appearances.

BRUNO. In light of the preceding, who could doubt it? A thoroughly subordinate mode of cognition holds sway throughout the whole sphere of knowing that we have just described—the knowing that is constituted by the relation of the finite, the infinite, and the eternal to the infinite power. We will call this sort of cognition 'reflection' or 'understanding.'[86]

LUCIAN. I am satisfied with the terms.

BRUNO. Shall we then count knowledge arrived at by means of syllogisms as reason's true cognition? Must we not instead regard it as merely a cognition mediated by the understanding?

LUCIAN. Apparently the latter.

BRUNO. Such cognition is nothing but the work of the understanding. For if you say that indifference inheres in the concept, but difference in the judgment, [300] while the identity of the two resides in the syllogism, even this last identity is one subordinated to the understanding. For reason indeed permeates all modes of cognition; within intuition, it is subordinated to the task of intuiting, and within the understanding, it is subordinated to understanding. And even if understanding and intuition are absolutely identical within reason, still in the syllogism they are united only for the sake of the understanding, for in the syllogism, the major premise corresponds to conceptual understanding, while the minor premise corresponds to intuition; the major is the universal, the minor the particular; in the course of the syllogism, however, they are pulled apart by the understanding, and are reunited in the conclusion solely for the sake of the understanding. Therefore it is a perfectly impious error to accept this form of reason that is subordinated to the task of understanding as reason itself.

LUCIAN. No doubt it is.

BRUNO. Now our forerunners gave the name 'logic' to the discipline that arises from the subordination of the whole of reason to the understanding. If we follow this usage, won't we be forced to view logic as merely a science of the understanding?

LUCIAN. Necessarily.

BRUNO. Then what hope is there for attaining philosophy for those who search for it in logic?

LUCIAN. None.[87]

BRUNO. So then, whatever science of the eternal you would obtain through this sort of cognition, it will be a knowledge limited to the level of the understanding, and it must forever remain so, mustn't it?

LUCIAN. We must believe so.

BRUNO. Now in the three forms of the syllogism, the absolute, considered from the side of form, [falls apart into three moments and] is reduced to an infinity of the understanding, a finitude thereof, and finally an eternity of the understanding; in just the same way, considered materially, the absolute is reduced within those syllogisms of reason made subservient to understanding, and it falls apart into soul, the world, and God; the understanding pictures these three moments as all separate and sundered from one another, which is the greatest possible disintegration of what is simply one within the absolute. Anyone who searches for philosophy in this mode of cognition, or who attempts to prove the eternal being of the absolute in this way or in any way whatsoever is on the wrong path.[88] We would have to judge that such a person has not even reached the doorstep of philosophy. [301]

LUCIAN. That is a fair judgment.

BRUNO. And furthermore, our verdict would have to be that what the greater part of previous philosophers, and almost all of those who call themselves philosophers today, have given out as a description of reason still falls within the sphere of the understanding. And so we shall have a place for the highest sort of knowing that is higher than they ever reached, for we posit reason as the sort of cognition whereby the finite and the infinite are seen within the eternal; we do not define it [the way mere logic would] as the cognition whereby the eternal is viewed within the finite or the infinite.

LUCIAN. I think you have proved our case.

BRUNO. But what do you think about this further issue: Can the highest sort of knowing be satisfied with merely viewing the finite as simply ideal, since the ideal is nothing other than the infinite itself? Or is it not rather the case that, since there is absolutely nothing outside of the eternal, it is as meaningless to talk about the finite being something for itself in the ideal order as it is to say it exists within the real?

LUCIAN. Indeed, that follows.

BRUNO. On our view, then, would an idealism that was idealistic only from the standpoint of the finite even deserve the name of philosophy?

LUCIAN. It does not look like it would.

BRUNO. But, in general, can any sort of knowledge be deemed absolutely true other than the sort that determines things just the way they are determined within the supreme indifference of the ideal and the real?

LUCIAN. Impossible.

BRUNO. My friend, everything that we call real in things is so through the things' participating in the absolute essence, but none of its images display it in its perfect indifference, except the one wherein everything attains to the same identity of thought and being that exists in the absolute, namely reason. It is reason alone that knows everything divine, for in knowing itself, it universally establishes its native indifference as the matter and form of all things. But never will anyone who cannot turn away from reflection attain to the intuition of reason's immovable identity. [302]

For the king and father of all things lives in eternal bliss, beyond all strife, more secure and more unreachable in his identity than in an unapproachable fortress.[89] But only for a person who more or less participates in this identity is it possible to perceive, even to some extent, the inner nature of this being that is in itself neither thought nor being, but simply the identity of the two. But still this inner mystery of the absolute's essence manifests itself even in the nature of finite things—the way he contains in himself nothing that is either a thought or a being, but is instead the identity of thought and being, set over them both, and untroubled by either of the two. Now, indeed, within reflection, the [indifferent] form of the absolute falls apart into the real and the ideal orders, but it is not as if they existed in the absolute previously; it should be recognized that the real and the ideal are elements in that which is their pure identity, though they are not themselves that identity.

Accordingly, to discern the eternal within things means to see thought and being united in them through its essence alone, but it does not mean positing concepts as effects of things, nor things as the effects of concepts; such a procedure puts one the greatest distance from the truth. For thing and concept are not united through the connection of cause and effect; they are united through the absolute, and, truly considered, they are but different aspects of one and the same thing. For nothing exists that is not expressed both finitely and infinitely within the eternal.

Nevertheless, it is difficult to express the inner essence of the eternal in mortal words, since language is derived from images and is created by the understanding. For we might seem to be correct in calling that which has no opposition in itself or above itself, but has all oppositions beneath itself, 'the existing one,' yet this peculiar instance of being includes in itself no contrast to knowing, and in every other context knowing is defined as the formal counterpart of being. For it belongs to the nature of the absolute that in it form is essential reality, and essential reality is form; now since the formal side of the absolute finds expression within reason as absolute knowing, its essential reality is expressed therein as well, and so, from the absolute point of view, there is no being that is left over as a remainder to be contrasted to knowledge. [303] Conversely, if we would attempt to define the absolute as absolute knowing, we could not do so without setting up an opposition between this absolute knowing and being, for, considered absolutely, true being is located only within the idea, and, conversely, idea is substance and being itself.

Again, it is only in relation to reason that the absolute can be posited as the indifference of knowledge and being, since only within this context can knowledge and being emerge as opposites. But the farthest removed from the true idea of the absolute are those philosophers who try to define the nature of the absolute as activity, in order to avoid speaking of it in terms of being.[90]

For the whole contrast between activity and being obtains only within the derivative image world, where, apart from the absolutely and sub-stantially eternal, the inner identity of the absolute's essence is perceived merely within the finite order, or within the infinite order, but in an equally one-sided manner in each of them, so that when reflection reunites the finite and the infinite worlds, identity is reborn as the [phenomenal] universe. But neither within the finite order nor within the infinite can the absolute be reflected without expressing the full perfection of its essential reality, and thus the identity of the finite and the infinite, reflected in the finite, appears as being, but in the infinite, it appears as activity. But this identity subsists within the absolute neither as being nor as activity, and expresses its reality neither under the form of finitude nor under that of infinitude, but under the form of eternity.

For within the absolute, everything is absolute, and so if the perfection of the absolute's essence appears in the real order as infinite being, and if it appears in the ideal order as infinite knowledge, then being is just as absolute within the absolute as is knowledge. And since each of them is absolute, neither of them is contrasted to an other outside of itself, but absolute knowledge is absolute being, and absolute being is absolute knowledge.

Since the boundlessness of the eternal essence is equally reflected in the finite and in the infinite, [304] both these worlds, into which appearance divides itself and within which it articulates itself, must have the same contents, since they form one reality. Therefore what is expressed in the finite or in being is one and the same as what is expressed in the infinite order or in activity.

Therefore what you perceive in the real or natural world as gravity is the same thing that is expressed in the ideal world as intuition, and the way finite things seem to be determined as relative identities and relative oppositions is one and the same with the way thought is determined as concept and judgment; in both cases, it is the separation of the universal and the particular, [occasioned by reflection,] that is responsible. Neither is the ideal as such the cause of any determination within the real order, nor is the real the cause of any determination within the ideal. Since the dignity of being a principle can be ascribed neither to the ideal nor to the real, neither of them is of higher value than the other, and neither of them can serve to explain the other; on the contrary, the orders of knowledge and of being are simply different aspects reflected from one and the same absolute.

And so the identity that underlies the opposition of the universal and the particular in things, and the very same opposition within knowledge as well, is truly and in itself neither being nor knowledge, if you conceive one in contrast to the other. But within each of these orders or worlds, whether it be the real or the ideal, where the absolute identity of opposites obtains, there is expressed, within the real itself or within the ideal itself, the full indifference of knowledge and of being, and this indifference is the same as the indifference of form and essential reality [within the absolute itself].

Now when the eternal identity of the finite and the infinite is reflected within the ideal order or in thought, it seems extended over a time span that is without beginning or end, but when it is reflected within the real order or in the finite, its identity is displayed perfectly, directly, and necessarily as space. And though it appears merely within the real order, still it shines forth as the identity of knowledge and of being.[91] For, on one hand, space, in its supreme transparency and rest, seems to be the highest type of being, that is, being which is self-grounded and perfect, and which never steps beyond its bound and never acts, but, on the other hand, space is at the same time absolute intuition, supreme ideality. And thus, whether you view it from the subjective side or from the objective, [305]—in its own perspective, this opposition is totally abolished—space is the supreme indifference of being and activity.

Moreover, among finite things, activity stands related to being the way soul does to body, and so, even if absolute cognition eternally exists in God and is God himself, it still cannot be conceived as an activity. For in him, soul and body, and thus activity and being themselves, all of these are forms that are subordinated to him, not inherent within him; and just as the absolute's essential reality, when reflected in the order of being, is the infinite body of the universe, the same essence reflected in thought or in activity, in the shape of infinite cognition, then, is the infinite soul of the world. Within the absolute, however, neither can activity obtain as activity, nor being as being.

If you could find the right words for expressing an activity that is as motionless as the deepest rest, and for a rest that is as energetic as the peak of activity, you would manage to some extent to approximate in concepts the nature of that most perfect being.

Yet it is just as unsatisfying to view the finite, the infinite, and the eternal within the real order as it is to perceive them within the ideal, and if someone does not intuit them within the eternal, he never beholds truth in and for itself.

But the division of the real and ideal worlds [that occurs within reflection], whereby the first expresses the complete reality of the absolute within the finite dimension, and the second expresses it within the infinite, also implies a division of the divine principle of things from their natural principle. And indeed, what pertains to the natural principle appears passive, while what belongs to the divine appears active, and so corporeal substances seem to fall within the domain of the natural principle on account of their passive and receptive nature, while light seems to be classed with divine things, because of its creative and active nature.

[But this contrast between passivity and activity, the natural and the divine, the real and the ideal, has no ultimate truth, since all oppositions are identified within the eternal.] Even the individual entity directly expresses the nature of the absolute in its very mode of being, whether it is located in that world subjected to the finite or in that subjected to the infinite; we can as little understand the individual entity as mere being or as mere activity as we can understand the absolute as merely one or the other. Now in the type of individual thing where soul and body are posited as equal and identical factors, there exists a copy of the idea, and just as the idea is being and essential reality itself in the absolute, [306] so too, in an individual of this type, this image displays the indifference whereby form is also substance and substance is form.

Among real things, the organism is this sort of individual entity, while in the ideal order, the beautiful work created through artistry is of this same type. For in the organism, light, or the eternal idea expressed within the finite, serves as the divine principle and is united to matter, the natural principle, but in the work of art, the divine principle is the light of this light, that is, the eternal idea expressed in the infinite order.[92] However, since the organism necessarily must appear as an individual thing, it forever stands in the same relation to absolute identity that bodies do inasmuch as they are heavy, namely, a relation of difference. Although activity and being are indeed always posited as identical in its mode of being (so that what acts is what exists, and, conversely, what exists is what acts), insofar as the organism is an individual entity, this identity is not self-achieved; rather, it is effected in the organism by an external identity, to which it is related as the ground of its existence. Therefore the two aspects of being and activity do not seem to coincide in a state of optimum rest within optimum activity in the organic being; they only converge upon causal agency, a state that is intermediate between being and activity, and an element common to both.

But the [ideal] world, where being seems to be established through activity, and where the finite is posited by the infinite, seems to stand opposed to the realm of nature, where activity arises in and through states of being, and the latter is considered simply as the world, the former as a realm constructed through freedom, the city of God, as it were.

By opposing nature and the world of freedom in this way, men became accustomed to viewing nature as if it were outside of God, and God as if he were outside of nature. And to the extent that they banished divine necessity from nature, they subjected nature to the unholy necessity they call 'mechanism,' and precisely by doing so, they turned the ideal world [of their deeds and social institutions] into the stage for a spectacle of lawless freedom.[93] At the same time, since they had defined nature in terms of inert and passive being, they thought they earned the right to define God (whom they exalted above nature) as pure activity, pure actuousity—as if the one of these concepts did not stand or fall with the other, neither having intrinsic truth.

Yet if you try to tell these people that nature is not extrinsic to God, [307] but has its being within God, they take 'nature' to mean the nature they have deprived of life by separating it from God; they think nature is something independent, or that it is really something other than its own self-effected creation.

But neither the natural portion of the world nor the free part are anything independent of the absolute, wherein they are not merely united, but are instead simply undistinguished. But it is impossible that they subsist inside their identity in the same way they exist outside of it, the one through mechanical necessity, the other through freedom. Nature, therefore, does not fall outside the province of the supreme power, the true God, nor does God transcend the true realm of nature.

Now within our own lives, we experience this indivisible identity of God and nature as destiny, but to behold it in direct, supersensible intuition is to be initiated into the supreme bliss, which is to be found only in the contemplation of the most perfect.

Now I think I have done what I promised you I would do, namely, disclose the groundwork of the true philosophy; I have done this only generally, and as far as my powers permit, but in different guises I have always sketched for you the figure of the one sole object of philosophy. [There are other questions that remain, for example,] how to proceed to build from these foundations, how to bring the sacred seed of philosophy to its fullest flower, how to cast such a doctrine into a form appropriate to it—but you may pursue these questions on your own.

ANSELM. But, my good man, it seems to me that we very much have to trouble ourselves about this detail of the forms of philosophy. For philosophy is not simply the endeavor to understand the supreme reality by means of universals alone; it attempts to portray this reality in strong, enduring lines, and with unwavering steadiness and lucidity, the way nature does. This is what elevates art to the status of art, and science to that of science; it is what distinguishes them from amateurism. And especially if a discipline's subject matter is most noble and splendid, as is philosophy's, as long as it lacks enduring form and shape, it will not escape corruption. [308] And though perhaps the least perfect forms have perished and the noble matter once bound to them has been set free, that matter must still be alloyed with what is base, be sublimated, and finally made wholly unrecognizable, [before it can reach its true shape], for philosophy is forever challenged to assume more enduring and less changeable shapes.[94]

But it seems that the metal of philosophy has never been more subjected to the whirl of change than in our time and among our people, an age which, at the same time, strives for the eternal and unchanging with the noisiest commotion. For while some people locate the matter of philosophy in what is simplest and least divisible, for others it has been transformed into water, for others into arid sand, and for still others it has become even thinner, more transparent, and more inconstant.

Thus it is hardly surprising that most people think philosophy incapable of anything but meteoric appearances, and that even the greatest forms of philosophy share the fate of the comets, for the common man does not count them among the enduring and eternal works of nature; he thinks instead they are just transitory apparitions of fiery vapors.

Furthermore, most people simply assume that there can be different philosophies, and that everyone who attempts to philosophize will necessarily have his own particular philosophy.[95] But overpowering time strikes down all who would produce an idiosyncratic philosophy; it forges them into one and the same chain, where each can move only as far as the chain will reach; whoever wants to stray the farthest, falls most profoundly under the rule again.

When closely examined, all these particular philosophies are seen to suffer from the same defect: They recognize only one mode of cognition as valid, one that reasons from effects back to causes. And since they are oriented solely toward the form of reason that toils in the service of the understanding, and they think they have proven that reason itself falls into unavoidable fallacies and empty contradictions, they feel justified in turning their fear of reason into the content of philosophy itself.[96] But if they would step beyond these limits, nothing would make them quake and tremble so much as the sight of the absolute, [309] except the prospect of attaining a categorical and apodictic sort of knowledge. Philosophers such as this could not take a single step forward from their standpoint without abandoning the finite and reasoning beyond it, something that must necessarily happen, if they are to arrive at anything that possesses being absolutely and through itself. But what such minds posit as the absolute would not turn out to be absolute, since they would always feel they had to posit some opposite along with it. And again, they could not conceive of any relation between their supposed absolute and its opposite other than that of cause and effect.[97] And so under all these forms, the sole origin and impulse [of pseudophilosophy] repeats itself, namely, the effort not to acknowledge the identity of the factors that lie separated in the understanding, the effort to turn the innate and insurmountable self-estrangement of the understanding into philosophy itself.[98]

All this applies to the rabble that 'philosophizes' today. Even the better achievements that the age has brought forth, those that it holds in highest esteem, reduce, for the most part, to a mere negativity, both in their style of presentation and their intellectual comprehension. They try to completely explain the finite from the side of form alone, although the eternal does not obstinately reject matter. Their whole philosophy consists in a demonstration that the sensible world, which certainly is nothing, is actually nothing, and this philosophy, categorical only in relation to the 'nothing,' they call idealism.

But the grand and true forms of philosophy have disappeared, more or less. Philosophy's subject matter is by its nature perfectly simple and indivisible, and only to the extent that a given form of philosophy embodies this simplicity will its contents be true and correct. Just as the earth's one center of gravity can be viewed from the four different directions of the compass, and just as the one primal matter shows itself in four metals, equally noble and equally indissoluble, so also has reason preeminently expressed its indivisible simplicity in four forms, which demarcate, as it were, the four directions of the world of philosophy. For the doctrine our contemporaries have labeled materialism seems to belong to the western hemisphere, while what they call intellectualism pertains to the Orient; and the southerly regions we can call the territory of realism, and the northerly ones, that of idealism. But the task which calls for our greatest effort is that of recognizing the one metal of philosophy, self-identical in all these forms, in the purity of its native state. [310] And I believe it is crucial for someone who would transcend them to become acquainted with these particular forms of philosophy and with their fate, though the review of these positions would be pleasant for anyone who has already surpassed them. And so, if it is to your liking, here is what I propose: Alexander should trace the history of that philosophical doctrine that recognizes the eternal and divine principle in matter, while I shall relate the essentials of the doctrine of the intellectual world; then Lucian and you, Bruno, can bring the contrasting positions of idealism and realism into our inquiry.

For it seems to me that we shall shape the edifice of our discussion into a perfect four-part vault when we show how the one idea, which we have learned is to be placed ahead of all others in philosophy and is to be sought above all else, was at the basis of all these types and systems, for reason expresses itself in a variety of shapes as it appears in [the history of] philosophy.

ALEXANDER. My friends, I can be quite brief about the fate of that teaching which borrows its name from matter, for its fate is the same as that which every other speculative doctrine has experienced over the course of time.[99] Its decline had its roots in the decline of philosophy itself. For what little the ancient tradition has handed down about the meaning of this doctrine is sufficient to inform us that it contained, in more or less developed fashion, the core of the highest speculative wisdom.

But in very early times, the true idea of matter was lost, and in succeeding ages, it was known to but a handful of men. For, in truth, matter is itself the identity of the divine and the natural principle, and thus absolutely simple, unchangeable, and eternal.

The successors of the ancient materialists, particularly Plato, understood by 'matter' the bare subject [or substrate] of natural, changeable things, and this is absolutely not the sort of thing that could be made into a philosophical principle. But what the founders of this doctrine called matter was the one reality that transcends all opposition, that within which the natural and the divine aspects of things first distinguish themselves and enter into opposition with one another.

Still later ages have confused 'matter' with 'body,' [311] and mingled that which is in its nature destructible and changeable with what is indestructible and immortal. And once this confusion occurred, it became easy to take raw inorganic stuff as the model of matter instead of the true, primitive matter. [Thus our common notion of matter is quite mistaken,] for we locate it under the concept of the inorganic, after we have already divided the organic and the inorganic; instead we ought to locate the idea of matter at the point where the organic and the inorganic are together and are identical. But precisely for this reason, this point is not to be seen with sensible eyes, but only with the eyes of reason.

We may picture the way all things issue from this unity in the following way: In itself, matter lacks all multiplicity. It contains all things in an undivided and therefore indiscriminable manner, as if they were one infinite self-enclosed possibility. Now the factor whereby all things are identical is simply matter itself, but that whereby they are different, and whereby each one is separate from the others, is form. Now the forms of things are all perishable, not eternal. The form of all forms, however, is eternal, and it is just as imperishable as is matter itself; this is the necessary or first form, and since it is the form of all forms, it is again identical with no particular form whatsoever. It is absolutely simple, infinite, unchangeable, and for just this reason it must be identical with matter. But this first form excludes no particular form, and so it is infinitely fruitful in forms, although matter is essentially barren. In picturing Eros as the child of Wealth and Poverty,[100] and in claiming that the world is created by him,[101] the ancients seem to have intimated just this relation that obtains between matter and the original form.

Thus the ancients located the infinite possibility of all forms and shapes within matter, yet matter is splendid in its poverty, and suffices for all alike. And since possibility and actuality are timelessly identical in the context of what is most perfect, so from all eternity all forms are expressed in matter and are actual at all times—or rather, are actual without any reference to time. [312]

Thus through the form of forms, the absolute can be all things, while through its essence, it is them all. Finite things as such are at each and every moment all that they can be at that moment, but not all that they could be according to their essence. For in each and every moment, the essence is infinite, and for that very reason finite things are entities whose form and essence are different, for their form is finite, their essence infinite. But the absolute, wherein form and essential reality are simply identical, is forever all that it can be, in every moment and all at once, without any temporal distinctions; there can be but one entity of this sort.

Through this same difference of essence and form, the existence of individual things becomes a temporal existence as well, for since in one part of their nature they are infinite, and in the other finite, the infinite part will comprise the possibility of everything potentially located in their substance, but the finite part will necessarily always be just a portion of that infinite possibility; thus arises the difference between form and essence in things. The finite part of a thing's nature can approximate its essential reality only in infinity. But this infinite finitude is time; the infinite aspect of a thing contains the possibility and the principle of time, while the finite aspect constitutes its actuality.

Now for itself the absolute is an absolute unity, perfectly simple, without any multiplicity, but with the differentiation of form and essence in things and the positing of time, the absolute passes over into appearance and becomes an absolute unity of multiplicity, the enclosed totality of things we call the universe. And so totality is unity, and unity totality, not differentiated, but one and the same.

Though we certainly might have described the form of forms by the terms 'life' or 'world-soul,' as others do, we wanted to avoid the misconception that the form of forms as soul of the universe would be opposed to matter in the way people usually oppose soul to body. So we must emphasize the fact that matter is not the body, but that wherein both the soul and the body exist. For the body is necessarily mortal and destructible, while the essential reality is immortal and indestructible. Considered absolutely, the form of forms is not opposed to matter, but identical with it, although in conjunction with an individual it necessarily and always posits some opposition, [313] since the individual is never wholly what it can be; the opposition it establishes is that of the infinite and the finite, that is, of soul and body.

Hence soul and body are themselves comprehended in that form of all forms, but this first form is everything, since it is simple, and for the very reason that it is everything, it can be nothing in particular; it is simply identical with the essential reality. Hence the soul is necessarily to be classified beneath matter [as one of its species], and it is on this level that it is opposed to the body.

In this way, as we have explained, all forms are innate in matter, for in all things, form and matter necessarily comprise one thing. This fact has moved some philosophers, who noticed how matter and form seek each other in all things, to express this truth pictorially: Matter, they said, desires form the way woman desires man, and is passionately attached to it.[102] But since, absolutely considered, matter and form are completely undifferentiable, others have followed the lead of the Pythagoreans, who called the monad the father and the dyad the mother of all numbers,[103] and they called form the father of things and matter their mother. They did so because matter appears receptive of difference when it is expressed within the finite order and becomes body, while it appears as a unity when it is expressed within the infinite and becomes soul. Of course, the point where matter and form are perfectly identical, where soul and body are themselves indistinguishable within form, is located above and beyond all appearances.

And now that we have succeeded in understanding how soul and body can be differentiated from one another within the unity of matter, we also grasp the fact that there is no limit to the elaboration of this opposition; but whatever excellence the soul and body might acquire in this elaboration, still this development occurs only within the all-encompassing and eternal principle of matter.

There is one light that illuminates all things, and one force of gravity that teaches bodies to fill space, and thus lends existence and essence to the creations of thought. Light is the day of matter, and gravity the night. And just as its day is infinite, so too is its night. [314] Within the universal life of matter, no form is generated in an external fashion, but only through the inner, living artistry that is inseparable from matter's essential reality. All things have one destiny, one life, one death. No one thing takes precedence over its fellows, for there is but one world, one plant, as it were, wherein everything that exists is merely leaves, or blooms, or fruit, differentiated not according to essence, but only according to rank; there is but one universe, and everything within it is splendid, truly god-like, and beautiful; but in itself, it is uncreated and equally eternal with absolute identity itself, since it is the latter's unfading and only-begotten offspring.

Since at every moment the universe is complete and perfect, its actuality perfectly proportioned to its potentiality, with never a lack or a defect, there is nothing at hand that could tear it from its immortal rest. It lives with an unchangeable and eternally self-identical being. All activity or motion is really only a mode of considering individual entities, and as such, it is but an elaboration of this absolute being which wells forth from its profound rest.

[Neither can the universe be moved, then] nor can it move itself, for it would have to move itself within space and time, but it contains all space and time, and is itself comprehended in no portion of space and in no temporal duration. [And if it cannot change its external configuration,] it cannot change its inner shape either, for all metamorphosis of forms, all enrichment or debasement of forms, pertains to the viewpoint of individual entities, just as change or motion does. If we could behold the universe as a whole, what would appear before our charmed and intoxicated eyes would be one steady face, unchangeably serene and self-identical.

But of that cycle of change and interaction [we see manifested in finite things and] which holds its being in and with the absolutely unchanging, we cannot say either that it had a beginning or that it had no beginning. For the whole order of change depends upon the eternal, not in the sense that it succeeds it in time, but in its very nature. Hence it is not finite according to temporal duration, but finite in its concept, and that means it is eternally finite. But no time span can ever measure this eternal finitude, whether it be a time that had a beginning or a time without a beginning.

But time, which has slain everything, and the culture of our era in particular—this age that has taught men to divorce the finite from the infinite, the body from the soul, the natural from the divine, [315] and to exile the sundered members to two totally different worlds—these two have killed the teaching of the eternal nature of the universe.[104] They have flung it into the common grave they dug for nature and have brought about the death of all science.

Once matter was killed and its bare image replaced the [living] reality, the notion almost automatically evolved that forms are all impressed upon matter from without. And since forms were thought to be purely external, and since there was thought to be nothing eternal over and beyond them, the forms had to be posited as unchangeable. In this way, the inner unity and affinity of all things was annihilated, and the world fragmented into an endless aggregate of fixed differences, until the general conception finally prevailed that the living totality of the universe is like a receptacle or chamber, in which things are placed in such a way that they do not participate in one another, nor live in community with each other, nor interact with each other.

Since men agreed that, in the beginning, matter was dead, it was decided that death was the principle governing all things, and that life was just a derivative phenomenon.

And after matter had succumbed to death, nothing remained but to banish the last witness to its vitality, that is, to transform light, the universal spirit of nature, the form of forms, into an equally corporeal entity, to divide it up [into particles, and to explain it] mechanistically, just like everything else. Now since life was extinguished in all the members and organs of the universe, since even the living manifestations that connect bodies to one another were reduced to lifeless motions, there now remained only the final and grandest task, namely, to bring nature, already dead in its innermost parts, back to life again, mechanistically.[105] Succeeding ages gave the name 'materialism' to this endeavor. One would think that the insanity of the project would have served to turn those who realized it back to the doctrine's original source, but instead it served to confirm the death of matter, to set it beyond all doubt. This mechanistic materialism has brought about such a crudity in our understanding of nature and its beings that it makes what we would otherwise call barbaric peoples look civilized when they worship the sun and the stars, or beasts, or individual natural objects! [316]

But life can never be absent from the universe, nor can it totally flee from the thoughts of men, and so, merely exchanging one form for another, life directly took flight from the realm of nature to an other, apparently different, world. Thus from the decline of the materialistic philosophy immediately issued a renewed life for that age-old doctrine of the intellectual world.

ANSELM. My friend, you are right in extolling the great age of this doctrine that all things in the universe possess their existence only through the causation and participation of natures more perfect and more excellent than they are.[106] And anyone who has reflected on the fact that knowledge of eternal things is found only among the gods would have good reason to surmise that this teaching stems from those ages when mortals kept company with the gods, for both in its place of origin and in those lands where it was first disseminated, this teaching was neither separated from the worship of the gods nor divorced from the conduct of a holy life, one in conformity with knowing them.

My friends, the hierarchy of being is threefold. The first level is that of appearances; they are nothing intrinsically real or true, for they depend upon the unities or monads that occupy the second rank. But each of these monads is but a living mirror of the archetypal world, which is indeed the sole reality.[107]

All true being, therefore, is located solely in the eternal concepts or in the ideas of things. The only idea that is truly absolute, however, is the sort of archetype which is not just a pattern for producing a copy in another medium, one that stands over against it as an opposite, but an archetype which is capable of uniting both exemplar and copy within itself. Every being that is an image of such an archetype directly receives both identity and opposition from it, but with a limited degree of perfection; it takes its soul from the exemplary aspect or pattern, but its body from the imaged aspect or antitype. But this latter, since it is eternally united to the exemplary aspect, is infinitely expressed within that union, and although it is finite, it is free of the disadvantages of finitude.

Thus the idea or absolute identity is what is unchangeable and not subject to duration; [317] it is substance, absolutely considered, and what we commonly call substance must be viewed as a mere reflection of the idea's substance.

But the monads or unities are derived from the ideas, for if we look to that which functions as substance in them, that is, to that which is intrinsically substance, the monads are the ideas themselves; but if we look to the element whereby they are individuated and separated from the identity of all things, this individuating factor is necessarily changeable, mortal, and destructible. But their substantial element endures even within appearances, namely the ideas insofar as they constitute what is real in the monads; thus the monads are like corporeal substances which endure, however much their form varies; essentially neither increased nor diminished by such changes, they are true to the nature of the unchangeable.

Therefore, if the idea is an infinite unity of the exemplary and the real worlds, a derivative unity or monad is generated from it when a concept chooses one individual from among the infinite abundance of the world of copies and connects itself to that object, and when it connects itself to an individual in this way, it stands related to it as soul does to body. Now the greater the portion of the antitypal world that is bound into this individual, the more the concept is able to intuit the whole universe within this individual, and to the extent that this happens, the individual copy or antitype approximates the nature of the exemplar, and thus the monad approaches the perfection of the idea, or substance.

But the element in the monad that serves as antitype or copy always and necessarily has a determinable nature, while its counterpart, the exemplary factor, has a determinative one. Now within the idea of all ideas, these two aspects are absolutely identical, and since this idea is the life of all life, the action of all action, (for, since it is action itself, it cannot be said to act) we can view the antitypal element as will, but the exemplary one as thought. And so, since there is a determinable element and a determinative one in everything, the former is the expression of the divine will, the latter of the divine understanding. Yet will and understanding have being, the one as well as the other, only insofar as they are manifested in created things; [318] they have no intrinsic being. But what unites the determining element in a thing with the determinable one is the imitation of the absolute substance itself, or the idea.

Now it is impossible to say where the realm of exemplars ends and where that of copies begins. For in the idea, each of the two is infinitely joined to the other, and, as a consequence, they necessarily belong together unto infinity, and [if they cannot be distinguished in the idea,] they cannot be dissociated in any given thing. Therefore what from one perspective seems to be the determinable element of a thing will in itself be a unity similar to that of an archetype, while what appears to be the determinable component of this unity will turn out to be, when considered in its essence, yet again a mixed unity of the determinable and the determinative. [From the first, it follows that the bodily elements of a thing are themselves monads, and from the second, that any apparently bodily segment of a thing is itself a monadic organization of lesser bodies.] For actuality within the world of copies is just as infinite as possibility is within the exemplary world; ever tighter connections arise between the two which link possibility in the copy world with actuality in the world of patterns. Accordingly, the more the determinable [or bodily] aspect of a being partakes of the infinite nature of the determinative, the more that being expresses the coincidence of possibility and actuality. And so no proof is neeeded to show that organized bodies, especially those that are most articulated and organic, are the most perfect things that we classify as determinable.

Now inasmuch as soul is immediately only the bare unity of a body which is necessarily individual and finite by its very nature, its representations are necessarily confused, indistinct, and inadequate. For in this capacity, substance [or the idea] does not appear as it is in itself; instead it appears only in relation to the contrast of the determinative and the determinable, not as their absolute identity, therefore, but as their finite conjunction.

The idea itself, however, or the substance of both soul and body, enters into an external relation to absolute substance because of the connection of soul to body, for this connection determines that the idea's cognition be limited first to the body and the soul, then to other things that are bound up with the concept of the body; in this way, the idea is subjected to time and duration. But the connection of soul and body also determines the idea's knowledge of itself, for it recognizes itself, absolute substance, only [externally or] as the ground of being, [319] and it perceives itself as such equally in itself and in other things outside itself; such a limited state, however, is the direct opposite of perfect cognition. For just as the idea itself is only an image of the true unity when it is conjoined to the determinate unity of body and soul, in like manner it becomes an image of all that is real in other things. In this way, the world of appearances arises from the monads.

But considered in itself, apart from the opposition of soul and body, every monad is perfect and is itself absolute substance, for substance is not relatively, but absolutely and intrinsically indivisible. Within each monad, it is the same identical absolute wherein possibility and actuality are one, and since substance is one by its very concept, and thus prohibited by its nature from participating in quantity, each of the monads is a perfect and self-sufficing world. There are as many worlds as there are monads, but since each one is equally complete and each one is intrinsically absolute, they are not differentiated from one another, but instead they form the one world.

Now if we look to what makes a monad independent and substantial, we see that it can admit nothing external. For, insofar as it is substance, the monad is absolute identity itself, that which comprehends everything in itself and produces everything out of itself, that which is never divided, the way even the forms of things are divided. Hence the productive agent in each and every monad is itself the perfection of all things, though there is also a limiting and individuating principle, which transforms what is eternal in the monad into a temporal series.

For the substantial element in each monad represents the universe in an eternally identical manner, while its particular nature reflects only as much of the absolute identity as is expressed in the monad through the relative opposition of soul and body. And since the degree of this relative opposition determines the greater or lesser perfection of both body and soul, each monad [more or less perfectly] represents the universe in a temporal manner, depending on the level of its development; thus each monad contains as much of the universe as is established in it by the individuating principle. In the same way, [320] each monad determines the ratio of its passivity to its activity, inasmuch as [in its particularity] it withdraws from fellowship with the eternal, where the ideas of all things subsist without affecting each other, each one perfect, all of them equally absolute.

Hence no substance, as substance, can undergo causal influence from any other substance, nor can it act upon another itself, for, as such, each substance is indivisible, complete, absolute, the one substance itself. The relation of soul and body is not that of one distinct item to a second; it is a relation of one identity to another, each of which, considered in itself, represents the whole universe according to its own particular nature. The one is not connected to the other through the law of cause and effect; rather, their respective representations of the universe agree in virtue of the eternally established harmony of things. But a body, as such, is moved by another body, for bodies pertain only to appearances. In the true world, however, there is no transition [from rest to motion, or vice versa], for what is substantially real there is unity, and unity, truly considered, is as little capable of being causally affected as it is in need of it; eternally self-identical, it continually creates the infinite out of the infinite.

But the One which possesses being absolutely is the substance of all substances, which is called 'God.' The unity of its perfection is the general locus of all the monads or derivative unities, and the absolute substance stands to these derivative ones the way its image within the realm of appearances, infinite space, stands to bodies, where, unaffected by the boundaries of individuals, it pervades all.

Only insofar as the monads' representations are imperfect, limited, and confused do they picture the universe as outside of God and as related to God merely as its ground, but insofar as their representations are adequate, they represent the universe in God. God is thus the idea of all ideas, the cognition of all acts of cognition, the light of all light. All things are derived from him and to him they return. For the world of appearances is only within the monads, and is inseparable from them, for only insofar as they perceive a distorted reflection of absolute identity is the universe in them in a sensible manner, composed of isolated things that are transitory and incessantly changing. But then again, only insofar as they produce the world of appearances [321] are the monads themselves separated from God; in themselves, they subsist in God and are one with him.

My friends, this exposition has touched only on the major points of the doctrine of the intellectual world, yet I believe it is sufficient to prove that this form of philosophy too leads back to the one absolute, which we have determined is the locus of everything that has being, wherein everything subsists without opposition, and in which alone is the perfection and the truth of all things to be intuited.

BRUNO. My friends, you intended that we consider the contrast of realism and idealism. The task still lies ahead of us, though the time draws near for us to part. So let us try to comprehend the most within the least, Lucian. Imagine yourself posing the question which is most basic to our inquiry: What sort of realism must be opposed to idealism, and what kind of idealism must be contrasted to realism?

LUCIAN. Before anything else, it seems we must state, in general, how idealism and realism can be distinguished. Since both aim at the highest sort of knowledge, and since this knowledge is necessarily just one thing, they cannot be distinguished through their objects. And if this knowledge is not of the speculative sort, either in one of them or in both, then in the first case, no comparison between them would be possible, and in the second case, it would not be worth the trouble to investigate their difference. But the one sole object of philosophy is the absolute.

BRUNO. Hence both for realism and idealism, the absolute is identically the object of the highest mode of knowledge.

LUCIAN. Necessarily.

BRUNO. Do you suppose, then, that their difference lies in the way they consider the absolute?

LUCIAN. I think so.

BRUNO. But how? Is there some difference or duality within the absolute? Isn't it necessarily and absolutely one, instead?

LUCIAN. There is no duality within the absolute itself, however there is one in the way we view it. [322] For insofar as we look to what is real in the absolute, we arrive at realism, but if we keep our eye on what is ideal, idealism results. Yet within the absolute itself the real is also the ideal, and conversely, the ideal is the real.

BRUNO. It looks like you will have to define what you mean by 'the real' and 'the ideal,' for, as we know, these terms are subject to quite different interpretations.

LUCIAN. For the purpose of this inquiry, then, let us take 'the real' to mean essential reality, and by 'the ideal' let us generally understand form.

BRUNO. So realism would arise from reflection upon the absolute's abiding reality, while idealism would result from fixing our gaze on the absolute's form.

LUCIAN. That is true.

BRUNO. But how is this possible? Did we not say that form and essential reality are necessarily identical within the absolute?

LUCIAN. With the very same necessity whereby essential reality is distinguished from form in finite things.

BRUNO. But how are they identical?

LUCIAN. Not by being joined or connected; instead each is for itself the very same thing, namely the whole absolute.

BRUNO. Then insofar as the one views the absolute in terms of essential reality, and the other in terms of form, necessarily and without contradiction realism and idealism consider one sole thing under both aspects—if, in general, we can call it a 'thing.' They both have the same object.

LUCIAN. Evidently they do.

BRUNO. But how would one designate such an identity? How would you best express an identity whose basis is not so much a conjunction of factors as a perfect equality therof?

LUCIAN. Well, earlier, and quite appropriately, it seemed to me, we designated this sort of identity as 'indifference,' and thereby we exactly expressed the way that it is all the same whether we consider the absolute as form or as essential reality.

BRUNO. But if the contrast between idealism and realism is the supreme opposition that is to be found within philosophy, [323] does not our discernment of this indifference suggest a philosophy without any oppositions, philosophy pure and simple?

LUCIAN. Without a doubt.

BRUNO. Then let us inquire further into this highest of all mysteries. Did we not establish earlier that the absolute itself was neither one nor the other of all pairs of opposites, that it was sublime identity, utterly nothing other than itself, and so completely absolute?

LUCIAN. Certainly.

BRUNO. But we agreed too that its form was the identity of both the one and the other of all opposites, namely an identity of ideality and reality, of the subjective and the objective, both with equal infinitude?

LUCIAN. We agreed.

BRUNO. But every identity of the subjective and the objective, conceived as active, is a cognition.

LUCIAN. That is self-evident.

BRUNO. Hence a cognition that is equally and infinitely both ideal and real would be an absolute cognition.

LUCIAN. Quite certainly.

BRUNO. Furthermore, an absolute cognition is not a thinking as opposed to a being; rather, it includes both thought and being itself, already absolutely united within it.

LUCIAN. Unquestionably.

BRUNO. Absolute cognition thus has thought and being under itself as subordinate concepts, not above itself as superior ones.

LUCIAN. Inasmuch as thought and being are opposites, it is necessarily superior to both of them.

BRUNO. And this absolute cognition stands in a relation of absolute indifference to the essential reality of the eternal.

LUCIAN. Necessarily, since it is the absolute's form.

BRUNO. But since form comprehends both thought and being as its subordinates, it will be impossible for us to make either thought or being into an immediate attribute of the absolute itself, in its essential reality. [324]

LUCIAN. Impossible indeed!

BRUNO. Viewing the absolute from the side of form, could we consider a philosophy to be a perfect realism if it makes thought and extension the immediate attributes of the absolute?—For this is the way [Spinoza's philosophy] is usually understood, the system that in other respects is accounted the perfect realism.

LUCIAN. Never again could we consider it perfect.

BRUNO. But what about those [idealists] who some way or another make thought pure and simple their philosophical principle and absolutely oppose it to being? I say we would simply have to classify them as philosophical adolescents.

LUCIAN. Well said!

BRUNO. Must we not necessarily give this account of absolute cognition, that it is a cognition wherein thinking is immediately also the establishment of being, and the positing of being is a thinking as well? [Are we not better off making this positive statement] instead of saying that within finite cognition, being appears as the nonpositing of thought, and thought appears as the nonbeing of being?

LUCIAN. It seems inevitable.

BRUNO. And in describing it this way, do we not establish at the same time that this absolute cognition is absolutely identical, simple, sublime, free of all duality or self-estrangement? For there is no opposition of thought and being within it.

LUCIAN. I agree.

BRUNO. Hence within absolute cognition, thought and being exist only in potency, not in act. That from which something is cut off does not need to contain the excised portion, but it can exist in absolute simplicity, [and this is precisely how things stand between absolute cognition and thought and being as separated]. Precisely because it is absolute, this cognition necessitates a separation between thought and being when it is related to the finite or to appearances in general; otherwise, as absolute, it could not express itself in finite things. Yet thought and being are both originally posited in and through their separation from one another, and neither were they present before the separation, nor are they present as such within absolute cognition. [325]

LUCIAN. Since this is the nature of things, I cannot help but agree.

BRUNO. But within the finite as such, can thought and being ever again be absolutely identified? Won't any identity of them that occurs within the finite always be a relative identity?

LUCIAN. That seems to be a necessary conclusion, since the form of finitude depends on the opposition of thought and being.

BRUNO. But even within the finite, is there not necessarily one point where thought and being are absolutely united, even though they are not indivisibly one? Would that not be the point where the absolute's essential reality as expressed within the infinite is perfectly exhibited within the finite or in being?

LUCIAN. We have deduced such a point, namely the self. It is necessarily the place where infinite cognition as subjective is connected to something objective, which exhibits cognition's completely infinite possibility within itself as actuality. It is the point where the infinite is enfolded within the finite.

BRUNO. But its infinitude notwithstanding, the connection of infinite cognition to something objective which expresses it within the finite order is necessarily a connection to an individual. Hence only within the idea and within intellectual intuition is there an absolute identity of thought and being; factually, though, within finite actuality, such an identity is always merely a relative one.

LUCIAN. That is evident.

BRUNO. Now since we generally termed such a determinate identity of thought and being 'selfhood,' we can call the very same identity 'absolute selfhood' insofar as it is perceived in intellectual intuition, but 'relative selfhood' insofar as it is relatively apprehended.

LUCIAN. We need have no hesitations on that score.

BRUNO. Now within relative selfhood [or empirical consciousness], objects are indeed established through the conjunction of objectively posited cognition and the infinite concept of cognition, but this happens only in and for the self's finitude, which is endlessly posited and determined. In the relative self, the opposition of the finite and the infinite is cancelled only relatively; relative truths arise, which indeed are infinite knowledge, yet merely relative knowledge.

LUCIAN. We are in agreement on this point too. [326]

BRUNO. Even though things are endlessly determined for appearance, in absolute selfhood or in intellectual intuition, they are not determined for appearance, but they are determined in conformity with their eternal character, and absolute knowledge results.

LUCIAN. It must happen that way.

BRUNO. But inasmuch as finite objects are endlessly determined through mere relative knowledge, they have being solely through this knowledge and for this knowledge.

LUCIAN. Of course.

BRUNO. And if we wish to interpret 'ideality' in the usual sense of the term, as merely the opposite of sensible reality, then idealism is a doctrine which does nothing more than deny the reality of the sensible world. But if this is so, and if things are defined in terms of sensible reality, all philosophy is necessarily idealism, and is necessarily opposed to realism, taken in the common sense of the term.

LUCIAN. Necessarily.

BRUNO. [But let us discuss a more specific form of idealism, one that takes its stand in the limitations of empirical consciousness.] From the standpoint of the mere relative identity of subject and object, the absolute identity of subject and object seems something totally independent, something unreachable through knowledge. Only within ethical activity is this absolute identity adapted to the limited character it possesses inside relative knowledge, that is, it appears to be something objective and completely independent of this knowledge, for the objective aspect of that which ought to be done seems to be something that is simply not a matter of knowing, since (according to this idealism's presupposition) knowledge is conditioned, while 'the ought' is unconditional. The objective nature of the ought's command secures the relation of difference that obtains between the absolute, on the one hand, and the territory of knowledge and cognition on the other. Thus original reality is banished from the domain of relative knowledge to that of ethics, and, in light of this, speculation is forced to migrate to the land of duty. And here, for the first time, the identity of thought and being appears categorically and absolutely, but since an absolute harmonization of possibility and actuality is never possible within time, this identity is not absolutely established or posited, but just absolutely demanded. For ethical activity, absolute identity assumes the guises of command and the infinite ethical task, while for thought, it takes the shape of faith, the end of all speculation.[108]

LUCIAN. I cannot bring any objections against the correctness of your conclusions. [327]

BRUNO. Just as in the one case of ethical activity, where the absolute identity of thought and being exists only in the form of the command, so it is in general. [This idealism thinks that] wherever the identity of thought and being exists, within nature, for instance, it exists only through the ought and for the ought, for this identity is the original substance not only of all action, but of all being as well. But only for ethics does nature assume a speculative significance, for generally this idealism views nature as but a tool or a means for action: On this view, nature does not act for the sake of its own divinity; indeed it seems to lack all purposiveness, either in itself or outside itself; this philosophy considers nature dead, the bare object and material for an action which does not spring from nature itself and which is located beyond nature.

LUCIAN. It all follows, just as you say.

BRUNO. Now won't a philosophy that takes relative knowledge as its standpoint and basis perfectly exhibit the essence of ordinary consciousness? Will it not be in complete conformity with empirical consciousness, and yet, for that very reason, not be philosophy in the least?

LUCIAN. That is wholly certain.

BRUNO. Will not this sort of idealism that has lost sight of absolute identity necessarily be the opposite of realism? For instead of making the absolute indifference point its principle, it adopts subordinate and relative indifference points, and subjects being to thought, and the finite and eternal powers to that of the infinite.

LUCIAN. There will be an inevitable conflict between realism and this type of idealism, since realism bases itself on the absolute's essential reality, while this idealism can be equated with nothing other than [the absolute's form or] absolute cognition.

BRUNO. And for this very reason, wouldn't such an idealism have as its principle not the ideal in itself, but only the ideal as it presents itself in appearances?

LUCIAN. Necessarily, for an idealism that would adopt what is essentially ideal as its principle would see that it is beyond all opposition to realism.

BRUNO. But the pure subject-object, absolute cognition, the absolute self, the form of all forms, this is the absolute's only-begotten Son, equally eternal with the absolute, not different from its essential reality, but identical with it. He who has the Son has the Father, and only through the Son does one come to the Father, and the teachings that come from the Son are the very same as those of the Father.[109] [328]

To come to know this indifference within the absolute—that character whereby idea is substance, the absolutely real, whereby form is also essential reality and reality is form, each one inseparable from the other, whereby form and reality are not just perfectly similar likenesses, but directly are one another—this is to discover the absolute center of gravity. To know this is to uncover the original metal of truth, as it were, the prime ingredient in the alloys of all individual truths, without which none of them would be true. This center of gravity is one and the same in realism and in idealism, and if the two are opposed, what is lacking is only that one system fails to acknowledge this indifference point or fails to present it completely, or that both do.

But concerning the shape of philosophical science, and the challenge to cultivate the sturdy seed of this principle of indifference to its fullest flower, the ultimate goal is to achieve a perfect harmony with the very framework of the universe, for philosophy should be a true copy of the universe. To this end, both for ourselves and for others, we can prescribe no maxim more excellent to constantly keep before our eyes than that contained in these words, handed down to us by an earlier philosopher:[110]

To penetrate into the deepest secrets of nature, one must not tire of inquiring into the opposed and antagonistic extremes or end points of things. To discover their point of union is not the greatest task, but to do this and then develop its opposite elements out of their point of union, this is the genuine and deepest secret of art.

Following the advice of this precept, we shall first discern in the absolute identity of essential reality and form the way both the finite and the infinite spring forth from its interior, the one necessarily and eternally in and with the other, and we shall grasp how that simple ray of light that shines forth from the absolute and which is the absolute itself appears divided into difference and indifference, into the finite and the infinite. Then we shall determine more precisely the mode of division and reidentification of these principles for every point in the universe, and we will follow this path upward until we see the point where absolute identity appears divided into two relative identities; in the one, we will recognize the point of origin for the real or natural world, in the other, that of the ideal or divine world. Within the first world, we shall celebrate the eternal incarnation of God; [329] in the second, the inevitable divinization of mankind.[111] And as we move up and down this spiritual ladder, freely and without constraint, now descending and beholding the identity of the divine and natural principle dissolved, now ascending and resolving everything again into the one, we shall see nature within God and God within nature.

Now when we have scaled this peak and behold the harmonious light of this wondrous cognition, we shall realize that this cognition is at the same time that which is real in the divine essence; then we shall be granted the favor of seeing beauty in its brightest splendor and not be blinded by the sight, and we shall live in the blessed company of all the gods. Then we shall catch sight of the kingly soul of Jupiter.[112] His is the power, but subordinated to him are the forming and the formless principles, which a god of the underworld reunites in the depths of the abyss; Jupiter, however, lives in the unapproachable ether. Even the destiny of the universe will not be hidden from our eyes, how the divine principle will withdraw from the world and deliver the matter married to form over to stern necessity; nor will the stories all the mysteries give out about the fate of a god and his death remain obscure for us, those tales of the suffering of Osiris, for example, and those of the death of Adonis.[113] But above all, our eyes will be turned toward the higher deities, and achieving participation in their sublime mode of being through contemplation, we shall be truly perfected and satisfied, as the ancients expressed it; for we shall live within this resplendent sphere not just as refugees from the lands of mortality, but as ones who have received the initiation into immortal excellences. But the fading night reminds us of this, friends, and the light of one solitary gleaming star. Let us go from here.

Notes

1. "ON THE NATURAL AND THE DIVINE PRINCIPLE OF THINGS."
The following passage from Plato will provide a preliminary explanation of the
title: "It is necessary to distinguish two kinds of causes, one of which necessitates,
the other a divine cause, and to seek after the divine in all things for the sake
of obtaining a happy life, so far as our nature will admit." *Timaeus* 68E–69A.

2. ". . . we cannot regard as true the kind of cognition etc." Anselm's
assertion that 'truth' must be something entirely severed from time or correspondence or falsifiability seems so radical today that it is nigh incomprehensible.
It is obvious that Schelling cannot subscribe to the Kantian limitation of our
knowledge to the empirically observable. Since he will claim that truth really
belongs only to the eternal ideas within the absolute, perhaps Schelling's thinking
was guided here by the connection Spinoza draws between adequate ideas and
truth.

> For no one who has a true idea is ignorant that a true idea involves the highest
> certitude; to have a true idea signifying just this—to know a thing perfectly or
> as well as possible. No one in fact can doubt this unless he supposes an idea to
> be something dumb, like a picture on a tablet, instead of being a mode of
> thought, that is to say, intelligence itself. . . . Just as light reveals both itself
> and the darkness, so truth is the standard of itself and of the false. (ETHICS 2,
> Prop. 43, schol.)

Important for understanding the *Bruno* is Spinoza's comment that ideas are not
dumb, but are themselves intelligences. Indeed both 'concept' and 'idea' are
dynamical notions, as Schelling uses them, the former signifying an act of
thinking, the latter the necessary and eternal subsistence of a thing within the
absolute. Trans.

3. ". . . things as they are exemplified in the archetypal understanding etc."
Kant first made the distinction between a (hypothetical) archetypal intellect and
our ektypal or image-dependent intellect. In describing the teleological explanation

of nature as the "as if" postulation of an intellect which determines the part by the whole and which establishes the particular by positing the universal, Kant says:

> According to the constitution of our understanding, a real whole of nature is regarded only as the effect of the concurrent motive powers of the parts. Suppose, then, that we wish not to represent the possibility of the whole as dependent on that of the parts . . . , but according to the standard of the intuitive (original) understanding to represent the possibility of the parts . . . as dependent on that of the whole. In accordance with the above peculiarity of our understanding, it cannot happen that the whole shall contain the ground of the possibility of the connection of the parts (which would be a contradiction in discursive cognition), but only that the *representation* of a whole may contain the ground of the possibility of its form and the connection of the parts belonging to it. . . . It is here not at all requisite to prove that such an *intellectus archetypus* is possible, but only that we are led to the idea of it—which too contains no contradiction—in contrast to our discursive understanding, which has need of images (*intellectus ectypus*) and to the contingency of its constitution. (*Critique of Judgment*, section 77, tr. Bernard [Hafner, New York, 1974])

Schelling certainly had the above passage in mind when he introduced the notions of archetypal intellect and archetypal nature (see below, 4:223). In doing so, he is taking as metaphysical and anti-Kantian stance as possible, for he is asserting that what could only be a regulative idea for the Kantian in fact exists and is the true locus of reality. Thus it is by way of deliberate, perhaps defiant, opposition to Kant's limitation of the employment of pure reason that the Platonic metaphysics of archetype and image finds its way into Anselm's discourses and that the *Bruno* as a whole is anachronistically cast as a dialogue of ancient and precritical metaphysical systems. Perhaps Kant's description of the 'archetypal intellect'—a mind that is organic, necessitating, and self-specifying—furnished Schelling his very model of the absolute. Trans.

4. ". . . wholly self-contained, and hence simply eternal." The distinction between time and eternity that Anselm makes here is quite important for the whole discussion that follows. Though it seems to be a plainly metaphysical assertion, which Fichte and Kant would be quick to label transcendent, the claim that truth pertains to eternity and not to time means that truth is not tied to mere phenomena or the level of appearances. Schelling's concept of eternity is not the heaven of archetypes that Anselm asserts within the dialogue, but the Spinozistic eternity of reason that Bruno advances. It can be said that Schelling always was a Spinozist, for, from the first, he carefully distinguishes being (*Seyn*) from existence (*Daseyn*) as that which is not characterized by time and that which necessarily is. On this basis, he ridiculed attempts to prove the existence of God, as in this passage from the 1795 essay, "On the Self as Principle of Philosophy,"

> It is equally remarkable that the majority of philosophers did not make use of the advantages offered by their language. Almost all of them use the words, *Sein, Dasein* and *Wirklichkeit* as if they were synonymous. Obviously the word 'being' expresses pure absolute being-posited, whereas 'existence' even etymologically signifies a conditioned and limited being-posited. Nevertheless one speaks commonly

of the existence of God, as if God could really exist. . . . (ESSAYS, 105, translation altered)

And in 1799, Schelling maintained this distinction between being and existence, saying, "Hence of the rational being as such, one can no more say that it has begun to exist than that it has existed for all time; the self as self is absolutely eternal, that is, outside time altogether." SYSTEM, p. 48.

Hegel echoes the theme in the 1801 Difference-essay, "The true suspension of time is a timeless present, i.e. eternity, and in it striving falls away and opposition loses its standing." DIFFERENCE, p. 134. And in the 1807 *Phenomenology*, Hegel presents time as the form of spirit's incomplete self-externalization, which nevertheless presupposes an internal and exhaustive self-grasp, namely, eternity:

> Time is the Concept itself that *is there* and which presents itself to consciousness as empty intuition; for this reason, Spirit necessarily appears in Time just so long as it has not *grasped* its pure Concept, i.e. has not annulled Time. It is the *outer*, intuited pure Self which is *not grasped* by the Self, the merely intuited Concept; when this latter grasps itself, it sets aside its Time-form, comprehends this intuiting, and is a comprehended and comprehending intuiting. (PHENOMENOLOGY, par. 801; translation altered)

See also pars. 679, 802, and 808, op. cit.

In the *Bruno,* Schelling is generally careful to maintain the distinction between the eternal subsistence of things in the absolute and their existence as individual entities within time. Accordingly I have translated the various forms of *seyn* as 'subsist,' 'have being,' or 'inhere', reserving the terms 'exist' and 'existence' for *Daseyn* and *existieren* alone. In many cases I have made it explicit that existence involves temporality. Trans.

5. "Right now that question does not concern us." It is unfortunate that Anselm sidesteps the question, for it is impossible to critically assess Schelling's philosophy of identity without a careful consideration of 'intellectual intuition,' Schelling's ladder to the absolute. Fichte had used the term to indicate the awareness of self-activity or self-constitution that is given in and along with empirical consciousness. In 1795 Schelling had explained this intuition as immediate and without any object, since the self is that which never can become object. In the 1800 *System of Transcendental Idealism,* he primarily defined it as abstraction from the stance of subjectivity.

In the early years of the System of Identity, 1801–1803, Schelling primarily characterizes intellectual intuition as (1) an abstraction from the particular character of empirical consciousness, as given here and now, and (2) as the capacity for holistic and integrating insight. The first corresponds to the universal personality of the creative genius [see below, 4:229]. Nowhere does Schelling provide a full and explicitly argumentative consideration of how these capacities lead to a philosophical intuition of the absolute or the eternal.

To illustrate the first characterization of intellectual intuition, we turn to a passage written late in 1802.

> That selfhood is the form in which the absolute grasps itself for immediate consciousness is a proposition quite intelligible in itself. But what is essentially real in selfhood is itself only the absolute. In intellectual intuition, which has as

its object this essential element freed from all limitations, the form disappears as *particular*. The opposition and merely relative identity of pure and emprical consciousness pertains only to the particular consciousness. (WERKE 4:355)

But a second passage from the same work suggests that intellectual intuition is a rather garden-variety intellectual function:

> The intellectual intuition which is not merely fleeting but remains as the unchanging organ [of reason] is the condition of the scientific spirit in general and all the parts of knowledge severally. For it is the general faculty of envisioning the universal within the particular, the infinite within the finite, both as brought to a living unity. The person who dissects a plant or animal body believes he immediately sees a plant or an animal body; really, though, he sees only the individual thing he calls plant or body. To see the plant in the plant, the organism in the organism, in short, the concept or indifference within difference is possible only through intellectual intuition. (WERKE 4:362)

The claims advanced in these passages are perfectly factual. It is true that sometimes, at least, our knowing can be disinterested and impersonal, and it is certainly true that we form conceptual wholes and integrate our perceptions by means of them. But they hardly demonstrate that an absolute totality of our knowledge can be attained or that there is some ultimately nonperspectival stance our knowledge can ascend to, a perspective upon all perspectives. These claims would equally well support the thesis that there are infinitely many degrees of generality and abstraction at play within our knowing, but no single Archimedean point. Thus we find that though the Hegel of the *Phenomenology* rejects Schelling's static method of 'potentiation' as but a repetition of a lifeless schema, he makes both the properties of intellectual intuition cited above positive characteristic of dialectical method. On the selflessness of 'conceptual' cognition, see PHENOMENOLOGY, pars. 72, 78; on the immediacy of conceptual or holistic insight, see pars. 73, 242, 257–258, op. cit. In the end we must admit that the mature Hegel's ceaselessly moving dialectic better captures the interplay of relativity and absoluteless in human knowledge. Only if knowledge achieves its objects everywhere and nowhere, that is, communally and historically, can it be said to be complete and absolute. But then it must still be recognized that its completeness is merely cumulative, and so its absoluteness merely relative. Trans.

6. ". . . not voluntarily indeed, but as enslaved to futility." Romans 8:20. Trans.

7. "Creation anxiously yearns etc." Romans 8:19. Trans.

8. "The created earth . . . is not the true earth." Though this passage sounds quite Neoplatonic, it is probably an echo of Socrates's mythic description of the true earth and the true heavens; see *Phaedo* 109E–110A. Schelling did not begin to read Plotinus until 1804, and was not introduced to the works of Proclus until 1820. Trans.

9. ". . . beauty is what the thing really is etc." In 1799 Schelling argued that the creative artist, whatever his conscious motivations and intentions, actually achieves more than he could ever intend. Unconsciously and instinctively, the creator of a great artwork achieves infinity. Beauty is therefore the infinite displayed within the finite work. See SYSTEM, p. 225. The following discussion

makes clear that 'what the thing really is' can only be its eternal concept or, in the language Bruno will introduce, its idea. Trans.

10. ". . . the way Socrates does etc." See *Phaedrus* 250A–C and 251A. Trans.

11. ". . pressed in upon resisting nature through the force of causes." Consult *Timaeus* 46E and 48A, where Plato differentiates the causality of reason which shapes the cosmos by looking to the 'form of the best' from the necessary and mechanical action of auxiliary causes, collectively called 'the wandering cause.' Trans.

12. ". . . eternal by its nature, even in the midst of time." In 1799 Schelling held that in fact there was but one work of art, since the content of every great work is one and the same, namely infinity.

> Infinity is exhibited in every one of its products. For if aesthetic production proceeds from freedom, and if it is precisely for freedom that this opposition of conscious and unconscious activities is an absolute one, there is properly speaking but one absolute work of art, which may indeed exist in altogether different versions, yet is still only one, even though it should not yet exist in its most ultimate form. (SYSTEM, 231)

Trans.

13. ". . . we proved the identity of philosophy and poetry." Schelling had asserted this identity before, in the conclusion of the *System of Transcendental Idealism*, but in such a way as to give art a distinct advantage over philosophy.

> Take away objectivity from art, one might say, and it ceases to be what it is, and becomes philosophy; grant objectivity to philosophy, and it ceases to be philosophy and become art.—Philosophy attains, indeed, to the highest, but it brings to this summit only, so to say, the fraction of a man. Art brings *the whole man,* as he is, to that point, namely to the knowledge of the highest, and this is what underlies the eternal difference and the marvel of art. (SYSTEM, 233)

As the following discussion shows, Schelling now thinks he conceded too much to art by focusing on the aspect of unconscious creativity. Whereas in 1799 he believed that philosophy lacks the power to consciously attain to absolute identity, Schelling now thinks it possesses that power, 'intellectual intuition.' Philosophy need no longer depend on the surrogate of aesthetic intuition. For the rather limited discussion of intellectual intuition within the *Bruno*, see below 4:301, 325–326, 327–328. Trans.

14. "This concept subsists in God etc." Throughout the *Bruno,* Schelling employs Spinoza's elaborate doctrine of soul or mind whereby (1) the soul-idea or concept inheres both in God and in itself, and (2) it functions as the soul of an individual thing inasmuch as it primarily represents changes in the condition of the material body. Spinoza had written:

> There exists in God the idea or knowledge of the human mind, which follows in Him and is related to Him in the same way as the idea or knowledge of the human body. (ETHICS 2, Prop. 20)

> This idea of the mind is united to the mind in the same way as the mind itself is united to the body. (ETHICS 2, Prop. 21)

Schelling had tried to imitate the deductive character of the *Ethics* in his 1801 *Exposition of My System,* and had only obscurbed his thought beneath layers of false rigor. Here he makes extensive and creative use of Spinoza's psychology to explain how the identity of the absolute is preserved even within the separated existence of the finite individual. See below, 4:278–288. Trans.

15. "In the same individual, but in an absolute mode etc." This double relation between beauty and the creative individual, here expressed so cryptically, was explained by Schelling in 1799 as a dialectic of conscious and unconscious forces within the soul of the artist. The absolute mode of relation that Schelling mentions in this passage corresponds to the work of the unconscious; it is "being possessed by the idea of beauty."

> This unchanging identity, which can never attain to consciousness and merely radiates back from the product, is for the producer precisely what destiny is for the agent, namely a dark unknown force which supplies the element of completeness or objectivity to the piecework of freedom; and as that power is called destiny, which through our free action realizes, without our knowledge and even against our will, goals *that we did not envisage,* so likewise that incomprehensible agency which supplies objectivity to the conscious . . . is denominated by means of the obscure concept of genius. (SYSTEM, 222)

It is precisely the workings of this subterranean force in the artist's psyche that is here criticized, as well as the fact that it works in and through the artist's personality. The philosopher, Schelling claims, is not beset by such limitations, but is able to intuit the concept in pure conscious inwardness. For similar remarks by Hegel on the limitations of the artificer and artist, the deficient quality of his self-consciousness, and the externality of his work, see PHENOM-ENOLOGY, pars. 693, 708. Trans.

16. ". . . one who defiles the mysteries." In the *Phaedrus,* Plato makes initiation into the mystery rites a symbol for the philosopher's vision of the forms, linking the etymologically related notions of perfection, initiation, and death together in a complex pun (see 249C). Schelling transforms the allusion into a symbol for intellectual intuition of the absolute. As a philosophical discussion cast in the form of a dialogue, and a discussion which is supposed to mediate a dispute, the *Bruno* is consciously modeled on the *Phaedrus,* and appropriately so, for one of the latter's major themes is friendship. The whole discussion of the origin of the visible universe (4:260ff.) seems to have the *Timaeus* as its pattern. Trans.

17. "Philosophy is necessarily esoteric etc." In the 1795 "Letters on Dogmatism and Criticism," Schelling described critical philosophy, with its emphasis on freedom as the foundation of all and the goal of all, as essentially esoteric:

> For the worthy, nature has reserved a philosophy that becomes esoteric by itself because it cannot be learned, recited like a litany, feigned, nor contained in dead words which secret enemies or spies might pick up. This philosophy is a symbol for the union of free spirits. (ESSAYS, 196)

In the Preface to the *Phenomenology,* Hegel criticizes Schelling for this sort of posturing. Science, he says, is esoteric only in its initial simplicity, before it has articulated the wealth of its contents:

Without such articulation, Science lacks universal intelligibility, and gives the appearance of being the esoteric possession of a few individuals. . . . Only what is completely determined is at once exoteric, comprehensible, and capable of being learned and appropriated by all. The intelligible form of Science is the way open and equally accessible to everyone. (PHENOMENOLOGY, par. 13) Trans.

18. "Thus Sophocles introduces one of his characters etc." In a fragment preserved by Plutarch, found in *Sophoclis quae exstant omnia,* ed. R. F. P. Brunck [4 volumes, Argentorati, 1786–1789] Vol. 4, 686.

19. ". . . men first learned that there is something unchanging etc." See Plato, *Phaedo* 78B–79E. In 1807 Hegel too asserts that the mysteries taught the nonbeing of sensuous things, in a passage echoing the language of the *Bruno:*
    In this respect we can tell those who assert the truth and certainty of the reality of sense-objects that they should go back to the most elementary school of wisdom, viz., the ancient Eleusinian Mysteries of Ceres and Bacchus, and that they have still to learn the secret meaning of the eating of bread and the drinking of wine. For he who is initiated into these Mysteries not only comes to doubt the being of sensuous things, but to despair of it. (PHENOMENOLOGY, par. 109) Trans.

20. "Now we notice that concrete things etc." See *Phaedo* 75A–B. Trans.

21. "The mysteries portrayed this knowledge etc." See *Phaedrus* 249E–250C. Trans.

22. "Second, that I may escape the evils etc." By acknowledging the reality of evil and imperfection right at the start, Bruno is dissociating himself from the simple Platonic dualism Anselm espoused (see 4:221–223 above). Whereas Anselm thinks in terms of simple oppositions such as time and eternity, soul and body, archetype and individual thing, Bruno will put forth an analysis of things in terms of three elements, the first two of which are antithetical opposites, and the third their union or identity. The difference is most clearly seen in the case of the relationship between concept and thing. Anselm presents them as simply opposed, while Bruno sees them as relatively opposed dimensions of phenomena, distinct aspects of the individual thing which are united in a third, the eternal idea that exists in the absolute. As the discussion unfolds it will become apparent that Bruno (Schelling's *persona*) is no dualist. Body and soul, matter and intelligence are but differently appearing levels of one and the same order of phenomenal reality. The only important duality is that of the absolute and phenomenal reality as a whole, or the duality of reason and reflection, and that duality *ought not* exist. In a sense, it indeed does not exist, for the difference between the inclusive reality of the absolute and the externality of appearance (the whole order of individuals) can be intuited only within the latter. It is the ideal being possessed by individuals as individuals within the absolute's form—a notion quite like the Medievals' divine intellect—that lends the phenomenal order or, as Bruno calls it, separated existence, the modicum of reality it has. Trans.

23. ". . . the idea of the absolute etc." Schelling's initial presentation of the concept of absolute identity is quite abstract and couched in the logical jargon that Fichte employed throughout the *Science of Knowledge*. Schelling's first announcement of the programme of identity philosophy, in the concluding section of the *System of Transcendental Idealism,* is more concrete:

> Now if this higher thing be nothing else but the ground of identity between the absolutely subjective and the absolutely objective, . . . which part company precisely in order to appear in the free act, then this higher thing itself can be neither subject nor object, nor both at once, but only the *absolute identity,* in which is no duality at all, and which, precisely because duality is the condition of all consciousness, can never attain thereto. (SYSTEM, 208–209)

Schelling reserves the full explanation of absolute identity as the indifference of the absolute's essence and its form for the conclusion of the dialogue. See below, 4:321–328. Trans.

24. ". . . if we do not adopt this identity of oposites etc." Schelling put forth a similar argument in the 1795 essay "On the Self as Principle of Philosophy":

> It is the character of finiteness to be unable to posit anything without at the same time positing something in opposition. The form of this opposition is originally determined by the opposition of the not-self [to the self] . . . The infinite self would exclude all opposites but without letting the exclusion establish them in opposition to itself. (ESSAYS, 84–85n, translation altered)

The issue that is at point in the following discussion is whether we can logically conceive an entity that is all-inclusive. Lucian argues that the principle of contrast is operative in all concept formation, and suggests that philosophy must follow the logic of meaning in setting up its principle too. No ultimate principle can be conceived or postulated without some opposite having to be postulated as well. Even if the opposite is some vanishing entity, like the not-self in Fichte's philosophy, the absolute principle will be affected by the opposition, and will be diminished or distorted. Bruno argues that philosophy's principle must be one and ultimate, an identity which includes difference rather than excluding it.

Though Fichte himself never advanced the arguments Lucian presents, Schelling accurately represents the Fichtean style of thinking, namely to follow the guidance of the laws of logic, even if they cannot be used for an empirical ascent to properly philosophical principles. Hegel presents a more precise account of Fichte's *Wissenschaftslehre,* and its 'Deduction of Presentation' in particular, in PHE-NOMENOLOGY, pars. 137–139. As Hegel describes it, the uniform expression of force (Fichte's primordial self) transforms itself into the opposition of in-dependent forces (self and not-self). But perceptual consciousness is unable to comprehend that force, the incipient form of selfhood, is nothing other than this diremption into independent opposites. Trans.

25. ". . . the identity of identity and opposition etc." The formula comes from Hegel's 1801 essay on Schelling and Fichte, where identity-philosophy is explained and defended in these terms:

> Philosophy must give the separation into subject and object its due. By making both separation and the identity, which is opposed to it, equally absolute, however,

philosophy has only posited separation conditionally, in the same way that such an identity . . . is also only relative. Hence, the Absolute itself is the identity of identity and non-identity; being opposed and being one are both together in it. (DIFFERENCE, p. 156)

Schelling adopts Hegel's terminology for the *Bruno,* and pushes the technical terminology of the *Exposition*—'absolute identity,' 'absolute indifference,' 'quantitative indifference,' etc.—off to the sidelines. Perhaps this was a conscious decision on Schelling's part to phrase the public attempt at reconciliation with Fichte in the language of Hegel's public criticism. Or perhaps Hegel had already voiced to Schelling his objections about using quantitative concepts to depict the absolute, a criticism voiced repeatedly in the writings and lectures of 1804–1806 and elevated into prominence in the *Phenomenology of Spirit.* There Hegel argues that philosophy must spurn any approximation to mathematical concepts or methods:

The principle of *magnitude,* of difference not determined by the Concept, and the principle of *equality,* of abstract lifeless unity, cannot cope with that sheer unrest of life and its absolute distinction. It is therefore only in a paralyzed form, viz. *as the numerical unit,* that this negativity becomes the second material of mathematical cognition, which, as an external activity, reduces what is self-moving to mere material, so as to possess in it an indifferent, external, lifeless content. (PHENOMENOLOGY, par. 46; translation altered)

See also pars. 271, 280, 286, 290–291 op. cit. Trans.

26. ". . . no . . . identity that is not distorted by difference." Lucian's demand that difference be inbuilt into absolute identity follows the pattern of Fichte's solution of the dialectic of infinitude and finitude in the self, namely, conceding that difference is somehow native to the self:

But if the not-self is to be able to posit anything at all in the self, the *condition for the possibility of such an alien influence must* be grounded beforehand, prior to any actual effect from without, in the *self as such, in the absolute self;* the self must originally and absolutely posit in itself the possibility of something operating upon it; without detriment to its absolute positing of itself, it must leave itself open, as it were, to some other positing. Hence, if ever a difference was to enter the self, there must already have been a difference originally in the self as such; and this difference, indeed, would have had to be grounded in the absolute self as such. (SCIENCE, 239–240)

Trans.

27. ". . . the practice of armchair philosophers etc." A reference to Reinhold and Bardili. See Hegel's DIFFERENCE, 187–190. Trans.

28. "Then you cannot seriously maintain etc." It is not immediately clear why Lucian gives in on this point and agrees, for the argument leading up to this conclusion is obscure.

The crucial point of the argument is that Lucian/Fichte thinks that identity and difference must be causally related. In his 1801 critical attack on Fichte, Hegel blamed the failure of his philosophy on the way he interprets logical relations as causal ones:

The basic character of Fichte's principle, as we have shown, is that the Subject-Object steps out of its identity and is unable to reestablish itself in it because the difference [i.e. the contrast of pure and empirical consciousness] gets transposed into the causal relation. The principle of identity does not become the principle of the system; as soon as the formation of the system begins, identity is abandoned. (DIFFERENCE, 155)

Schelling takes over this criticism and amplifies it in a letter of 3 October 1801, which ends with a terse announcement to Fichte of the publication of Hegel's "Difference" essay:

Whether I make the series of conditioned beings real or ideal is, speculatively considered, of no moment. For in the one case as in the other, I do not transcend the finite. You thought you fulfilled all the demands of speculation by making the finite ideal, *and this is the chief point of our difference.* From the third fundamental principle [of the *Science of Knowledge*] onwards, that whereby you attain to the sphere of divisibility, reciprocal limitation, to finitude in other words, your philosophy is a continuous series of finitudes—a higher causal order. The true annihilation of nature (in *your* sense) does not consist in granting that it is real only in an ideal sense, but in bringing the finite into absolute identity with the infinite. That means that one grants no sense whatsoever to the finite outside of *the eternal,* whether in the real (common) understanding of the terms or the ideal (your position). (BRIEFE 2, 353–354)

Bruno's argument against Lucian's contention that difference distorts identity presumes Fichte's bent to turn logical relations into causal ones, and it presumes Schelling's and Hegel's criticism as well. The argument can be reconstructed as follows: If identity and difference are conceived as things, as limiting and restricting one another, then they are causally interrelated. But mathematics hardly posits unity and multiplicity as opposed 'things' that causally interact. Indeed, multiplicity must depend on unity—this is Schelling's omitted premise. Therefore difference must in some way depend on identity, even though the two are conceptually opposed. For neither is the integrity of unity destroyed by its conceptual contrast to multiplicity, nor is identity's identity tarnished by its conceptual contrast to difference. Construed this way, the present argument turns Lucian's first objection (see 4:236) against himself.

The initial series of arguments (4:235–238) suggests, but does not plainly state, that the relations that obtain between identity and difference, or between the absolute and the finite individual, must be conceived nonentitatively if they are to be correctly stated. Difference must be conceived as a dependent modification of identity, individuals as dependent modifications of the absolute, whose individuality is established and maintained only from their own point of view. The closest Schelling comes to spelling out this position is found in Anselm's interpretation of Leibniz's monadology; see below, 4:316–321. Schelling might have had recourse to Spinoza's doctrine of modes to help him state this clearly, though there is some danger in explaining the obscure by the obscure. Trans.

29. "For things that are absolutely and infinitely opposed etc." This argument might compete with the conclusion of Plato's *Parmenides* for the title 'paradigm of nonsense.' It shows the influence of the line of thought Hegel developed in the 1801 Difference-essay. On Hegel's view, the understanding can but make conceptual distinctions; its function is to analyze reality in terms of fixed

oppositions. Thus its law is the principle of noncontradiction. Reason, however, is what reunites everything that the understanding analytically sunders, and it reaches totality by way of antinomy. Its law is precisely the principle of contradiction:

> Logical cognition, if it actually does advance toward Reason, must be led to the result that it nullifies itself . . .; it must recognize antinomy as its supreme law. (DIFFERENCE, 180)

> The union of opposite concepts in the antinomy—which is a contradiction for the faculty of concepts—is the assertoric and categorical appearance of the inconceivable. . . . The antinomy is the true revelation of the inconceivable in concepts, the revelation that is possible through reflection. (DIFFERENCE, 185)

Schelling does not generally argue in this highly paradoxical Hegelian fashion, but Hegel himself employed the model of the 'rational paradox' as the tool of philosophical reflection up until 1805. The transitions that are found in the Jena *Logik, Metaphysik und Naturphilosophie* (1804–1805) are not transitions that the mature Hegelian system would find rational. They involve no mediation. Instead they are antinomies, a direct joining of opposites. Isolated passages in the first half of the *Phenomenology* betray Hegel's use of the infinite or the infinite judgment as the model of conceptual rationality as late as 1805–06. As the following passage indicates, Hegel's 'infinity' is quite close to Schelling's 'indifference':

> This simple infinity, or the absolute Concept, may be called the simple essence of life, the soul of the world, the universal blood, whose omnipresence is neither disturbed nor interrupted by any difference, but rather is itself every difference as also their supersession; it pulsates within itself but does not move, inwardly vibrates yet is at rest. It is self-*identical,* for the differences are tautological; they are differences that are none. (PHENOMENOLOGY, par. 162; translation altered)

See also pars. 160–161, 344, op. cit. Trans.

30. "The identity of thought and intuition." Schelling is quoting from a letter composed by Fichte on 31 May 1801, but first sent on 7 August, that is openly critical of Schelling's *Exposition of My System.* Fichte had written,

> [Philosophical science] cannot be founded on and proceed from some instance of being, but it must originate in a seeing. (Everything connected to a mere thinking and which, as a consequence, is akin to the *real ground,* is *being,* even if one calls it reason.) So too, the identity of the ideal ground and the real ground must be presented as the identity of intuition and thought. (BRIEFE 2, 341)

In his *1801 Exposition of the Science of Knowledge,* Fichte defined his terms more closely:

> This resting within unity and being for itself, which, as is evident, can itself happen only within the absolute freedom of knowing, is *a thought.* In contrast, the wavering in the manifold of separate factors is *an intuition.* . . At any rate, the fact remains, as we explained above, that knowing is located neither in the unity nor in the multiplicity, but in and in between both. For neither is the thought a knowing, nor the intuition; only both of them in their union constitute knowing. (F. WERKE 4, 25–26)

For echoes of the last sentence, see 4:253–255, 299 below. Trans.

31. "One intuition is determined by another etc." One naturally expects to read, 'an intuition is determined by its object,' but, in addition to taking a phenomenalistic stance on the reality of objects, Schelling is working within the framework of Spinoza's metaphysics, where thought and extension form absolutely distinct though correlated orders:

> When things are considered as modes of thought, we must explain the order of the whole of nature or the connection of causes by the attribute of thought alone, and when things are considered as modes of extension, the order of the whole of nature must be explained through the attribute of extension alone. (ETHICS 2, Prop. 7, schol. Cp. 1, Prop. 28)

Schelling utilizes Spinoza's separation of the two orders of attributes to argue that things and concepts, or being and knowing, are distinct but ontologically equal orders wherein the absolute expresses itself in individuals. Both orders are equally phenomenal. This doctrine implies, as in Spinoza, that every individual has been a psychic and a somatic aspect, though the psychic dimension need not be conscious. Trans.

32. ". . . the concept remains one and unchanged etc." For Schelling, a concept is simply an act of thinking. "Every thinking is an act, and every determinate thinking a determinate act; yet by every such act there originates for us also a determinate *concept*. The concept is nothing else but the act of thinking itself, and abstracted from this it is nothing." SYSTEM, 24–25. In the same work, Schelling defines the end or purpose of an action as 'the concept of the concept,' i.e. a representation of a thinking outside of my thinking (172, 178). The discussion that follows makes plain that concepts are infinite, but empty, or, in the words of Kant, "Thoughts without content are empty, intuitions without concepts are blind." *Critique of Pure Reason* A51/B75.

Despite the radically dynamic sense the mature Hegel assigns to *Begriff,* isolated passages in the 1807 *Phenomenology* exhibit Schelling's understanding of the concept as an abstract generality, devoid of intrinsic content. For example:

> Natural consciousness will show itself to be only the Concept of knowledge, or in other words, not to be real knowledge. But since it directly takes itself to be real knowledge, this path has in fact a negative significance for it, and what is in fact the realization of the Concept, counts for it rather as the loss of its own self. (PHENOMENOLOGY, par. 78; translation altered)

Trans.

33. "What a splendid and lofty idea. . . ." Schelling's reply to Fichte's criticism of the 1801 *Exposition* (see note 30) begins on this laudatory tone, but strenuously attacks Fichte's contention that philosophy must start from a *seeing,* not a *being:*

> The identity of the ideal and real grounds = the identity of thought and intuition. With this identity you express the supreme speculative idea, the idea of the absolute whose intuiting consists in thinking and whose thinking consists in intuiting. . . . Since this absolute identity of thought and intuition is the supreme principle [of philosophy] and is actually conceived as *absolute indifference,* it is necessarily at the same time the supreme instance of being—the highest being, not the finite and determined being, say that of an individual corporeal thing, which always expresses a determinate difference between thought and intuition.

In this case, the ideal and the real mutually distort one another. The undistorted indifference of the two is located in the absolute alone. As the shortest way to the intuition of this absolute indifference, and thereby to the highest being necessarily and immediately conjoined to it, I ask you to consider absolute space, which is exactly the intuition of the supreme indifference of ideality and reality, supreme transparency and clarity, the purest case of being we intuit. For you, being is completely synonymous with reality, indeed with actuality. But preeminent being no longer has any opposite, for it is itself the absolute identity of the ideal and the real. (BRIEFE 2, 348) Throughout the *Bruno,* Schelling polemically insists that it is space, not empirical consciousness, that provides the best model for understanding the absolute's identity within difference. See below 4:263–264, 304–305.

34. ". . . those self-proclaimed philosophers etc." Fichte is hardly congratulated when it is claimed his philosophy outstrips the achievements of Reinhold and Bardili. See Hegel's DIFFERENCE, 174–195. Trans.

35. "I think I see it quite clearly etc." Fichte himself was not as pliable as his literary stand-in. Early in the *1801 Exposition of the Science of Knowledge* he sharply separates philosophical analysis of absolute knowing from any talk of the absolute itself:

First, there is something quite important that must be said about the direction of our inquiry. It is clear enough from the mere concept of an absolute knowing that it is not the same as *the absolute.* Every second word added to the expression 'the absolute' cancels absoluteness purely as such; it lets the absolute stand only in the perspective or the relation signified by the modifying second word. The absolute is neither knowing nor is it being, nor is it identity, nor is it the indifference of knowing and being. It is purely and simply the absolute. Since within the science of knowledge . . . we cannot come any nearer the absolute than to knowing, the science of knowledge must proceed not from the absolute but from absolute knowing . . . Perhaps the absolute can never enter consciousness in a pure state, as it is in and for itself, but only in the context in which it is presented, namely as the *form of knowing.* (F. WERKE 4, 12–13) Trans.

36. ". . . what dominates all philosophical talk etc." I translate *Form* [literally, procedure] as 'dialectic,' since Schelling is plainly thinking of Platonic dialectic. On the relation of the absolute's 'form' to its essential reality, see 4:258–259 below. Later in 1802 Schelling coined the term *Ineinsbildung* for this dialectical process which is not an arbitrary procedure of mere human understanding, but is itself the absolute's form. Form is the process whereby the absolute maps its essential and identical reality onto both the natural and spiritual orders, by building them into one another. See WERKE 4:380, 394, 415.

There is no graceful translation for *Ineinsbildung.* The term suggests 'imagination' (*Einbildungskraft*) and 'making uniform' (*Einbildung*). I have elsewhere translated the term as 'in-vention,' which, despite its awkwardness, at least suggests that Schelling modelled his idea of the absolute's form on Christian Neoplatonism's notion of the divine intellect or the creative Word as the original locus of creation. See "Schelling's Neoplatonic System-Notion," in *The Significance of Neoplatonism,* (SUNY Press, Albany 1976), pp. 275–300. Trans.

37. ". . . as Plato has Socrates say etc." In a passage from *Philebus* [15D–E].

38. "Now we differentiate 'idea' and 'concept' etc." In *Faith and Knowledge*, written shortly after the *Bruno* was penned, Hegel freely adapts the latter's terminology—the triads of the finite, the infinite, and the eternal, and of intuition, concept, and idea—to criticize subjective idealism, and Fichte in particular, for its inability to attain to an integral unity of human experience. This form of philosophy is willing to remain at the level of the concept, and is thus only a general reflection of empirical reality:

> The fixed principle of this system of culture is that the finite is in and for itself, that it is absolute, and is the sole reality. According to this principle, the finite and singular stands on one side, in the form of manifoldness. . . . On the other side there is the very same absolute finitude, but in the form of the infinite as the concept of happiness. The infinite and the finite are here not to be posited as identical in the Idea, for each of them is for itself absolute. So they stand opposed to each other in the connection of domination; for in the absolute antithesis of infinite and finite, the concept is what does the determining. However, above this absolute antithesis and above the relative identities of domination and empirical conceivability, there is the eternal. (FAITH, 60)

Trans.

39. ". . . it looks like everything is upside down etc." This is the first mention, as far as I know, of the inverted world concept or the idea of standing reality on its head, the polemical tool widely employed by Hegel, Feuerbach, and Marx. Schelling here claims that it was Fichte who first stood reason on her head in the analysis of substance in the *Science of Knowledge*. In 1794 Fichte argued,

> The accidents, synthetically united, yield the substance; and the latter contains nothing whatsoever beyond the accidents: the substance, on analysis, yields the accidents, and after a complete analysis, there remains nothing at all of substance beyond the accidents. We must not think of an enduring substratum, or of some sort of bearer of accidents; any accident you care to choose is in every case the bearer of *its own* and the *opposing* accident, without the need of any special bearer for the purpose. (SCIENCE, 185)

By rejecting every vestige of the appearance/reality dichotomy, including Schelling's contrast between finite cognition and the idea, the mature Hegel will make inversion fundamental to the conceptual grasp of reality. "Existence is really the perversion of every determinateness into its opposite, and it is only this alienation that is the essential nature and support of the whole. . . . The alienation will alienate itself and the whole will, through this alienation, return to its Concept." PHENOMENOLOGY, par. 491; translation altered. See also pars. 157, 521. Trans.

40. "Therefore we do not require any time-concept etc." A seemingly paradoxical claim. Schelling seems to conflate Spinoza's claim that time pertains to the imagination while reason comprehends only the necessary and the eternal with Kant's view that time pertains only to appearances, being the form of all intuition as such. Spinoza wrote,

> It is of the nature of reason to consider things as necessary and not as contingent. This necessity of things it perceives truly, that is to say, as it is in itself . . . It

is of the nature of reason to consider things under this form of eternity. Moreover the foundations of reason are notions which explain those things that are common to all, and these things explain the essence of no individual things, and must therefore be conceived without any relation to time, but under a certain form of eternity. (ETHICS 2, Prop. 44, Coroll. 2)

Note that although Schelling claims we do not need any concept of time to think the finite as such, he makes time essential to the limited comprehension of individuated existence that we can obtain. Time is in a sense the cause of individuation, though an individual's own internal possession of time (the highest case of which is consciousness) constitutes its self-identity, the perfection of its individual existence. See below, 4:261–265. Trans.

41. "A finite being is thus an actuality etc." The concepts of possibility and actuality enter the discussion abruptly, without prior deduction or justification. In 1795 Schelling had argued that Kant's modal categories—possibility, actuality, and necessity—were not categories at all, but a summary of the whole table of categories. They are a schematization of the original forms of thought—being, not-being, not-being determined by being—and so belong to the province of logic. Consult "On the Self as Principle of Philosophy," ESSAYS 114, 118n. Trans.

42. ". . . this divorce of possibility and actuality etc." Schelling said essentially the same thing in 1795:

> For the absolute self there is no possibility, actuality or necessity, since whatever the absolute self posits is determined by the mere form of pure being . . . If there were any possibility and actuality at all for the infinite self, all possibility would be actuality, and all actuality possibility. For the finite self, however, there is possibility and actuality. "On the Self as Principle of Philosophy," (ESSAYS 120; translation altered)

Trans.

43. "Even things that do not exist now etc." Schelling is here following Spinoza, who said,

> The ideas of non-existent individual things or modes are comprehended in the infinite idea of God in the same way that the formal essences of individual things or modes are contained in the attributes of God. (ETHICS 2, Prop. 8)

Trans.

44. ". . . though in itself equal to the infinite etc." A paraphrase of Philippians 2: 6–8. Schelling and Hegel are equally fond of Trinitarian and Christological metaphors. Hegel echoes the 'suffering God' theme in the *Phenomenology*'s best pun: "This form [artistic activity] is the night in which substance was betrayed and made itself into Subject." PHENOMENOLOGY, par. 703. See also par. 532. Trans.

45. ". . . you will overleap the territory of human knowing etc." Hegel echoes Schelling's complaint about the ambiguity of Fichte's principle in *Faith and Knowledge*. One and the same principle, he says, is forced to play two roles, but if the self is both the absolute and the principle of empirical consciousness, then as absolute it must be empty.

This acknowledged incompleteness of the absolute principle and the acknowledged necessity of going on to something else . . . form the principle of the deduction of the world of sense. Because of its absolute deficiency, the completely empty principle [Ego = Ego] from which Fichte begins has the advantage of carrying the immediate necessity of self-fulfilment immanently within itself. It must go on to something other [than itself] and from that to something else in an infinite objective world. (FAITH, 157)

Hegel suggests that Fichte's 'self' is solely an empirical principle, Schelling that it seems to be purely an absolute one. They would both declare with one voice, "You cannot have it both ways." Lucian clears up this ambiguity as the argument proceeds. If the self is but a principle in and of consciousness, then its claim to be an absolute and self-sustaining principle is nullified, for the self is merely a relative identity, opposed by its counterpart, being. The upshot of the argument (cf. 4:256–257) is that consciousness is not the absolute. The absolute can only be the identity of consciousness and being, an identity which is simultaneously the essential and grounding reality behind both phenomenal orders, but which, for that very reason, is neither consciousness nor being. Trans.

46. ". . . I recognize it as the principle of knowing, no more." To Schelling, Fichte's very Kantian methodological caution is an inability to transcend the finite, a decision to remain at the standpoint of empirical phenomena. See the passage from Schelling's letter of 3 October 1801, quoted in note 28 above. Trans.

47. ". . . that which I do not know?" This is an odd sounding definition of being, but a perfectly logical one in the Fichtean perspective, which views all objectivity as ultimately derived from the not-self. For the not-self cannot be intuited, and as a philosophical concept, it cannot be thought either, only postulated. In 1807 Hegel seems to adopt this Fichtean perspective when he argues, "What merely *is,* without any spiritual activity, is, for consciousness, a Thing, and, far from being the essence of consciousness, is rather its opposite; and consciousness is only *actual* to itself through the negation and abolition of such a being." PHENOMENOLOGY, par. 339. In his popular presentation of Fichte's philosophy in 1799, Schelling made the same point less paradoxically: "The objective is simply that which arises without consciousness." SYSTEM, 219–220. Trans.

48. "For being is just as real as knowing, etc." The whole debate between Schelling and Fichte on methodology and first principles (4:252–257) seems inconclusive. Fichte holds that empirical consciousness furnishes evidence for an absolute consciousness, so his philosophy postulates an absolute as an absolute self, but utilizes this posited self only for the investigation of empirical consciousness. Methodologically, this is correct and careful, for on Fichte's terms, the only postulation that is self-validating is self-positing.

Schelling argues that Fichte's stance is too limited. Since the self given in and with empirical consciousness is merely a relative identity, or what Hegel called a subjective Subject = Object (See DIFFERENCE, 155), it must be complemented by another relative identity, being or the objective Subject = Object.

On these terms, the dispute cannot be settled. For (1) Schelling fails to fully explain what intellectual intuition is, and thus provides no methodology for an ascent to the absolute. In contrast, Fichte is quite clear about what self-intuition and self-positing mean. But (2) Fichte is apparently willing to countenance talk about an absolute other than or beyond absolute consciousness. He thus admits an absolute that is in principle hidden from philosophical inspection; see F. WERKE 4, 12–13. The only resolution of the dispute possible is not Schelling's position, the strong thesis that the absolute is the indifferent union of consciousness and being, but the weaker thesis that, apart from consciousness, there is neither being as such nor knowing as such. As the following passage makes plain, the standpoint of methodological idealism is the only common ground Fichte and Schelling can share. But using idealism as a mode of explanation, Fichte must confine his philosophy to a phenomenological investigation of empirical consciousness, while Schelling, doing the same, attempts to transcend the phenomenal and so produces a metaphysics of identity. Trans.

49. ". . . there is no being as such nor knowing as such." In 1801, Hegel summarized Schelling's philosophy of identity and pointed out the ground of its congruence with Fichte's in the following words:

> These two opposites, whether they are called self and nature, or pure and empirical self-consciousness, or cognition and being, or self-positing and opposition, or finitude and infinity, are together posited in the Absolute. Ordinary reflection can see nothing in this antinomy except contradiction; Reason alone sees the truth in this absolute contradiction through which both are posited and both nullified, and through which neither exists and at the same time both exist. (DIFFERENCE, 174; translation altered)

This passage is remarkable in that it clearly states the central thrust of all post-Kantian idealism, while it ignores subtle differences in position. One can imagine Fichte, Schelling, and Hegel signing this statement as an official document, and then, of course, resuming polemical bickering before the ink was dry. The greatest disagreement would be between Fichte and Hegel, essentially two moralists with opposite views, one demanding that spirit abolish nature, the other that it be integrated with nature to achieve wholeness once again. Schelling would be in between, having no moral point of view, but only a metaphysical programme, a proposal for a metaphysics that would unite the philosophical study of nature with the study of consciousness. Trans.

50. ". . . form is always adequate to the essential and abiding reality etc." In the *Bruno,* Schelling fails to adequately explain the form-essence distinction he employs, nor does he show how this categorial distinction applies both to the absolute and to individual entities. The latter task is crucial, for unless Schelling can show why the distinction between essential reality and form of development should apply to the absolute as well as to individuals, Spinoza's absolute monism would seem a more logically consistent metaphysics than the relative monism of the identity-philosophy. For what sets Spinoza and Schelling apart is the fact that the former did not explain how substance includes individual entities, while the latter attempted to explain the link between the absolute and phenomenal individuals. Indeed, one of the most interesting features of the

Bruno is its energetic attempt to retain ontological commitment to individuals while at the same time asserting their inclusion in the absolute.

As the argument evolves (4:257–260) it appears that the form-essence distinction is tied to the paradoxical nature of the finite as such: that is, that it is both finite and infinite. (1) That the absolute contains the finite is what distinguishes its form from its identical essence. Form here means the ideal evolution of individuals, or the establishment of the limited essences that will exist in separation *when* they separate and distinguish themselves. (2) Because the finite and the infinite coexist in the absolute's form, its essence (identity) is identical with, or nondifferent from, its form. (3) When individuals withdraw from the absolute, they actually differentiate the finite and infinite and establish the thing or material aspect in opposition to its concept or soul. (4) The form of individuals' separated existence is being in time or temporality as such. Therefore, (5) the absolute's form is an ideal and timeless evolution of individuals, while the individual's is a temporal development, wherein finite actuality in attempting to express infinite possibility for itself becomes an unstable series of individuals excluding one another. In short, the absolute's form is inclusion, assimilation of difference into indifference, while the individual's form is the establishment of difference as actual. Later in 1802, Schelling began to talk about this positing of difference in the mythic language of a fall (*Abfall*) from the absolute. Trans.

51. ". . . this absolute eternity, which we could term a rational eternity, etc." Schelling is thinking of Spinoza's third and highest form of knowledge, knowing *sub specie aeternitatis*. Spinoza had written:

> Things are conceived by us as actual in two ways—either insofar as we conceive them to exist with relation to a fixed time and place or insofar as we conceive them to be contained in God. . . . But those which are conceived in this second way as true or real we conceive under the form of eternity, and their ideas involve the eternal and infinite essence of God. (ETHICS 5, Prop. 29, schol)

Schelling explains this eternity of reason in a letter to Fichte, written on 3 October 1801:

> You apply the adjective 'incomprehensible' to the real ground of the separate condition of individuals. Indeed it is incomprehensible for the reflective understanding that attempts to grasp it from an inferior position . . . But it is not incomprehensible for reason which posits absolute identity or the indivisible togetherness of the finite and the infinite as its first principle and proceeds from there. For reason is neither finite nor infinite, but is eternally and identically both. This *eternity of reason* is the authentic principle of all speculation and of true idealism, and it is what negates the causally organized series of finite beings. This reason-eternity essentially (*natura*) precedes all time. Conversely, it exists before [each and every moment of time] in no other way than the way, now and forever, it is prior according to its nature. (BRIEFE 2, 351)

Trans.

52. ". . . while indifference corresponds to soul etc." On the relation of soul and body in organisms and in conscious individuals, see below, 4:278–288. Trans.

53. "Its expression in the order of things etc." Each of the phenomenal orders, the finite series of objects and the infinite series of concepts or acts of thinking, equally expresses the absolute. Since the two series are strictly parallel, an individual thing expresses the absolute just as much as an act of consciousness does. Schelling's thought is here guided by Spinoza:

The order and connection of ideas is the same as the order and connection of things . . . . Whether we think of Nature under the attribute of extension or under the attribute of thought or under any other attribute whatever, we shall discover one and the same order or one and the same connection of causes, that is to say, in every case the same sequence of things. (ETHICS 2, Prop. 7 and schol)

The parallelism of the opposed phenomenal orders insures the reality of nature, for, combatting Fichte's restriction of reality to the domain of consciousness, Schelling wants philosophy to comprehend the reality both of nature and of spirit. In the deduction of the visible (or phenomenal) universe that follows, the structures of consciousness emerge out of those embedded in nature, without any discontinuity. The mechanical motion of inorganic nature, the life of organisms, and the field of rational consciousness have the same laws, in the sense that they exhibit the same order, pattern, or structure—the relative identity and opposition of the finite and the infinite, or, in simpler terms, of the material and the mental. Schelling's metaphysics of identity is thus panpsychistic, but it is also pansomatic. Every individual entity is thus both spiritual and natural. It follows, among other things, that soul is just as mortal and bound to the conditions of time as is body. See below, 4:282–283.

For Hegel's argument that world-history alone, not organic nature, is the appropriate link between the absolute and individual consciousness, see PHE-NOMENOLOGY, par. 295. This is the sole passage in the *Phenomenology* where Hegel's criticism is directed at the form of Schelling's system rather than his method. But in par. 807, Hegel speaks of nature in terms quite similar to Schelling's, calling it the "eternal externalization of its [Spirit's] *continuing existence* and the movement which reinstates the *Subject.*" Trans.

54. ". . . as the tradition handed down by the ancients etc." This is an echo of Plato's *Timaeus,* 50C–D:

For the present, then, we must conceive of three kinds—the Becoming, that 'Wherein' it becomes, and the source 'Wherefrom' the becoming is copied and produced. Moreover, it is proper to liken the Recipient to the Mother, the Source to the Father, and what is engendered between these two to the Offspring.

In the *Bruno*'s presentation of philosophy of nature, Schelling marries his views on nature to an imitation of the general structure and the style of the *Timaeus.* To this is due many of the curious features of this treatment, for example, the preoccupation with the stars or heavenly spheres, and also the omission of many phenomena such as magnetism, electricity, and chemical interaction, phenomena that occupy an important place in Schelling's other sketches of the philosophy of nature. Trans.

55. ". . . compared to mortal men, undying gods etc." Compare Aristotle, *Metaphysics* 1074^{b}1–3: "Our forefathers in the most remote ages have handed

down to their posterity a tradition, in the form of a myth, that these bodies are gods and that the divine encloses the whole of nature." See also *Timaeus* 40B–D. Trans.

56. ". . . the line is more an activity than it is an entity etc." This passage parodies Fichte's postulation of an absolute self. In the "Second Introduction to the Science of Knowledge," Fichte argued that philosophy must proceed from a primary datum that is both fact and act:

> It is therefore not so trivial a matter as it seems to some, whether philosophy starts out from a fact or an Act (that is, from a pure activity which presupposes no object, but itself produces it, and in which the acting therefore immediately becomes the *deed*). If it proceed from the fact, it places itself in the world of existence and finitude, and will find it difficult to discover a road from thence to the infinite and the supersensible; if it sets out from the Act, it stands precisely at the point joining the two worlds, from whence they can be surveyed with a single glance. (SCIENCE, 42)

Schelling's remarks on the role of postulates in geometry are interesting in their own right, both for the constructivist view of mathematics they imply, and because they precede by a scant twenty one years the invention of non-Euclidean geometries by Bolyai and Lobachevskiy. The fact that alterations in Euclid's fifth postulate produce alternate geometries demonstrates how much postulates differ from universal facts. When Schelling speaks of geometers "postulating the line," he seems to refer indiscriminately to all five Euclidean postulates. Trans.

57. "For time is a continually moved etc." A paraphrase of Plato's famous definition of time in *Timaeus* 37D–E. Trans.

58. "Thus every single thing exhibits the whole universe etc." Schelling does not provide a very detailed explanation of the potencies or powers in the *Bruno*, though he makes extensive use of the concept. In the 1801 *Exposition of My System of Philosophy*, Schelling presents the powers as repeating patterns or structures which express absolute indifference within individuals either as identity or as differences or as indifference. The powers function as the forms of appearance as such, or the forms of phenomena in general. Thus every finite thing or class of things will indeed express the absolute subject-objectivity, but it will do so in one of these three forms, hence as subjectivity or as objectivity or as subject-objectivity. The powers are ordered in a hierarchy: A^1, the real power, A^2, the ideal power, and A^3, the eternal power. Each one of these potencies itself has three moments—(1) relative identity, (2) relative difference, (3) relative totality.

Now in translating these notions into the language of the *Bruno,* where the powers are named 'the finite,' 'the infinite,' and 'the eternal,' Schelling encounters an ambiguity about the order of the potencies. The contrast between the real and the ideal, especially when applied to the phenomena of nature, seems to define the finite as A^1 and the infinite as A^2. But the conceptual contrast of possibility and actuality, especially when applied to the phenomena of consciousness, seems to make the infinite $= A^1$ and the finite $= A^2$, for Schelling seems to hold (1) that possibility grounds actuality and (2) that possibility is infinite or infinite compossibility, while actuality is limited. Schelling seems aware of the difficulty himself, for in speaking of the natural world, he arranges the powers in a ladder going from the finite, to the infinite, to the eternal. In speaking of the domain of consciousness, however, he presents their order as the infinite, the finite, and the eternal.

The following table is a highly synoptic one showing how the potencies order and arrange Schelling's discussion of the worlds of nature and of consciousness:

LEVELS OF PHENOMENA	THE POWERS		
The Absolute:	The Finite	The Infinite	The Eternal
Metaphysical or modal categories:	Actuality	Possibility	Necessity
Consciousness:	Intuition	Thought (i.e., Concept and Judgment)	Syllogism
Intuition:	Sensation	Conscious awareness	Reason
Thought (i.e., Concept):	Plurality, Boundary, Cause and Effect	Unity, Reality, Substance and Accident	Totality, Determination, Universal Reciprocity
Syllogism:	Hypothetical Syllogism	Categorical Syllogism	Disjunctive Syllogism
Organisms:	Body	Soul (i.e., concept of an individual)	Union of body and soul
Universal principles of nature:	Gravity	Light	Reason
Inorganic matter:	Space	Time	Gravity/ Light
Time:	Duration (i.e., mechanical motion)	Organic Instinct	Consciousness
Space:	Breadth	Length	Depth

I have not attempted to introduce Schelling's treatment of the stars and their motions into this table, though the table will make clear why he calls them the perfect and preeminent individuals. For the stars comprehend and embody all the universal principles of nature, namely gravity, light, and reason. For a developed account of Schelling's philosophy of nature, see J. Esposito, *Schelling's Idealism and Philosophy of Nature* (Lewisburg, Bucknell University Press, 1977). Trans.

59. ". . . sensitive and intelligent animals." Schelling is following Plato, who made the world itself an animal endowed with intelligence:

> On this wise, using the language of probability, we may say that the world came into being—a living Creature truly endowed with soul and intelligence by the providence of God. (*Timaeus* 30B–C)

Trans.

60. ". . . disclosed to us by a divine intelligence." These are Kepler's laws. One must understand them in their purity and free them from later mechanistic and empiricistic distortions before one can approach their speculative meaning. On this score, I can appeal with confidence to the previous efforts of a friend [G. W. F. Hegel, *De Orbitis Planetarum*, 1801]. What is positive in the interpretation of the laws advanced here corresponds to the general schema of construction that dominates this conversation. For Kepler's three laws are generally related to one another as indifference, difference, and totality, that which reconstitutes the identity of the two. And in this way, the laws perfectly express the whole living body of reason and form a self-enclosed system. This much might serve as a guide for interpreting Bruno's discourse on the heavens. Further explanations of the significance of these laws will be furnished elsewhere.

61. "But these are absolutely equivalent forms etc." Gravity is not conceived by Schelling as one force among others; it is the totality of mechanical forces. In 1799 he wrote:

> In the phenomena of magnetism, all material traces are already disappearing, and in those of gravitation, which even scientists have thought it possible to conceive of merely as an immediate spiritual influence, nothing remains but its law, whose large-scale execution is the mechanism of the heavenly motions. (SYSTEM, 6)

The law of universal gravitation, discovered by Newton, unifies and brings to totality Kepler's laws of planetary motion. See below, 4:271–272. Trans.

62. "For the circle is . . . the most perfect expression of reason." Plato connects circular motion about an axis with intelligence in a passage on the divinity of the stars:

> Of these two movements, that confined to one place must in every case be performed about a center, after the fashion of a well-turned cartwheel, and it is this which surely must have the closest affinity and resemblance that may be to the revolution of intelligence. (*Laws*, 898Af)

On the "revolution of intelligence," see Plato's proof of soul's immortality, *Phaedrus*, 245C–246A. Trans.

63. ". . . the whole universe is divided into two regions etc." Plato distinguishes the fixed stars and the planets as unwandering and wandering deities respectively:

> From this cause, then, came into existence all those unwandering stars which are living creatures divine and eternal and abide forever revolving uniformly in the same spot; and those which keep swerving and wandering have been generated in the fashion previously described. (*Timaeus*, 40B)

Schelling's account of the heavenly bodies and their motions is confused because he is trying to marry an account of the rational system of motion contained in Kepler's three laws to a rather thoroughgoing imitation of the *Timaeus*. Kepler's laws, however, describe the motion of the planets, while for Plato the perfectly rational motion was to be seen only in the fixed stars, that is, in the revolution about their own centers which keeps them perpetually in the same place. In addition to this confusion, the whole discussion of celestial movements is fragmentary and lacking in organization, either written in haste or betraying its origin in disconnected aphorisms. I have taken the liberty of inserting explanatory comments and transitions into the text. Trans.

64. ". . . all the stars together constitute a line etc." This idea of an axis of the universe may have been intended as an application of Kepler's third law, which states that the ratio between the cube of a planet's mean distance from the sun to the square of its orbital period remains constant for all the planets. The odd names 'square' and 'cube' applied to the second and third potencies may also be a reflection of this law which expresses the fundamental idea that the planetary bodies form a system, not just an aggregation. Trans.

65. ". . . everything was arranged according to proportion and number etc." Plato writes,

> Thus it was that in the midst between fire and earth God set water and air, and having bestowed upon them so far as possible a like ratio one towards another . . . he joined together and constructed a Heaven visible and tangible. For these reasons and out of these materials, such in kind and four in number, the body of the Cosmos was harmonized by proportion and brought into existence. (*Timaeus*, 32B–C)

Trans.

66. ". . . the heavenly spheres were populated etc." Schelling applies Plato's vision of the universe as a whole being a cosmic animal to each of the stars individually.

> For the original of the universe contains in itself all intelligible beings, just as this world comprehends us and all other visible creatures. For the deity, intending to make this world like the fairest and most perfect of intelligible beings, framed one visible animal comprehending within itself all other animals of a kindred nature. (*Timaeus*, 30D)

Trans.

67. ". . . it forever strives . . . to become one body and one soul." Schelling echoes the closing words of the *Timaeus*:

> We may now say that our discourse about the nature of the universe has an end. The world has received animals, mortal and immortal, and is fulfilled with them,

and has become a visible animal containing the visible—the sensible God who is the image of the intellectual, the greatest, best, fairest, most perfect—the one only-begotten heaven. (92C) Trans.

68. ". . . the soul of an individual existing thing." Schelling's conception of the relation of body and soul closely follows the psychology that Spinoza elaborates in Book 2 of the *Ethics*. Its chief features are: (1) that soul is an idea, a concept in Schelling's terminology, that which the mind forms purely as a thinking thing; (2) that soul and body express precisely the same reality, the one substance, but each strictly within its own order; (3) that the soul or mind is primarily the idea of the body; (4) that there is no causal interaction between soul and body.

Schelling reshapes this doctrine of the independence and seeming interdependence of the conceptual and material orders of phenomena by employing Kant's modal categories. The concept or soul of a thing establishes the ground of possibility for what the body actually expresses, since, as an individual concept, it is an act of thinking just that reality that the body expresses. But neither side is real and substantial in itself. Only their identity or necessary togetherness is real, that is, the eternal idea or its image within the individual. Trans.

69. ". . . the idea functions as the intuiting agent etc." The conceptual or infinite aspect of an animal comprehends a greater share of the domain of the possible than that of an inorganic thing because it is the concept of an organic body, a body related in some way to all other bodies and in direct interaction, at least, with all of its immediate environment. Thus the animal's concept is fit to be a knower or an ideal expression of the web of existing organic affinities.

For Spinoza's doctrine that mind or soul is essentially the idea of the body, see *Ethics* 2, Props. 11–12, 20; also 3, Prop. 10. For his argument that all bodies are complex, in interaction with, and affected by others, see *Ethics* 2, lemmas and postulates; also 1, Prop. 15, schol. From these positions follows this proposition, relevant to Schelling's description of the organism: "The human mind is adapted to the perception of many things in proportion to the number of ways its body can be disposed." *Ethics* 2, Prop. 15. For a more complete explanation, see "The Human Mind as 'Idea' in the Platonic Tradition and in Spinoza," *Diotima*, Vol. 8 (1980), 134–143. Trans.

70. ". . . the body's concept . . . includes these external determinants etc." Following Spinoza's reasonings in *Ethics* 2, Schelling here explains how absolute cognition turns into a representation of the thing's external environment when it functions as a thing's concept or soul. Spinoza establishes (1) that the essence of matter is unknowable [2, lemmas 4 and 5; Prop. 16, coroll. 2; Prop. 19], (2) that all finite bodies are complex and in interaction [2, the lemmas and postulates], (3) that all states of mind are complex, since the mind is the idea of the body [2, Props. 9, 15, 19, and 29]. He concludes that there can only be confused knowledge of the body and of its environment: "The human mind does not know the human body itself, nor does it know that the body exists

except through ideas of modifications by which the body is affected." [2, Prop. 19].

But the confused state of knowledge limits both the mind's idea of the body and that of itself too: "The idea of any modification of the human body does not involve an adequate knowledge of the human body itself." [2, Prop. 27]. And "the idea of the idea of any modification of the human body does not involve an adequate knowledge of the human mind." [Prop. 29]. Thus for Spinoza, the mind as idea or pure act of thinking becomes radically finite, unaware of the real nature of things and of itself as well.

Guided by this line of thought, Schelling agrues that the soul-concept, precisely in functioning as the soul of an individual thing, becomes a double soul, one properly infinite, and another finite and restricted to the comprehension of bodily states. The two aspects of soul are opposed as thought and intuition respectively, and it is their identity that constitutes consciousness; see below, 4:281–288. This 'double soul' notion does not come from Spinoza directly, though it grows out of his contrast between inadequate and adequate knowledge. Trans.

71. "Indeed consciousness has no reality in the sight of the absolute etc." On the face of it, this is a shocking statement for an idealist to make, but it is fully justified by Schelling's insight that neither consciousness nor the world of objects is ultimately real. Fichte takes consciousness to be ultimately real, but Schelling insists it is merely phenomenal. See Hegel's remark, cited in note 49 above. Trans.

72. ". . . the contemplation of what is most excellent." An echo of Aristotle: "Hence the possession of knowledge rather than the capacity for knowledge is the divine aspect of mind, and the act of contemplation is what is most pleasant and best." *Metaphysics* 1072^{b}22–23. Trans.

73. ". . . nor is even that soul of souls, the infinite concept of soul etc." An echo of the terminology Spinoza used to indicate mind's reflexive self-awareness. Spinoza wrote,

> The idea of the mind is united to the mind in the same way as the mind itself is united to the body . . . . For, indeed, the idea of the mind, that is to say, the idea of the idea, is nothing but the form of the idea insofar as this is considered as a mode of thought and without relation to the object, just as a person who knows anything by that very fact knows that he knows, and knows that he knows that he knows, etc. (ETHICS 2, Prop. 21)

What Spinoza here calls 'the idea of the idea' and Schelling 'the soul of souls' is afterwards called 'the infinite concept of all concepts' or 'infinite cognition;' see below, 4:285ff. All of these terms indicate the moment of self-awareness in knowing whereby the self can form an idea or concept of itself. Self-awareness is a concept *of* a concept because mind or concept is primarily a representation of a body or material thing. Trans.

74. "Rather, it is a function of its own intrinsic finitude etc." Finite entities are limited by being causally conditioned, and this holds good for the conceptual or psychic order as well as for the order of material things. Thus the soul-concept becomes finite not by being related to the finite existing individual,

but by being determined by other determinate concepts. Spinoza stated this principle of serial determination as follows:

> An individual thing, or a thing which is finite and has a determinate existence, cannot exist nor be determined to action unless it be determined to existence and action by another cause which is also finite and has a determinate existence . . . ." (ETHICS1, Prop. 28)

Trans.

75. ". . . it exists in eternal communion with God." Schelling is here following Spinoza, who held that although the human mind cannot know except insofar as it is primarily the representation of changes of state in the body, the mind-idea nonetheless eternally exists in God.

> In God, nevertheless, there necessarily exists an idea which expresses the essence of this or that human body under the form of eternity . . . . The human mind cannot be absolutely destroyed with the body, but something of it remains which is eternal. (ETHICS 5, Props. 22 and 23)

This eternal existence of the idea or soul-concept must be conceived to be unconscious or nonconscious, both for Spinoza and for Schelling. Neither conscious knowing, nor activity, nor freedom can be ascribed to the absolute as such, and still less can their contraries; see below, 4:302–309. Trans.

76. ". . . as if looking through a mirror." A paraphrase of 1 Corinthians 13:12. Trans.

77. ". . . infinite cognition exists . . . under the form of difference and indifference." The ensuing discussion makes clear that the concept's existence as finite-infinite or as different-indifferent means that, on the one hand, it exists as an infinitely discriminated series of conditioned intuitions (in Spinoza's language, ideas of the body's states), and on the other, that it exists as a wholly general, and in fact empty, unity of thought. It is self-consciousness or the act of knowing that joins the two and mediates the contradiction of the concept being both one and multiple, or infinite and finite. Hegel will later embrace the same doctrine: "But further, self-consciousness is the relation of its pure consciousness to its actual consciousness, of what is in the form of thought to what exists objectively; it is essentially *judgment*." PHENOMENOLOGY, par. 495. It is highly ironic—and Schelling was probably quite conscious of the irony— that the Fichtean definition of consciousness is derived from Spinoza's analysis of the relations of mind and body. That the philosopher who Fichte once called the perfect dogmatist reaches the very same description of empirical consciousness that the transcendental idealist does pointedly undercuts the latter's claim to possess a superior philosophical standpoint. Trans.

78. ". . . the one concept that makes the world disclose its riches etc." In 1799 Schelling wrote,

> Kant, in his *Anthropology*, finds it remarkable that as soon as a child begins to speak of itself by the word 'I,' a new world appears to open up for it. In fact, this is very natural; it is the intellectual world that opens up to the child. (SYSTEM, 31)

Trans.

79. "What we call the self etc." This passage paraphrases Fichte's words in the 1794 *Foundations of the Entire Science of Knowledge:*
The self's own positing of itself is thus its own pure activity. The *self posits itself,* and by virtue of this mere self-assertion it *exists;* and conversely, the self *exists* and *posits* its own existence by virtue of merely existing. It is at once the agent and the product of action; the active and what the activity brings about; action and deed are one and the same, and hence the 'I am' expresses an Act, and the only one possible . . . (SCIENCE, 97)
Trans.

80. ". . . thought becomes its own object within the finite." This is the way Schelling expressed the Fichtean standpoint in the *System of Transcendental Idealism:* "Self-consciousness is the act whereby the thinker immediately becomes an object to himself, and conversely, this act and no other is self-consciousness." SYSTEM, 24; see also 36. The mature Hegel will return to the Fichtean position of the primacy of self-consciousness: "But Spirit becomes object because it is just this movement of becoming an *other to itself,* i.e. becoming an *object to itself,* and of suspending this otherness. And experience is the name we give to just this movement . . . " PHENOMENOLOGY, par. 36. Trans.

81. ". . . the laws and conditions for finite things etc." Compare Hegel's description of the term of philosophical endeavor: "But the *goal* is as necessarily fixed for knowledge as the serial progression; it is the point where knowledge no longer needs to go beyond itself, where knowledge finds itself, where Concept corresponds to object and object to Concept." PHENOMENOLOGY, par. 80; translation altered.

Bruno's announcement brings to a close the long discussion of the double nature of soul and the definition of consciousness as a union of the concept as intuiting with the concept (in its other function, namely) as reflexive self-awareness (see 4:278–290 above). The purpose of this discussion was to demonstrate to Fichte that Schelling still shares a common idealistic standpoint with him. Fichte would undoubtedly object that a deduction of self-consciousness from the conditions of an ensouled organism violates his principle that philosophy must start from a seeing, not a being. Schelling has at least demonstrated, however, that there can be a harmony and a continuity between the philosophy of nature and Fichte's transcendental stance. Schelling reserves direct criticism of Fichte's position for his treatment of the opposition of reflection and reason. See below, 4:301–307; also 325–327. Trans.

82. ". . . whoever knows also immediately knows that he knows etc." This paraphrases Spinoza, *Ethics* 2, Prop. 21. See note 73 above. Trans.

83. "Thus the three powers . . . determine the number of concepts." The deduction of categories that follows in fact deduces only nine categories; it presumes what Kant called the categories of modality. Schelling simply identifies possibility, actuality, and necessity with the potencies, that is, with the infinite, the finite, and the eternal respectively. Schelling's procedure here presumes an argument he advanced in 1795, when he proposed that the modes be eliminated from Kant's table of categories:

Material (objective) possibility, actuality, and necessity do not belong among the original forms which precede all synthesis. For they express materially what the original forms express only formally, that is, they express it in relation to an already accomplished synthesis. Therefore these three forms are not categories at all, since categories really are the forms through which the synthesis of the self and the not-self is determined. But these three together are the syllepsis of all categories. (ESSAYS p. 114; translation altered)
Trans.

84. "Some even dig down underneath appearances etc." In his 1801 *Contributions to a Survey of the State of Philosophy*, K. L. Reinhold postulated three absolutes—thinking, the application of thinking, and a matter to which thought is to be applied. It is the latter to which Schelling refers. Hegel describes the connection between the materiality of Reinhold's principle and its multiplicity as follows:

This materiality which is partly nullified by thinking, and partly fits into it, is postulated . . . . Matter cannot be what thinking is; for if it were the same, it would not be another, and no application [of thought] could take place because the inner character of thinking is unity. Hence the inner character of matter is just the opposite, in other words, it is manifoldness. DIFFERENCE pp. 186–187.
Trans.

85. ". . . the immovable and harmonious fire-heaven etc." See Plato, *Timaeus*, 31B, 40A. Trans.

86. "We will call this sort of cognition 'reflection' etc." Schelling's notion of reflection remains ambiguous throughout the *Bruno* where it is sometimes used in the context of Platonic image metaphysics, and sometimes used in the sense given it by Hegel in *The Difference Between Fichte's and Schelling's System of Philosophy*. Hegel defined the term as follows: "Reflection in isolation is the positing of opposites, and this would be a suspension of the Absolute, reflection being the faculty of being and limitation." DIFFERENCE, 94. In a passage written in 1802, Hegel explains how reflection is synonymous with the limited cognitive faculty that Kant called the understanding,

Inwardly, then, the understanding is, and should be, a speculative Idea, inasmuch as universal and particular are one in it. For the positing of the opposites in the judgment should be *a priori*, i.e. necessary and universal, which is to say that the opposites should be absolutely identical. But the matter comes to rest with the 'should.' For as opposed to empirical sensibility, this thinking [as conceived by Kant] is once more [only] an activity of the understanding. The entire deduction is [merely] an analysis of experience and it posits an absolute antithesis and a dualism. (FAITH, p. 78; translation altered)

Though Schelling adopts his colleague's terminology, he takes over only half of the idea it conveys, for while Hegel viewed reflection as the work of reason, a process of division and particularization which ultimately undoes even itself, Schelling views reason and reflection as disconnected opposites. In DIFFERENCE, Hegel continues the passage cited above as follows:

But reflection as Reason has connection with the Absolute, and it is Reason only because of this connection. In this respect, reflection nullifies itself and all being and everything limited, because it connects them with the Absolute. But at the same time the limited gains standing precisely on account of its connection with the Absolute. (DIFFERENCE, p. 94)

Schelling maintains a sharp and static division between the sort of cognition found in intellectual intuition (or reason) and the sort found within reflection. Hegel's full notion of reflection, even in the period of collaboration on the *Critical Journal,* is a dynamic one, characterized by negativity and self-reference; reflection, or the positing of limits, ultimately transcends limitation by reflecting on itself, that is, negating the limitations it has established. In 1807 Hegel explicitly criticizes Schelling for ignoring the self-suspending character of reflection:

> Reason is, therefore, misunderstood when reflection is excluded from the True, and is not grasped as a positive moment of the Absolute. It is reflection that makes the True a result, but it is equally reflection that overcomes the antithesis between the process of its becoming and the result. (PHENOMENOLOGY, par. 21)

Trans.

87. ". . . what hope is there for attaining philosophy etc." C. G. Bardili proposed the program of reducing philosophy to logic in 1800. K. L. Reinhold seconded the idea in 1801. Consult Hegel's DIFFERENCE, 108–109, 186, 189. Trans.

88. ". . . who attempts to prove the eternal being of the absolute etc." Schelling had always been persistently critical of any philosophical effort to prove an ultimate principle. Typical of his criticism is this comment made in 1795:

> Everything demonstrable presupposes either something already demonstrated, or else the ultimate, which cannot be further demonstrated. The very desire to demonstrate the absolute does away with it, and also with all freedom, all absolute identity, etc. (ESSAYS, p. 87)

In 1799 Schelling proposed the intriguing idea that human history is a demonstration, not of God's existence, but of his *presence:*

> God never *exists,* if the existent *is* that which presents itself in the objective world; if He *existed* thus, then *we* should not; but He continually *reveals* Himself. Man, through his history, provides a continuous demonstration of God's presence, a demonstration, however, which only the whole of history can render complete. (SYSTEM p. 211)

In a striking passage from the "Philosophical Letters on Dogmatism and Criticism," however, Schelling places ontological proofs of God's necessary existence in a favorable light:

> It seems almost unintelligible that people criticizing the proofs for the existence of God could have overlooked for such a long time the simple, intelligible truth that for the existence of God only an ontological proof could be given. If there is a God, he can be only *because* he is. . . . While Spinoza did not offer a proof of an absolute being, but simply and absolutely asserted it, our modest philosopher wanted to prove the very actuality of God. . . . It is significant enough that even language has distinguished very precisely between the *actual* (that which is present in sensation, that which acts upon me, and upon which I react), the *existing* (that which is there at all, i.e., in space and time) and the *being* (which is by itself, absolutely independent of all temporal conditions). Having completely confused these concepts, how could anyone have an inkling of the intention of Descartes and Spinoza? While these two spoke of absolute being, we foisted upon them our crass concept of actuality, or at best, the pure concept of *existence.* And

this, though pure, is nevertheless valid only in the world of appearances and is absolutely empty outside of it. (ESSAYS, 174n)

In this passage Schelling seems to have anticipated recent discussions that view the ontological proof as a modal proof, one that establishes either the impossibility or the necessary existence of a deity, but which totally excludes the options of contingent nonexistence and of contingent existence as well. Consult C. Hartshorne, *The Logic of Perfection* (Open Court, 1962). Trans.

89. "For the king and father of all things etc." See Plato, *Epistle 2,* 312E–313A and *Epistle 6,* 323D. Compare *Timaeus* 28C and 41A. Trans.

90. "But the farthest removed from the true idea of the absolute etc." This criticism is aimed squarely at Fichte's claim that the category of activity encompasses both the finite and the infinite, both the sensible and the supersensible. See the passage quoted in note 56 above. Schelling argues below that activity is not truly the point of indifference joining the finite and the infinite. It is merely a relative indifference point, the appearance of the conceptual order within finite things. Trans.

91. ". . . space . . . the identity of knowledge and being." Compare Schelling's deduction of space and time as the work of reflection mapping absolute identity onto the real and ideal worlds with the justification of the Kantian forms of intuition that Hegel offered a few months later in *Faith and Knowledge:*

> This shows that the Kantian forms of intuition and the forms of thought cannot be kept apart at all as the particular, isolated faculties which they are usually represented as. One and the same synthetic unity . . . is the principle of intuition and of the understanding. . . . Kant is therefore quite right in calling intuition without form [i.e., concept] blind. For in [mere] intuition [without form] there is no relative opposition, and hence there is no relative identity of unity and difference. . . . The opposition is not suspended in sensuous intuition, as it is in intellectual intuition; in the empirical intuition *qua* sensuous the opposition must emerge; so it keeps its standing even in this state of immersion. Hence the opposites step apart as two forms of intuiting, the one as identity of thinking, the other as identity of being, the one an intuition of time and the other of space. (FAITH, 70; translation altered)

Trans.

92. "Among real things, the organism etc." For a more detailed analysis of the similarity of the organism in nature to the work of art in the spiritual realm, see the *System of Transcendental Idealism,* 226–227. Trans.

93. ". . . a spectacle of lawless freedom." A reference to the Reign of Terror. This passage criticizes the French Enlightenment for separating the natural and spiritual worlds, for rendering living nature into a dead machine devoid of the spontaneity of life and freedom, while, on the other side, removing all constraints of law and order from the realm of spontaneous action. In 1799 Schelling had argued that freedom and order are not antithetical, but naturally belong together:

> The universal rule of law is a condition of freedom, since without it there is no guarantee of the latter. For freedom that is not guaranteed by a universal order of nature exists but precariously. . . . (SYSTEM, 203)

Arguing that an unconscious purposiveness orders human history, Schelling says,

> Only if an unconscious lawfulness again prevails in the arbitrary, that is, wholly lawless actions of men, can I conceive of a finite unification of all actions towards a communal goal. (SYSTEM, 206)

Compare Hegel's expansive treatment of the Enlightenment in PHENOMENOLOGY, pars. 538ff., especially pars. 549, 562, 589 and 592. Trans.

94. "For philosophy is forever challenged etc." Hegel takes over this theme in *Faith and Knowledge* and elaborates this idea of a processive transformation and realization of philosophy in the famous passage wherein he speaks of a 'speculative Good Friday' as the condition for a philosophical resurrection of an integral human culture:

> In their totality, the philosophies we have considered have in this way recast the dogmatism of being into the dogmatism of thinking, the metaphysic of objectivity into the metaphysic of subjectivity. . . . The soul as a thing is transformed into the Ego, the soul as practical Reason into the absoluteness of the personality and the singularity of the subject. The world as thing is transformed into the system of phenomena, . . . whereas the Absolute as [proper] matter and absolute object of Reason is transformed into something that is absolutely beyond rational cognition. . . . The metaphysic of subjectivity has brought this cultural process to its end. Therewith the external possibility directly arises that the true philosophy should emerge out of this [completed] culture, nullify the absoluteness of its finitudes, and present itself all at once as perfected appearance, with all its riches subjected to the totality. (FAITH, 189)

See also PHENOMENOLOGY, par. 2. Trans.

95. ". . . everyone . . . will have his own particular philosophy." Hegel had vigorously attacked Reinhold in 1801 for advancing this idiosyncratic view of philosophy:

> . . . for according to Reinhold, the history of philosophy should serve as a means, "to penetrate more profoundly than ever into the spirit of philosophy, and to develop the idiosyncratic views of one's predecessors . . . in new views of one's own." (DIFFERENCE, 86)

But Hegel replies,

> The essence of philosophy, on the contrary, is a bottomless abyss for personal idiosyncracy. In order to reach philosophy it is necessary to throw oneself into it *à corps perdu*—meaning by 'body' here the sum of one's idiosyncracies. (DIFFERENCE, 88)

Schelling and Hegel agree that intellectual intuition consists in abstraction from what is subjective, in the abandonment of a strictly personal stance. See note 5 above. Trans.

96. ". . . turning their fear of reason into the content of philosophy itself." This harsh remark appears to be directed against Kant, though it is probably directed against 'Kantians' who refuse to see an absolute principle of systematic philosophy in Kant's writings, and see instead only a sermon on the weakness of human reason. On two occasions in 1795, Schelling attacked these dogmatic pseudo-Kantians and their reduction of the *Critique* to the well-worn cliché that reason is too weak to achieve its proper ends:

Our spiritless age trembles before every authentic force that stirs in man. Therefore the representatives of the age promptly tried to tone down the first great product of this philosophy, . . . to reduce its doctrine to the humiliating tenet that the limits of objective truth are not set by absolute freedom but are a mere consequence of the well-known weakness of man's mind. . . . ("On the Self as Principle of Philosophy," ESSAYS, 68)

See also "Philosophical Letters on Dogmatism and Criticism," ESSAYS, 160–161. Hegel is equally harsh on Kant in the *Phenomenology*, where he labels Kant's critical epistemology "fear of error" and remarks, "What calls itself fear of error reveals itself rather as fear of the truth." PHENOMENOLOGY, par. 74. See also par. 617, op. cit., where Hegel calls Kant's moral philosophy "a whole nest of thoughtless contradictions." Trans.

97. ". . . they could not conceive of any relation . . . other than that of cause and effect." These remarks are aimed at Fichte, who posited an absolute not-self alongside the absolute self, and then tried to work out their relation through empirically valid categories such as determination, causality, and reciprocal determination.

In 1801, Hegel pointed out that the flaw in Fichte's *Science of Knowledge* consisted in his interpreting substantial relations and relations of identity in terms of cause and effect:

The causal relation between the Absolute and its appearance is a false identity, for absolute opposition is at the basis of this relation. In the causal relation, both opposites have standing, but they are distinct in rank. The union is forcible. The one subjugates the other. The one rules, the other is subservient. The unity is forced, and forced into a mere relative identity. The identity [of self and not-self] which *ought* to be absolute *is* incomplete. Contrary to its philosophy, the system has turned into a dogmatism. . . . (DIFFERENCE, 115)

See also 138, 155, op. cit. Trans.

98. ". . . the innate and insurmountable self-estrangement of the understanding." This echos Hegel's 1801 "Difference" essay:

Self-estrangement [*Entzweiung*] is the source of the *need for philosophy;* and as the culture of the era, it is the unfree and given aspect of the whole configuration. In [any] culture, the appearance of the Absolute has become isolated from the Absolute and fixated into independence. . . . The understanding [*Verstand*], as the capacity to set limits, erects a building and places it between man and the Absolute, linking everything that man thinks worthy and holy to this building, fortifying it through all the powers of nature and talent and expanding it *ad infinitum*. . . . But in its striving to expand itself into the Absolute, the understanding merely reproduces itself infinitely and so mocks itself. Reason reaches the Absolute only in stepping out of the manifold of parts. (DIFFERENCE, 89–90; translation altered)

Trans.

99. ". . . about the fate of that teaching etc." Scholars will perhaps not need to be reminded that the presentation of the history of materialism that follows closely approximates the particular manner Giordano Bruno employed to expound his teachings on the universe, especially in the ingenious abstract

of his work, *On the Cause, the Principle, and the One,* which Jacobi presented as an appendix to his *Letters on the Doctrine of Spinoza.* The following passages from Giordano Bruno may be viewed as illustrations of Alexander's exposition, and as parallels thereof. (The only dissimilarity is that Bruno explains soul as identical to the form of a thing [loc. cit., p. 269], whereby it becomes impossible for him to attain to the supreme indifference point of matter and form with complete clarity. Alexander, on the other hand, maintains that soul itself is one of the opposites within form, and that it is accordingly subordinate to form):

> From all accidental forms we must distinguish the necessary, eternal, and first form, which is the form and source of all forms. (p. 282)

> That first universal form and the first universal matter: How are they united, inseparable, different, and yet only one entity? We must seek to unravel this enigma. (p. 283)

> The complete possibility of the existence of a thing cannot precede its actual existence; just as little can it survive after actual existence ceases. If it were possible for a complete possibility to be actual without actual existence, things would have created themselves and would have existed before they existed. The first and most perfect principle comprehends all existence in itself. It is able to be all and it is all. In it, therefore, active force and potency, possibility and actuality, are undividedly and indivisibly one. Not so for other things, things that can be or not be, that can be so determined or otherwise determined. Every man is in every moment all that he is in that moment, but he is not everything that he generally could be according to his substance. The being which is all that it can be is the one unique being alone, and it comprehends all other beings within its existence. (p. 284)

> The universe or uncreated nature is likewise everything that it can be, in fact and all at once, since it includes within itself all matter along with the eternal and unchanging form of its varying configurations. But in its development from moment to moment, in its particular parts and states, in individual beings, in short, in its externality, it is no longer what it is and can be. It is but the shadow of the image of the first principle, wherein active force and potency, possibility and actuality, are one and the same. (p. 285f.)

> We have eyes neither for the height of this light nor for the depths of this abyss, wherefore the holy books combine the two extremes and say with such sublimity, "Darkness is not darkened for you. Night is illuminated as is the day. *As your darkness is, so is your light.*" (p. 287) [Job 13:8; Psalm 139:12,15].

> One should guard against confusing the matter that the sensible and supersensible worlds have in common with matter of the second kind, which alone is the underlying principle of natural and changeable things. (p. 287)

> Insofar as it contains in itself the multitude of forms, this matter that underlies incorporeal and corporeal things as well is a manifold entity. But, viewed in itself, it is absolutely simple and indivisible. Since it is all things, it can be nothing in particular. I admit it is not easy for everyone to comprehend how something can

possess *all* properties and *none,* how it can be the formal essence of everything and yet have no form itself. For the worldly-wise know the old saying, "It is impossible that a something be identical with the totality." (p. 290)

100. ". . . Eros as the child of Wealth and Poverty." See Plato, *Symposium* 203B–C. Trans.

101. ". . . the world is created by him." See Aristotle's account of Parmenides, *Metaphysics* 984ᵇ24–31. Trans.

102. "Matter . . . desires form etc." See Plato, *Timaeus* 50D and Aristotle, *Metaphysics* 988ᵃ4–6. Trans.

103. ". . . the Pythagoreans, who called the monad the father . . ." See Aristotle, *Metaphysics* 987ᵃ29–988ᵃ17; also *De Anima* 404ᵇ16–27. Trans.

104. "But time, which has slain everything etc." This passage and the rest of Alexander's discourse echoes the criticisms Hegel voiced in 1801 of the self-estranged nature of reason when it functions as understanding:

> The other presupposition [of philosophy] is the fact that consciousness has stepped forth from the totality and the totality is split in two, into being and not-being, into concept and being, finitude and infinity. From this perspective where everything is split in two, the absolute synthesis is a beyond; it is the undetermined and shapeless as opposed to the determinacies of the split. (DIFFERENCE, 93; translation altered)

See also p. 95, where Hegel explains that the work of the understanding is to separate and oppose the determinate and the indeterminate, the finite and the infinite, being and not-being, and to leave them simply opposed.

Note that the critique of mechanistic materialism that Alexander voices expands Schelling's logical critique of reflection (see 4:297–301, 305–307 above) into a scientific critique. Mechanism is incapable of explaining biological phenomena, thinks Schelling, and any adequate biology would force us to replace the mechanistic model of nature with a vitalistic or dynamical one. In 1799, Schelling wrote:

> The necessary tendency of all natural science is . . . to move from nature to intelligence. This and nothing else is at the bottom of the urge to bring *theory* into the phenomena of nature.—The highest consummation of natural science would be the complete spiritualizing of all natural laws into laws of intuition and thought. (SYSTEM, 6)

Few biologists today would be sympathetic to this description of their endeavor, but there are exceptions. See M. Polanyi, "Emergence," in *Tacit Dimension* (Anchor, New York, 1966) and E. Harris, *The Foundations of Metaphysics in Science* (Humanities Press, New York, 1965), 288–447. Trans.

105. ". . . to bring nature, . . . back to life again, mechanistically." In 1801, Hegel had accused Fichte's philosophy of endorsing this empiricistic mummification of nature:

> From this highest standpoint [of reflection] nature has the character of absolute objectivity, that is, of death. . . . The products of reflection, such as cause and effect, whole and part, etc. must now be predicated in their antinomy of this [unconscious] determining of self by self. In other words, nature must be posited

as cause and effect of itself, as being whole and part at once etc. In this way, nature takes on the semblance of being alive and organic. (DIFFERENCE, 140–141) See also pp. 193–194, op. cit. Trans.

106. ". . . all things in the universe possess their existence etc." Anselm indeed espouses Leibniz's intellectualism. In his exposition of it, however, he seems constrained by its primary limitation, the fact that it proceeds from the concept of the monad [rather than from that of God]. But perhaps the reader may ask whether Leibniz's doctrine is not actually reinterpreted here and raised to a higher significance, whether, in and amongst the complications and inelegance occasioned by this first limitation, one cannot see glimpses of the true philosophy at various points within Anselm's discourse. One such point is his statement that outside of God, there can only be inadequate representations of things. This question is all the more natural, since generally and *even to this day,* Leibniz's doctrine remains totally misunderstood, even in its chief points such as the preestablished harmony (which concerns the way soul and body are united), the relation of the monads to God, and so forth. Such misunderstandings are current even among philosophers who embrace Leibniz's thought or who would trace their philosophy back to Leibniz, though he is himself not without fault for their currency. I would venture to say that nothing could be found in Anselm's speech that could not actually be substantiated by individual passages from Leibniz, that I need not take flight and invoke the spirit of the intellectualistic system [in the absence of the letter]. Concerning the existence of the monads or unities within God, for example, or the teaching that for adequate or rational perception, everything exists in God, one might look to various pronouncements that can be found, partly in the *New Essays [Concerning Human Understanding]* themselves, and partly in their supplement entitled, "On Malebranche's Theorem that We See All Things in God."

107. ". . . each of these monads is but a living mirror etc." For the most part, I translate *Einheit,-en* as 'monad(s)' in this section devoted to Leibniz's metaphysics. Throughout the *Bruno,* Schelling uses *Einheit* rather than *Identität* to signifying 'identity.' Perhaps he wished to employ a rather neutral term, and thus furnish a common ground for discussion of Platonic unity, Leibnizean monads, as well as his own absolute identity. One might be critical of Schelling's project of translating his identity-philosophy into the language of earlier metaphysical systems on this score, for these translations are based on equivocation on the term *Einheit.* Schelling nowhere claims, at least, that Plato, Bruno, Spinoza, or Leibniz understood by their systems exactly the content of his identity-philosophy. Trans.

108. ". . . faith, the end of all speculation." In this passage and subsequent ones, Schelling directly criticizes Fichte's philosophical stance, following the path he sketched out in a letter to Fichte on 3 October 1801:

> In your philosophy, you turn the necessity to proceed from a seeing, [not a being,] into a series of thoroughly conditioned [states of consciousness] which no longer has anything to do with the absolute. In my opinion, philosophy can treat the consciousness or feeling [you speak of] just as little as geometry can. You must have sensed this, for already in the *Vocation of Man* you transferred the speculative

over to the sphere of faith, since you could not actually locate it in your knowledge. In that work, you as much as said that what is authentically and primitively real, that is, the truly speculative, is nowhere to be seen inside knowledge. (BRIEFE 2, 350)

Hegel mounts a similar line of attack on Fichte in *Faith and Knowledge*, 153–187. In 1795 Schelling launched a similar polemical attack on the pseudo-Kantians at Tübigen, theologians who sought to take advantage of Kant's admission that God, immortality, and happiness were practical postulates necessary for morality. As in the passage cited above, Schelling's point is that faith ought not be beyond the reach of speculation, that speculation should not put itself out of business by locating its object in an empty beyond:

> Now you need no longer engage in crafty proofs difficult to grasp; we have opened up a shortcut for you. What you cannot prove, you mark with the stamp of practical reason. . . . It is well that this proud reason has been humbled. Once she was sufficient unto herself; now she recognizes her weakness, and patiently awaits the guidance of a higher power which will promote your favorites farther than a thousand strenuous vigils could advance the poor philosopher. (ESSAYS, 162)

Trans.

109. "He who has the Son has the Father etc." John 15:15, 1 John 2:23. Trans.

110. ". . . these words handed down to us by an earlier philosopher." The philosopher is Giordano Bruno, once again. The words cited here (from the afore-mentioned abstract, p. 303) would serve well as the creed of true philosophy.

111. ". . . we shall celebrate the eternal incarnation of God etc." Perhaps an echo of Hegel's "Difference" essay. In explaining the ladder of the forms of consciousness that Schelling's 1800 *System* depicted, Hegel had said:

> The original identity must now unite both [consciousness and matter, in all the forms of their evolution] in the self-intuition of the Absolute, which is becoming objective to itself in its completed totality. It must unite them in the intuition of God's eternal human incarnation, the begetting of the Word from the beginning. (DIFFERENCE, 171)

For Schelling's speculative interpretation of the Christian dogma of the Trinity, see 4:252, 327 above. See also Hegel's 'conceptual' interpretation of the Trinity as essence, otherness, and being-for-itself in PHENOMENOLOGY, pars. 769–772. Trans.

112. ". . . we shall catch sight of the kingly soul of Jupiter." "Then in the nature of Zeus you would say that a kingly soul and a kingly mind were implanted through the power of the cause . . ." Plato, *Philebus* 30C–D. Trans.

113. ". . . the stories . . . about the fate of a god and his death etc." Compare 4:252 above, the reference to the finite potency as a suffering god. This whole passage, rich in the language of mythology, recalls the religious language of the closing words of Hegel's 1801 essay:

> That which has died the death of dichotomy, philosophy raises to life again through the absolute identity. And through Reason, which devours both [the

finite and the infinite] and maternally posits them both equally, philosophy strives toward the consciousness of the identity of the finite and the infinite, or in other words, it strives towards knowledge and truth. (DIFFERENCE, 195)
Trans.

Index